The Films of
Brigitte
Bardot

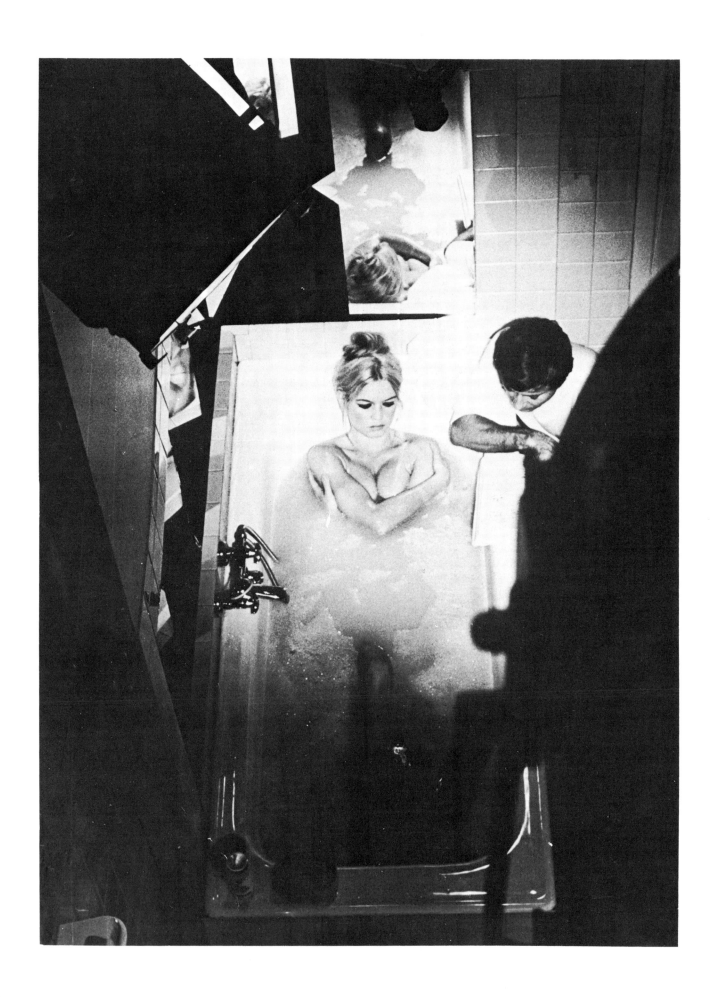

The Films of
Brigitte Bardot

By Tony Crawley

A CITADEL PRESS BOOK
Published by Carol Publishing Group

Acknowledgements

More people have chronicled the films, the fame, the figure, fortunes, foibles and fellas of Mlle. Brigitte Bardot than of any other post-war screen legend: from poets and intellectuals to critics and satirists. It is, therefore, patently impossible for me fully to acknowledge all the muses having influenced my journey through *Bardolatrie*. Where possible, though, all such scribes have been duly credited: to any inadvertently missed out, my apologies and my thanks. Closer to the steam of the typewriter and photo-probing digits, I owe quite immeasurable debts to the following for their direct assistance and encouragement: George Axelrod, Betty Box, Christine Gouze-Renal, Olga Horstig-Primuz, Ralph Thomas and, most particularly, Roger Vadim/the British Film Institute librarians; Mme. L. Camus, Unifrance-London; Gianni Comencini, Cineteca Italiana, Milan; John Kobal, of the inestimable John Kobal Collection, London; Paulette Lachaud, Françoise De Beaucoudrey, Unifrance-Paris; Luis Roos, Danish Film Museum, Copenhagen/*Cinémonde, Cinema X, Game, Lui, Paris-Match, Playboy* and *Première* magazines/Frank Selby, Rex Features; Charles Simons, Camera Press; Paul and Helle Bolton, Sungravure Syndication/Peter Cargin, Frederick Chance, Barbara De Lord, Barry Edson, Tim Evans, Brian Fitter, William Hall, Colin Hankins, Bob Herrington, Ted Nunn, John Pipkin, Simone Pré, Serge Ruettard, Marc Sharratt; my editors for their trust and patience; my designer for his enthusiasm; and not least, the toil of Nicole in both interpretation and accentuation, and the youthful stoicism of Nicholas and Delphine, for missing more weekends than can be repaid.
Merci!

First Carol Publishing Group edition 1994

A Citadel Press Book
Published by Carol Publishing Group
Citadel Press is a registered trademark of Carol Communications Group
Editorial Offices: 600 Madison Avenue, New York, N.Y. 10022
Sales and Distribution Offices: 120 Enterprise Avenue, Secaucus, N.J. 07094
In Canada: Canadian Manda Group, P.O. Box 920, Station U, Toronto, Ontario M8Z 5P9
Queries regarding rights and permissions should be addressed to Carol Publishing Group, 600 Madison Avenue, New York, N.Y. 10022

Edited by Tom Hutchinson
Designed by Jeff Tarry

Carol Publishing Group books are available at special discounts for bulk purchases, for sales promotions, fund-raising, or educational purposes. Special editions can be created to specifications. For details, contact Special Sales Department, Carol Publishing Group, 120 Enterprise Avenue, Secaucus, N.J. 07094

Manufactured in the United States of America
ISBN 0-8065-1477-9

10 9 8 7 6 5 4 3 2 1

For Pilou and Totty—without whom, etc.

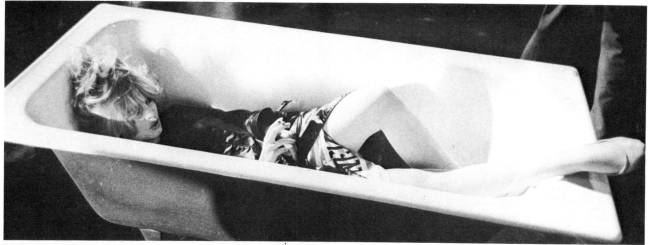

Contents

Bébé Doll:
the fesses that launched
a thousand strips....

Brigitte Bardot is no creation—more a recreation. No manufactured, Svengali dream-wish fulfilment, not of Vadim, nor anyone else. She is a state of mind, body and spirit. An attitude of body, as critic Raymond Durgnat specified; and a delight in it. A product, not entirely rare, of her time—not ours. Of Paris under the Nazi heel, of the Occupation and the preoccupation with treacherous Vichy politicking, black-market bitterness and the post-'45 French youthful delight in slick American commercialism. In order to sell by demand, first a demand has to be created—and *that* is where Roger Vadim strolled in. With him, and in the company of several like-minded attitudinists, the lucidly amoral, splendidly disdainful creature to be labelled BB was already self-established before Vadim drew it into the light of cinema projection. For some, the myth has stilled; the attitude remains, however, having drastically liberated much of the world's mores and, thereby, its tensions. She is past 40 now, an almost sacrilegious statement, not that many will, or can, believe it to be true. Attitudes do not age as fast as flesh. 'I am Brigitte Bardot,' says she. 'And that Brigitte Bardot—the one I see in the magazines and the newspapers, the one up on the screen, that Brigitte Bardot will never, for example, be 60.' Nor she will.

Her devastating image—and note, she mentioned the Press media version of it before the screen's—is time encapsulated for ever. Like Garbo—yet more blatantly, courageously; living dangerously in the ever-staring public eye—Bardot is untouched by age or reason and endures for her most ardent or even lukewarming devotees, the same as she always was, and surely, always will be. The essence of youth. Ageless youth. Her youth; our youth. A hank of hair, lank of leg, never considered classically beautiful (whatever that may mean), but with a mouth, a male chauvinist pig's dream of a mouth, and an androgynous figure of unbridled, and suggestively ambiguous, sensuality. This is the girl who washed away the pimples of global adolescence . . . while still struggling with eczema herself. She made growing up a distinct pleasure, chasing off post-war restraints and attacking the ruling-class hypocrisy with a warming, thrilling gusto. That girl is now a woman, she could be a grandmother before the end of this decade; yet the image, the mouth, the perfectly proportioned frame, reek no less of sexual musk. She remains no less a siren, no less a fond dream of an entire generation . . . or three.

It would not be beyond belief to nominate Bardot as the most famous Frenchwoman since Jeanne d'Arc. And without wishing to resort to the norm in filmic pomposity, cinema history can certainly be compartmentalised as *pré*-Bardot and *après*-Bardot. One can talk of few other artists in like manner. No other woman in particular has accomplished such revolutionary changes in style of films and indeed within all fashions and facets of global society as Bébé. She was at the vanguard of the brave new world of permissivity on-screen—and even more so, off it. The world was slow in catching up with her lead, but match her it did. In a life crowded with events—and men—she has lived enough for ten, twenty women or more. She has outlasted, outclassed, her so-called creator, outlived, outgrown, her supposed scandals (none of which broke up a home or a couple), and she has now attained a tenor of respectability, both abroad and in her homeland, that would have been considered risibly satiric in the 50s. Of late, she has begun a marked return to her bourgeois beginnings, in philosophic views if not in her essential free mode of living. This is not to suggest she has become

hypocritical in middle age—such an opponent of cant could hardly fall to that level. It is simply that the bourgeoisie she abandoned and now rejoined had gradually escalated itself to her level of honesty and freedom. 'I may be dead tomorrow, so I live for today. Tomorrow is a different day.' And this is this rôle for which she will always be remembered. She has

played it, to the hilt, for 23 years: a star of life itself rather than of the screen or any of the entertainment media.

If she never found acting second-nature to her, neither was it as traumatically horrendous as for Monroe. In her early trivial rôles, there is a definite, if appealing clumsiness about her, deriving more

from boredom than unease, and normally rescued by that puppy-like energy and eagerness to please, to strive above plots thinner than her costuming. She has, in the main, alternated between lightweight comedies, the harem-scarum, stripteasing with a mirthful joy in the distinct pleasures of her own torso—and heavy, often turgid, scripts, the sexual catalyst of tragedy, offering her indolent, almost documentary, challenge to the forever double-standard forces of respectable morality.

She succeeded in both strata as, clearly, herself; proving that while the screen is ever hypnotic, all the world is her stage. All the people . . . merely Bardolateers.

11

The BBeginning: Débourgeoisification

'*Love on the screen is neither physical nor spiritual, but something between the two. It is sensuality to the point of pleasure or nausea—or sensuality to the point of the most insupportable disgust. On the one hand, the lewdness of the physical becomes acute, even painful; on the other, it becomes something indeterminate, something not quite blue and not quite white—with the almost imperceptible taste of well-watered milk. The cinema always employs an uncertain interpretation of love, and never permits us to know whether what we are witnessing is ideal love, passionate love, carnal love, or love of some other well-known category. It leaves us with a vague sense of malaise.*'
—**Thomas Mann**

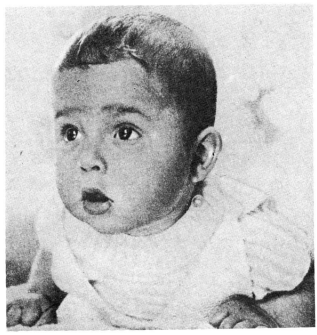

Infant. The baby Bébé and the . . .

Bald, save for three black hairs on the world's most instantly recognisable and copied blonde head, she was born on September 28, 1934; a big baby, 3 kilos 500 grammes, arriving in typical French style, in time for lunch at home, 35, avenue de la Bourdonnais. This was the family home in Passy, between the Seine, the Champ de Mars and the Eiffel Tower, centrepoints in the capital she would dominate as cinematic queen, and celebrity second only in appeal to that of the nation's post-Occupation saviour, De Gaulle. Their two figures stand physically and mentally at opposite ends of the epitome of *la vie française*, poles apart though in considerable awe of each other; the god-like ruler and the goddess, the greatest export-earner of the nation.

A Libra therefore, and she would have much need of the even temper the sign usually signifies. The French dote on astrology and it is a matter of family, even journalistic, record that the infant Bardot's horoscope in the *Petit Parisien* promised all girls born that day an artistic future, much travel and good health. What is less known is that the baby, to be known as just that—*Bébé*—made her first film appearance within minutes of gulping air. Her father photographed her with his new cine-camera toy. He filmed her first gestures, that is, not the actual birth; les Bardot were fundamentally too bourgeois by

Schoolgirl. In bow, braces and glasses.

13

nature to have even ruminated on that possibility. She also made the papers immediately—the birth appeared in the prerequisite columns of *Le Figaro*.

Brigitte was the Bardots' first child, and named after her mother's favourite doll. The family had an insufferable penchant for nick-names, and soon enough Brigitte was Bricheton, or more simply Bri-Bri. Her father, Louis Bardot—Pilou—was chairman and managing director of his own business at 18, rue du Pilier, in Aubervilliers. Bardot & Co. may sound like her own finishing school for young lovers, but was a company producing liquid air and acetylene— a clue, perhaps, to her own appetite for high-octane living. The family later moved to the rue de la Pompe. This is where, amid Louis XIV furniture and cream moquette carpeting, Brigitte grew up in comparative luxury, war or no war. Positive luxury compared to most of her screen contemporaries. A family of three, plus maid and nurse, in seven fifth-floor rooms, while Monroe was pushed from adoptive pillar to hastily married-off post, and Loren was one of nine crammed into four sweltering Pozzuoli rooms. Brigitte had a room of her own, in white, with an Empire sofa, a Romantic period dressing-table, a green divan, candelabra, her cat, Crocus, and two birds in a cage.

Her first sentence was delivered in English due to a British nurse, with whom she breakfasted each morning before bidding *bonjour* to her parents and going off for her daily constitutional and playtime in the nearby Bois de Boulogne. Her sister, Marie-Jeanne—Mijanou—was born in 1939, by which

14

Plaits. For *l'enfant terrible* tom-boy.

Pointe. For the ballet pupil of twelve.

time Bri-Bri was, on her own testimony, growing up very plainly indeed: in glasses, due to astigmatism, braces on her teeth and suffering almost permanent psychosomatic eczema. 'A monster,' she says. 'Perhaps it was being so ugly that made me try harder.' Life then was orderly and precise, the personification of respectability. Lunch every day was at 1 pm sharp; dinner at 8 pm exactly; in her later teens she would be allowed out late on Saturdays, as long as she obeyed Pilou's midnight curfew. When the summer heat drove the family from the city, there was the Norwegian chalet, *circa* 1870, to flee to in Louveciennes, near Versailles, and ski-ing was a must every winter at Meribel; a pattern Bardot has stuck fast to all her life, with her La Madrague summer home at St. Tropez, and the Le Chouan chalet at Meribel for *sports d'hiver*.

As a child, she was shy, sheltered, loved by strict, if doting, parents and spoilt by her grandparents, with more than sufficiency of expensive toys to provide a taste of more of the same in the future—when men became her playthings. M. Bardot was wealthy enough to send her to the élite Hattemar private school, an education she found both severe and indulgent. Not the background to breed ambition, then, apart from a paternal hope for the inevitable good match. 'It left me unprepared for life as I found it,' she has said. Neither school nor family instructed her in the facts of life, for example: 'My parents replied as well as they could without telling me lies. But I was quite ignorant . . .' Vadim, it could be said, changed all that. Not quite. Or at least not yet. He merely took

over, radically so, from Maman's own ambitions for her daughters, and for Bri-Bri in particular.

Mme. Anne-Marie Bardot—Totty—was a cultured woman from her own upbringing in Milan, where she studied music and dance. She was similarly rigorous with her girls and desirous of the same background, sent them for dancing lessons to Recco, a dancer at the Opera, and later into Mme. Bourget's classes in the rue Spontini. Bri-Bri went on to the Conservatoire Nationale de Danse under Boris Kniaseff; Leslie Caron was another pupil. The French saw the gamine Caron plucked from their midst by Gene Kelly, and ever chauvinistic about their stars, they did not like it; Bardot understood, and never flew from her Paris-based career.

With time, as well as two fairly ordinary-looking girls on her hands, Totty opened a small boutique in two

rooms on the rue de la Pompe; she sold hats and soon became an admirer of new designer Jean Barthet. And so it all started in late 1948, the first preliminary chess-like moves towards fame; started not by Vadim, the ogre to come, but by Totty herself, who owned to instincts about some kind of future success for her ugly-duckling first-born. Brigitte was shining in ballet class (she won more dancing than scholastic exams), and her mother suggested a ballet theme to Barthet for his first collection of hats, to be staged at the Drouand David Gallery: No. 36, *Entrechats* . . . No. 37, *Jetée-battue* . . . *et al*. Bri-Bri would be dancing model, of course. Barthet jumped at the notion; Brigitte, just 14, dressed in tutu, black ribbon and a rose in her corsage, modelled, feeling, so she said, rather silly. The audience thought otherwise; among them, the editress of the fashion magazine, *Jardin des Modes*. She asked Totty to allow her daughter to model some more—for a magazine teenage fashion spread. Totty was delighted with the result, complete with cover, which appeared later in 1949; less pleased, though, when the more prestigious *Elle* magazine rang up and asked for Brigitte to fill in for a missing cover-girl. Mme. Bardot did not hold with the cover-girls; it just was not the done thing in her circle. However, she obtained a promise that no names would be used. *Elle* suggested using initials only and so BB was born. She was paid 5,000 old francs and spent it on pigeons and a book for Pilou.

The cover appeared on May 2, 1949, and Brigitte was thrilled, any schoolgirl would be, and kept taking roundabout routes home from school, stopping at the multivarious newsstands and showing off the cover to her *copines*. Film director Marc Allégret saw it and found a dream realised; here, he thought, was his new Simone Simon, the girl he had made into a star with his film of the Vicki Baum tale, *Lac aux dames*, in 1934—the year Brigitte was born. Simone, never around long enough to become dubbed SS (and for obvious reasons, come the Occupation), had been described by critics as a child-woman with a winning, innocent depravity: the mould for the Bardot we know, love/hate today, the Bardot that Vadim is usually credited with having created. Allégret did it first and was in high hopes of repeating his formula; like Simone, Brigitte already had 'it' and Vadim simply took Allégret's dream, Bardot's instinctively sexpressive body, and merged them in an explosive cocktail promotion. Allégret was impressed enough with the girl in *Elle* to send his assistant off in search of her. The assistant, a young film and literary buff, who in the manner of all assistants, did everything and nothing for Allégret, was the son of a French mother and a Kiev-born diplomat. His father had died in front of him from a heart-attack at the breakfast table, when he was eight. A Byronic type, with the innate Russian indulgence for displaying his suffering, his soul, and soon enough, his women, to the world at large, his name was Roger Vladimir Plemiannikov. He, too, preferred diminutives, taking the shortened form of Vladimir: Vadim.

As their legend soared, Vadim was increasingly credited with noting Bardot in *Elle* himself, and persuading a reluctant patron to test her. The truth, in fact, is exactly the reverse, and Vadim has never veered from it. Allégret found Brigitte in *Elle,* asked Vadim's opinion, and received his usual non-committal answer: interesting. 'I didn't have any special opinion . . . then I wrote the little letter to her parents, asking if she'd like to meet Allégret.' Maman was horrified! She had feared all along that being a cover-girl would lead only to a bad end, and for Totty, no end could be deemed much worse than *le cinéma*. Brigitte, content with dreams of a manne-quin's career, was simply flabbergasted. 'I never saw myself as a star. Because as a child I was timid and self-effacing.' If it had not been for her grandfather—Boum Papa, of course; and by far the most fascina-ting man in her life up to this point—the film exercise would never have been even flexed. 'My parents were scared of films, but my grandfather, like the man of intelligence he was, said "Going into films will not make her a lost child".' He did not live long enough to see his prophecy collapse; saw the initial fame but died when she was 23 and making *Et Dieu créa la femme*—she could have greatly bene-fitted from Boum Papa's counsel in the turbulent years after that.

Totty was soon to rue the day she gave into *Elle*'s original entreaties, particularly when Vadim came to call. In the neat-as-a-pin Bardot family manse, Vadim *circa* 1950 cut a frightening figure—for the parents.

He was that dread image of the bohemian world, unshaven, in black turtle-neck sweaters. A demi-journalist, a quasi film-maker. And he actually dared say *tu* to Brigitte. Pilou and Totty recognised him as one of the hungry young men of Paris they had heard and read of, and, more than likely, feared. A reactionary, existentialist product of the St. Germain-des-Prés crowd, forerunner of *le beatnick* and the hippy, and throwback in part to the dealers of the Occupation. What the Americans would call a promoter. A hustler.

To Brigitte, he was 'as handsome as a god', with charm aplenty to win over Mme. Bardot as well. Set against the idea of her daughter entering the sinful movie world she may have been—and she was, she was—Totty dutifully trotted Bri-Bri along to meet Marc Allégret. Pilou was dead set against it; Totty saw no harm, she felt certain her girl would never make an actress. 'She will not make the movie, I know,' Totty told Vadim, 'but I won't stop and frustrate her. It's better she makes her own experi-ence. After, she will be able to marry the banker I am thinking of for her.' Not, then, an entirely success-ful encounter. Allégret did not rate mother or child; he liked the girl's mouth 'except she talked with her Mother's dental plate'. He agreed to test her all the same, and Vadim volunteered to prepare her. At the time, he was living in the apartment of his actor friend, Daniel Gélin, and Brigitte would arrive there each day direct from school for coaching. They then made the screen-test together, Allégret directing.

Once again: zero. Nothing came of the test, nor the film it was made for: *Les lauriers sont coupés/The Laurels Are Cut*. The film career of the cover-girl known as BB seemed over before it had begun.

Vadim did not relent so easily. There was something of the visionary in him even then, because, superficially at least, there seemed little cause for his courting the plainish schoolgirl with the haughty disdain of a moneyed childhood. 'I was,' she even admits, 'a complete little brat when he met me.' He knew her better—longer—than Allégret; during the coaching sessions of Gélin's place, Vadim saw her more relaxed, less nervous, more herself. He found her pretty, quite tantalising—or her potential was, at least. 'I wasn't immediately sexually aroused: for me, you have to have something to look forward to in sex. I do not like women who are totally aware of their beauty or their looks. There is nothing less sexy than a woman who knows what effect she has on a man.

'Two things struck me about her, then. First, her style. She had a way to be very free with her body. And her mind. When I say free with her body, I'm talking about the way she will walk, move, look at people, sit. She was a fantastic classic dancer—and she had the sort of grace and elegant movement that good, classic dancers have. She was also, for a little bourgeoise, in a certain way very revolutionary. She will approach life, any kind of problem, with a really free mind, which was interesting. And she had a very good sense of dialogue. Just a few words—and she was on the point. Great spontaneity. That is one reason for her success . . .'

As Brigitte recalls it, her first probable steps towards a film career, instead of a model's, coincided with her 15th birthday discovery of a further inch on her bust. 'No joking matter. I rushed to my mirror and dared it to tell me I would not make a mannequin. Inch by inch, I surveyed every detail of my body. A tiny waist—yes, that would be all right. Legs—yes, they were all right, as well. But my bosom! They'd never accept a bosom like mine. I had twice too much. And with my 19-inch waist, it looked ridiculous.' Not to Vadim. For him, she embodied the living image of *The Wise Sophie*, the heroine of his first novel written as a boy. 'The way she spoke —almost it seemed, in whole phrases from my book.' She began calling herself, and signing all her love letters to him as 'your little Sophie'. And he never stopped calling at the rue de la Pompe.

One anecdote from his *copains* has him feeling particularly suicidal over life and the lack of a film-directing break. He went through his little black book to seek some Tender Loving Care. *Rien!* He was down to the last notation when he spied the Bardot name and number: JASmin 82-86. He called her up. The timing could not have been better. Both parents were away in the Landes, and Brigitte and Mijanou were being looked after by their grandmother. She soon called the parents about this extraordinary young man coming around every night, filling the girl's head with endless lofty theories about films and sex, society and sex, the immortality of his generation, and what he was already beginning to call his 'sincere amorality'. .

Brigitte, he contended, had all the intangible right-stuff for the cinema. 'You have all the qualities of a

Pouce. One (model) girl and her thumb. Or how one of the world's most envied mouths was shaped.

Pose. The rising starlet—stars on holiday for her home-movie enthusiast father.

18

Family. Brigitte, still known as Bri-Bri or Bricheton, holidays at the Louveciennes chalet house with her heavily nicknamed kin: parents, Pilou and Totty, grandfather, Boum Papa, sister Mijanou—and, of course, a pet, Clown, the cocker-spaniel.

star. We shall work together to make you a success.'
She was nonplussed, she was no star, she thought; she had not the beauty of Jean Simmons, Ava Gardner, Maria Schell or Sophia Loren. 'My nose is a very bad nose. It is not shaped well. When I meet a man, it wrinkles up as though I were sniffing a bowl of milk. My mouth is not a good mouth; the lower lip is heavier and more swollen than the other.' Twenty years on, she still denigrates her looks—cheeks too round, mouth too large, eyes too small. 'I have,' she said recently, 'never thought I was beautiful, even when I was at the height of my fame.' Vadim recalls coming home to find his wife in tears at the mirror: it was her 21st birthday, she was old, she said, ugly—hideous!

The teenage Brigitte was more aroused by the man than his dreams. 'He was fascinating; he knew so much and seemed so free.' Not so, Brigitte. Her parents, aghast at their growing relationship, forbade her from seeing him. Vadim, today, still has 30 letters or more from Brigitte of that period: very bold, outspoken, direct and erotic letters for a girl of such a cloistered upbringing. Vadim realised the only way to avoid the crime of seducing a minor was to marry her. Brigitte's wildly proclaimed intention of doing just that was smote mightily by Papa Bardot who could not stand 'that boy—*c'est un zazou!*' Why, she had not reached her majority yet, nor even accomplished her baccalaureate. She never did, graduating instead from the Vadim Finishing School for Dream Girls. They quickly became lovers, of course, despite both parents vowing to shoot Vadim dead if she succumbed to him.

Allégret was due to work with Vadim in London (where they had filmed *Blanche Fury* in 1947); he wanted to take Brigitte with him. *Non,* said the parents and that was final, cuddly nicknames or not. Almost literally final for the girl. She chose to stay home the night Mijanou persuaded her parents to take her out to see the Notre-Dame floodlighting. Their car had not got much further than the Place du Trocadero, when Mme. Bardot felt a maternal presentiment and insisted on returning *immédiatement.* They found Brigitte unconscious, face downward by the kitchen gas oven. She had almost gone. 'All my life is his for ever. He is the only man I will ever want.' The parents relented. She could marry, but not until she was 18. 'Something in her broke,' writes Vadim in his autobiography, 'and she has never been the same since.' He blames her parents for forcing her to prove her love for him, condemning her to a three-year wait. 'At 15, it seemed like a life sentence. The three-year strain of being apart left a permanent mark on her.' Three months after that birthday, December 20, 1952, at the Town Hall of the 17th district and thereafter at the church of the Notre-Dame

Model. An early magazine modelling shot—gazing at the riches to come . . .

Marriage. Vadims and Bardots pose—stiffly—for the album in December, 1953, three months after Brigitte's 18th birthday.

de Grace in Passy, Vadim—'my first love . . . took me out of my bourgeois prison'—plighted his troth and was given his dream-wish girl, and proceeded to garnish her own attitudes, and his, into a kind of intercontinental nihilistic missile aimed at the hypocrisy of her class. She had the body and did with it as she felt; he had cunning, an agile, even devious brain, and the opportunist's flair for publicity. All they ever really lacked in concert was soul.

Once more, they were hardly assisted by Pilou's incredible strictness. After the civil marriage ceremony, he made up a camp bed for Vadim downstairs and ordered the couple not to sleep together—until after the church service next morning. 'Until then,' recalls Vadim's book, 'in his eyes, we were not married. At first, Brigitte thought it was a joke. When she realised her father was serious, she nearly choked.' They didn't need to look far for a target when they later made their names, pricking such terrifying pomposity.

Six years later on location in Spain for the second time, Brigitte was to say: 'I feel that I have missed out in life. I should never have made movies but now I'm in the rat race. At 18, I should have married someone stable, a real companion. We should have had children, a villa at Arcachon, and a lot of togetherness without dramatics. That would have been so marvellous. But in love, I have never counted. . . . People have blamed me for leaving Vadim, to whom I owe everything. It is true. Maybe I have hurt him, but perhaps I was not completely in the wrong.'

Roger Vadim began laying plans for his bride long before the actual wedding. He sent her to René Simon's drama school from where she won her first two films. Vadim insists he had nothing to do with obtaining the films, despite his various contacts. Brigitte had to make her start herself. She got little more than £220 for her début, *Le trou normand/The Norman Hole*. An empty hole as it turned out in 1952; it has still barely seen the light of day outside Paris, never seen at all in Britain, although it led to her British début, and was imported to the United States during the height of the BBoom, when it seemed Americans would queue and pay good money to see BB slides flashed on a screen.

The kind of outrage that was to cling to her firmly from the mid-50s onwards began as early as her second film, *Manina, la fille sans voile/Manina, Girl Without Veils*, also in 1952. In Casablanca, a priest tore down the movie posters depicting an all but naked Bardot; her itsy-bitsy bikini in the film was easily two sizes too small and almost certainly chosen by Vadim before she went on location to Tangiers. Papa Bardot was furious at the news. He had only allowed her to go abroad on the strict understanding there would be nothing offensive in

Preparations. For the big day.

Congratulations. From Marc Allégret.

the film. (There wasn't; just his daughter, blooming in her skimpy bikini and a split-second nude glimpse.) After winning a court order to preview the film for himself, M. Bardot secured some cuts, making sure the released *Manina* was not *sans voile* too much, or too often.

Released seven years later in Britain under the limericky title of *The Lighthouse Keeper's Daughter* (and *The Girl in the Bikini* in America, 1959), the film hardly set the box-office ablaze with customers or fury. Unifrance, the national film promotion office, however, selected Bardot as one of their '*espoirs d'aujourd'hui, vedettes de demain?*' 'A roguish face, full of character, 18 years of age and already married, she is one of the youngest starlets in French films.' Similarly nominated were such newcomers as her *Trou normand* co-star Nadine Basille, Genevieve Page, Magali Vandeuil, Barbara Laage . . . where are they now?

Vadim made sure his journalist friends—the *Paris-Match* building was their meeting place—got hold of Papa's outburst, and quickly exploited every other publicity trick that came his way to keep his wife in work, his promotion bubbling. There were, though, plenty who felt he was wasting his time. Veteran critic Paul Reboux was scathing: 'She is not pretty. Her lower lip is too thick. She has enormous eyes and the face of a skivvy.' Raymond Cartier in *Paris-Match* (not all the staff was friendly) said her acting was bad, diction deplorable, rôles lamentable and her beauty less than indisputable. Vadim told her not to worry as long as they wrote about her. He was not providing *le cinéma français* with just another typical *vedette française*: no new Martine Carol, for example. His thoughts were more inspired, like the

Cahiers du Cinéma critics, by the revitalised Hollywood dream machine, and the refreshingly new genre of *les films américains* beginning their battle royal with the TV seduction of their vast audience; a style and freedom that would, in turn, be heavily influenced by Vadim himself. Once he started directing, his work owed much to the impact of Joshua Logan's films, *Picnic* and *Bus Stop*. (Ironically, Logan is a godfather of Vadim's third wife, Jane Fonda, and directed her own screen début in 1960.) Though adoring the Hollywood panache, Vadim abhorred the conveyor-belt mentality methods. He did, however, eventually work in Los Angeles, and invited Bardot to join him: the only time she nearly agreed to film in Hollywood. Despite offers of 250,000 dollars per picture and upwards, plus percentage of profits, she always said no to America, the reason she is still Bébé today and not Doris Day.

For Brigitte, the first year of the marriage was the happiest. They had no money, life was exciting and Vadim was perfect. He talked magnificently and she was proud to be with him. 'Our love was so marvellous and so reciprocal. I used to wake up at night just so I could look at him. Little by little, the foundation of our love diminished. I was away from home much of the time—filming. At first I missed Vadim terribly. Later, I became used to our separations.' He had arranged most of them. Vadim was married to the movies with Brigitte as his eagerly compliant mistress. He thinks all wives should be mistresses first, but spent so much time with his 'wife', that he lost his 'mistress', almost encouraged her infidelity to a string of successively less involved men. What else from the man who quite simply invested his entire future into his wife's succulent young body. 'You are,' he insisted, 'going to be the respectable married man's unattainable dream.'

Certainly his determination far outweighed her ambition, of which, quite clearly, she had none. She did not enjoy her early films (nor did anyone else) and would have quit movies, except she wanted to please Vadim. 'Times were very tough at the start and I was often on the point of throwing it all in. Vadim alone guided me, sustained me, consoled me, gave me the love and the affection I needed and taught me to be courageous, and above all willing. Everything I know, I am, I owe to Vadim.'

In their small flat in the rue Chardon-Lagache—which her parents had given them along with Totty's tatty old Citroën—he toiled at changing his bride in small, subtle ways. Some less so. He taught her slang, to eat with her fingers, to turn her toothy smile into a sullen, sexual pout; improving what the Americans would call her corkscrew walk, and encouraging her to stroll naked around their rooms. 'Whenever I walked or undressed or ate breakfast, I always had the impression he was looking at me with someone else's eyes—and with everyone's eyes. Yet, I knew he was not seeing me, but through me, his dream. At that time I was enjoying myself, amused by what I thought his innocent eccentricities. I didn't realise myself how much he was playing with fire and, even though he is cynical, he didn't either. . . . He worked hard for me, arranging meetings with important film people, and dreaming up all manner of publicity stunts to establish me in the eyes of the public. He was, in part, a father to me. Or a brother. He taught me what life was all about and the terrible effort it needs to grow up; I was very wild and he made me into a sociable being.'

She made two more films in France (including her first American feature, *Act of Love*, in which her rôle was shorn by two-thirds; Totty had to see it twice to notice her at all); then another couple, including being second choice and general stand-in for *Helen of Troy*, in Italy—where she shared hotel quarters with Ursula Andress, another unknown refugee from the Vadim-approved St. Germain-des-Prés bohemian sect. Ursula was dating the Vadims' friend, noted French star Daniel Gélin, at the time. 'He had kidnapped her from school in Switzerland,' recalls Vadim. Gélin was making *Woman of Rome*, and Vadim was in and out of the city on another Allégret assignment, *Femina*. The trip brought Brigitte's total of movies to seven by the end of 1953. Her father preferred her one and only venture into the theatre, a far more respectable institution for the bourgeoisie. Brigitte created the rôle that Dany Robin later took over (and not, as is generally reported, vice versa) in *L'Invitation au château* by Jean Anouilh. He chose her himself and remembers her well—'an angel, simple, natural, spontaneous'. She was not struck by the stage. 'I can't do the same thing every night, the same gestures . . . it's like putting on dirty panties every day.' Anouilh adored her enough to pen an original screenplay for her, *The Ginger Cat*—never made, despite her love of its

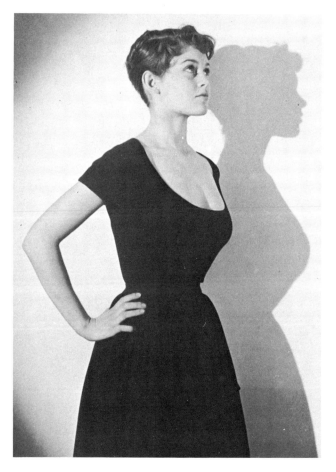

premise. 'I really am a cat,' she often purrs, 'transformed into a woman'.

Vadim continued his sales-*putsch*, making it clear that he was selling a personality, not an actress, indeed not even a personality but a phenomenon. 'Brigitte doesn't act—she exists.' He photographed her and showed what he called the printable shots around his Press pals, hinting broadly about the others, his strictly private collection, and even they were nothing—nudge, nudge—compared to seeing those curves in movement, in motion. The photographers either appreciated his feelthy-postcard candour or adored Brigitte for her own remarkable *joie de vivre*. Or they simply needed someone new in their lenses, because they nominated Brigitte as the girl of the hour. They could not photograph her during the 1953 Cannes festival, going to the rare extent of clubbing together to pay her hotel bill to keep her in town a few days more. She was a nobody at Cannes: and she stole the show from the established names, with graceful bikini posing on the beach. She won a greater triumph during the traditional visit to the US Navy in the bay. All aboard the aircraft carrier *Midway* they went: Kirk Douglas, Anne Baxter, Lana Turner, Olivia de Havilland, Lex Barker, Mel Ferrer, Edward G. Robinson, Raf Vallone, Leslie Caron, Sylvana Mangano, Vittorio De Sica. Gary Cooper was mumbling words of thanks to the crew when the French photographers pushed their favourite on the makeshift stage. 'Her raincoat slipped from her shoulders,' ran Raymond Cartier's *Paris-Match* report, 'she emerged in a tight-fitting teenager's dress and with a toss of her head sent her pony-tail flying. There was a second of silence, just enough for the electric discharge to pass the crowd of males and the figure in the floodlights. Then the *Midway* was engulfed in a single shot of lightning and a crash of thunder: thousands of flashbulbs and shouts of admiration that exceeded in volume all the previous acclaims put together.'

As American critic Dwight MacDonald commented, the geneticists who bred BB were looking to the American market. There on the *Midway* was Vadim's future audience in microcosm. The tide had begun to turn. His girl was something, after all.

His coaching stepped up. Brigitte remembers him instilling the facts of her new life: 'You can't get anywhere without working for it. So far, you've had some little success because of your beautiful body . . . but there's so much more to you than that. You must be conscientious, work hard and know how to use that body to advantage, how to show it off.' He taught her how—via one art-form the French had adopted from America and definitely improved upon: striptease. How to show all her body, yet not quite

Cannes. Brigitte the starlet was the cameramen's delight at the festival of '53. Kirk Douglas had to join her on the beach to be photographed at all.

all, plus various other erotic moves and modes he was improvising upon. He also took up the Monroe factor, getting Bébé to act more empty-headed than she was. Her intelligence rating was above-average; good in French, Latin and particularly in ancient history. 'We worked,' recalls Bardot. 'How we worked. Gradually I overcame my fear, I played more parts, better parts, even if they were smaller parts in other people's films.'

Four films followed in 1954, two only of any import to the BB-line. First, one written by Vadim at last, for Marc Allégret, *Futures Vedettes/Sweet Sixteen*; like Allégret's classic Simone Simon vehicle it came from a Vicki Baum novel and allowed Vadim, the master-exploiter, free rein in presenting his child-bride on-screen the way he envisaged. Next, her invitation by no less an august arm of the dwindling British film industry than the similarly run-down Rank Organisation—to replace Kay Kendall in *Doctor at Sea*. Producer Betty Box had seen Bardot's pretentious début film in a Riviera cinema, and had noted her enormous impact in the Continental film magazines (as she was to repeat with various of the copy-BB's, Elke Sommer, Mylène Demongeot, Claudia Cardinale). The British Press, easiest in the world for a pretty girl to conquer, loved her from her opening malapropism at London Airport: 'I've brought several nightdresses because I' hope someone will invite me out.' The photographers popped flashes and eyes,

the norm from then until now, and fought to capture her for every front page in town. Vadim was astonished. Anouk Aimée, he remembered, had been in London before Bardot and her coverage had been scant in comparison. 'But that is really the secret of Brigitte. The impact she has on people. You know, there is a certain kind of person who arrives in a room and you don't know for what reason—you are talking to someone else, maybe—but you feel this presence and you have to turn your head and watch this person. Maybe to criticise, maybe to compliment. But you *have* to turn and watch. Brigitte had this kind of quality. A real break with the tradition of the actress at this time. It did not mean she was a great actress—her style was quite different. And totally natural.'

Her impact upon the staid Pinewood studios was to prove exactly the same. 'People would stroll on the set to look at her and we couldn't get them off again,' recalls director Ralph Thomas. 'For weeks, all the men in the studio were going around with cricks in their necks, you know. She really has the most fabulous legs.' They actually got to see much more than the legs. In one sequence, the star of the comedy, Dirk Bogarde, catches Bardot unawares, showering in his cabin. Bogarde stutters, 'I suppose I'll be seeing more of you presently.' He did. Everyone did on the set. A firm believer by this time in the Vadim-fed naturalism of life and filming, Brigitte strongly objected to the mock-undies she was given to avoid nudity in the shower. *Pourquoi?* For, well, your protection, luv. *'Non—vraiment?'* Cinematographer Ernest Steward complained, too: the coveralls showed through the shower curtain, no matter which way he lit the set. That was cue enough for Brigitte. She solved the problem simply by tearing off the panties and nipple-covers, and shooting the scene nude. *'Very* daring at that time,' comments Ralph Thomas. 'But she was always proud of her body—an exquisite creature.' Daring it was; and even if no more flesh than a shoulder and her lately labelled Pekinese face were to be seen peeking around the shower curtain, it probably constituted the first naked actress in a British film studio.

Both Box and Thomas, and after them the British public, were delighted with her performance. 'Before long,' said Thomas, 'she will be one of the biggest stars in the business.' A hackneyed line, but rapidly true in this instance. The couple would have leapt at any chance of starring Bardot again; frankly they could never afford her. Not that Brigitte forgot them. She writes to them still and sends Christmas cards. Vadim, too, always credits the British with really having discovered his girl and putting her on the world screen map.

Pin-up. After Cannes, the lensmen never stopped queuing and the sultry shots flooded world magazines.

With the British-generated fuss over Brigitte—to say nothing of the dumb American censors attacking her walk as too provocative in the otherwise harmless film; and this one year after Monroe's swinging derrière filled the CinemaScope screen in *Niagara*—the French took a new look at Vadim's protégée. And she was starred in a film that exemplified the French genre of the period: *La lumière d'en face/ The Light Across the Street*. A *petit*-film to the French—'a hot wife with a cold husband', ran one review—it was a mammoth eye-opener to the British. Critics recognised the deficiency of home-made films, of what the more straight-jacketed British directors had not (or dared not) photograph: the vibrant inner sexuality of the girl suddenly likened to animals of one feline nature or another. Until the set piece with

Vadim one year and four films later, *Lumière* constituted Bardot at her most erotic, a sweltering frustrated child-bride with a tragically impotent husband and a virile neighbour. She oozed rampant sensuality from every pore . . . and this before Vadim really began to exploit her sensual gifts. He noted their impact. 'It was, I remember, considered a kind of B *érotique* movie then,' comments Vadim. 'And it was popular in the way people today will go to see a pornographic movie. It was not bad; there is some interesting feeling in it.'

Veteran René Clair featured her next, exhorting her comedic flair for the subplot of *Les Grandes Manœuvres*; his pupil, Michel Boisrond, began his directing career, and the first of his three and a half excellent films with Bardot, with *Cette sacrée gamine*.

This was called *Mam'zelle Pigalle* in England, which meant her next import, *En effeuillant la marguerite* which really meant *Plucking the Daisy,* was smartly retitled *Mam'selle Striptease.* She was an amateur ecdysiast in a second Vadim script for, by and with Allegret. Between the two, she played Poppea in *Mio figlio Nerone/Nero's Week-end* in Rome where, on Vadim's say-so—it's said so—she milked as many headlines as possible out of a supposedly nude bathing scene, by demanding milk in the tub, asses' or otherwise, instead of the producer's cut-price mixture of whitewash!

The French critics were no kinder, but across the English Channel, the new *Mam'zelle* items, coupled with the *Doctor at Sea* impact, and the major triumph of *Lumière,* meant she had conquered new land. Vadim helped write the publicity notes for *Lumière,* including this portrait of the wife he was about to share, openly, with the world:

'She is more advanced than children of earlier generations. Along with this, she has blank spots. She knows Egyptian history down to the smallest detail, but I had to teach her that rats don't lay eggs and that the moon always presents the same side to the earth.

'She cannot fry an egg, but she covered the chairs and divans at home as well as a professional could. She drives her car in Paris with all the assurance of a taxi-driver, but she fears spirits which become invisible monsters. It is to protect her from these monsters when I am working that I bought her the cocker spaniel, Clown. Here in order after Clown, is what Brigitte likes most in the world: other dogs, birds, the sun, money, the sea, flowers, period furniture, grass, kittens and mice. I did not dare ask her where she placed me, perhaps between the grass and the kittens . . .'

He would have to write no more hand-outs. Brigitte's contract for two more films with the since dead producer of *Lumière* was taken up by a promoter even smarter than Vadim: Raoul J. Levy, not yet 30, financially ruined five times and ever ready for a new gamble. He naturally conferred with Vadim and offered him *carte blanche* on the film the latter had running through the back of his mind, a heady cocktail mixture of the fantasy and reality of his four-year-old marriage to his hoydenish discovery, a film with BB about the wild girls of Paris . . . which finished up

Art. The Vadims used paint as well as cameras. He sketched her as the Sophie of his first novel (top); she saw him, and indeed herself, with far more lustre.

Promoter. By June '56, the Vadim duo became a torrid trio with the inking of contracts with producer Raoul J. Levy.

Cannes. The Vadims return to the festival of '55. While shooting their sexplosion just around the corner...

as one about one wild girl only, and of St. Tropez, a lazy fishing village, quiet and still in the sun since the Allies landed there in the D-Day back-up campaign. 'In those days,' Levy told *Cosmopolitan*, before it too changed in the post-BB permissive world, 'we were just three penniless bums who couldn't get ourselves arrested. We went to Columbia Pictures about a release. They threw us out. We came right in again—through the window!' Their stumbling block was obvious: no star. The German actor, Curt Jurgens, was considered 'hot' at that time, and Vadim and Levy chased him to Munich, and impressed him by taking over an entire floor at the Four Seasons Hotel. They had no money to pay for it. Why worry—they had no storyline for Jurgens, either. They saw him as a probable Onassis figure—a good excuse to hire a yacht for the shooting. And Jurgens loved boats. He fell for their quickly improvised story and promised them just 15 days of his over-committed schedule.

Columbia agreed to finance them *if* they really had Jurgens buttoned up. No cash until he showed. This put a blight on all manner of routine pre-production chores, including the relatively important area of having a script written. Jurgens, minus any form of

scenario, cabled them to forget him—with 14 days to go to his starting-date. 'Vadim and I got to work,' recalled Levy, 'and wrote one ourselves in four days.' Jurgens arrived, so did the money, and shooting began in an exceedingly haphazard manner. After his promised 15 days, Jurgens departed and doubles had to replace him in long-shots and re-shot sequences. Improvisation remained the keyword throughout—and Bardot has never stuck to a scenario text since. She prefers, like many Method actors, to make words fit the characterisation and not vice versa. And since a Bardot characterisation is, or most certainly was, merely Bébé herself—she wrote her own dialogue as she spoke it. In any event, her actions spoke much louder than any written lines.

As far as Vadim was concerned, Britain had been conquered, and British taste was not so very far removed from that of America. The time then, 1956, was ripe, indeed it could not have been better—and Vadim and Bardot let rip with the biggest sexplosion the European screen had seen since or before the war. With his title, Vadim acknowledged who held the copyright on his 'creation': *Et Dieu créa la femme*.

33

The Fiery Fifties: Vadimification

'What was he to make of Brigitte? A vamp? No, men just returned from five years of war were no longer disposed to be taken in by the obvious wiles of a social climber, a gold-digger or a female spy. A young virgin? That could imply a purity ill-suited to the nature of and hardly likely to be appreciated by the men of the 1960s. A lascivious child, perhaps? A nymphet, a Lolita? But that wasn't Brigitte at all; she was a true woman. Very young, yes. Perverse? Wicked? Not exactly. Rather audacious, immodest, but with the innocence of a young animal. There lay the secret of reaching the most blasé spectator: so much sheer naturalness simply couldn't be ignored.'
—André Maurois, in *Playboy*

In 1951, only 350 British cinemas screened foreign-language product, usually X-rated. Six years later, as the BBoom began, the total was in excess of 4,000. 'The reason more people went to see X films,' stated the then British Censor, Arthur T. L. Watkins, 'is because the public is growing up.' Mr. Watkins and his decidedly non-liberal British Board of Film Censors, alas, were not among them. At his office in Soho Square—the most apposite of addresses—he took one look at *Et Dieu créa la femme* and blew his august top. He refused any kind of certification point-blank, akin to banning the film entirely. Later, encouraged no doubt by its markedly unfevered reception in Paris, he agreed to certain cuts and the film opened. There seemed even then, let alone in hindsight, little worth the blunt scissoring. Bardot was undressed for less than five minutes in all (if that), and as Vadim argued long into the night, only in wartime did humans tend to mate fully clothed. Censor-hacked or not, *Et Dieu créa la femme* is the definitive watershed film of the 50s for the French and the international cinema; even though some termed it simply a water-closet film. More than Bardot herself, the film bred the new-wave in Paris and thereafter in every major film-making capital, utilising unfettered expressions of sexual, at times sensual, realism—an effect reverberating still.

In the sparsest terms, the film is the tale of a shimmeringly on-heat adolescent girl, openly encouraging three brothers and one sugar-daddy to try and quench her fire. Bardot strips, teases, pouts (of course), dances, writhes, rocks, rolls: a constant invitation to coïtus. Quite naturally, the movie created a firestorm wherever it played (outside of France, that is), praised for its youthful truths, put down as a sex-opera without music or morals, adored by sensualists, attacked by the clergy with the kind of vehemence denying their deity's major attribute of forgiveness. Jehovah's Witnesses condemned Bardot to eternal damnation, and in one New York township three opposing religious factions launched ecumenical union a full decade early, in order jointly to ban the film from their brethren's sight.

Although quickly dismissed in France, it soon became a new entry in the record books of box-office bonanzas—earning in America alone, the equivalent of more than 250,000 exported Renault Dauphines. Long before the end of the 50s, it had made a colossal impact upon the mores and morals of the cinema, the world . . . and of Brigitte Bardot herself.

Censors kept using nudity as their ploy to defeat the film's other objects. Vadim recalls one French censor screaming that 'the scene where she jumps off the bed naked' had to go. There was no such scene! Vadim ran the sequence through a moviola, slowly, to prove his point: BB was wearing a sweater. 'But he honestly believed she had been nude because he wanted to believe it . . . to see it.' So did her audiences. Throughout her career, Brigitte has rarely been viewed fully naked, preferring to be the quintessence of teasing arousal; yet her most ardent of followers will talk of one nude sequence or another, a d take hours of convincing before realising they, too, saw only what they wanted to see.

What really rattled the world censorship groups was not what Bébé did or did not reveal physically—but mentally. What affronted them and, on average, their middle-aged, middle-class values was this girl's 'wicked' attitude towards sex: thoroughly masculine by orientation. There are those, Jane Fonda among them, who stoutly proclaim the film as being the first cinematic blow for women's liberation. 'She may have been portrayed as a beautiful sex object,' Fonda told *Playboy*, 'but Brigitte Bardot ruled the roost. She kicked out any man she was tired of and invited in any man she wanted. She lived like a man in Vadim's films.' Outside them, as well.

Vadim's game-plan was more revolutionary in impact than concept. Inspired by a leading lady he knew more intimately than anyone, he made a dialectically sound merging of two of the screen's most traditional personas: the ingénue and the femme-fatale, the gamine and the vamp. In short: Allegret's child-woman, and before him, Pabst's, and more recently, Ingmar Bergman's in *Summer With Monika*, which Jean-Luc Godard likened to the Vadim vehicle. To consolidate further his fusion of forces, Vadim mixed in innocence with sensuality—or depravity, depending upon which side of the censorial fence one fell off from.

Vadim had taken his cue from his master, de Sade;

Team. Bardot on Vadim: 'It's never any good trying to impress him with mood or hot tempers. If you fly into a rage he won't hit back. He'll take it and not turn a hair. He's always in complete control. In a different way that's why he's such a good director. He knows exactly what he wants. No one can tell him. You never wonder: Is he right? Because it's him, you know it must be. Even when we made our early pictures together and he was virtually unknown, he'd tremendous confidence in himself. And he knows how to handle me in front of the cameras better than anyone . . . he understands me very well.'

Team. Vadim on Bardot: 'We've known each other so long that I'm the only person who can tell her anything. She has to be surrounded by people who treat her like a queen—which I don't. I'm the only one she respects—and she knows I love her. Our love has nothing to do with passion. Brigitte is now an old *copine* [pal] . . . I feel like a brother towards her, would do anything to help or protect her. I never thought she'd retire for good for she has become a good actress. She had temperament when I found her. Now she has talent.'

even the Bardot character was named Juliette. And Vadim's message was that the rôle had been no acting performance at all. This was the real thing! Brigitte was Juliette, not vice versa, and the scandal tales from the location seemed to prove the argument. She was, as André Maurois wrote for *Playboy*, 'a *petite*, sulky, tousled beast of the jungle . . . No vamp nor woman of *élégance* . . . By preference, she lived in the nude.' If she wore anything, it would be blue jeans, sweater or a plain, cotton dress.

'Her role,' declared Vadim, selling the movie without stint, 'allowed her to open herself completely and show what she has within her of anguish, of dynamism, of sexuality, confidence and lack of conscience . . . passion without excesses and entirely free in her sexual behaviour.' She was, he insisted, representative of the psychosis of the post-war French generation. Brigitte followed his lead and told all interviewers that *oui, bien sûr*, she was as amoral as Juliette. 'I correspond to the sort of girl who personifies our epoch. The Mae West type would be out of touch for now. I'm the kind of girl every man in France has a chance to meet. I play myself— I'm not good enough to play somebody else. That's why I like simple, wild, sexy parts. I must resemble my generation—that's why they've adopted me so nicely.'

Her generation vigorously denied the analogy; they were, many of them said, far more serious in mind and work, and thought naught of the Vadim-Bébé world, allied as it was to that of Françoise Sagan and other artists they equally distrusted. Actually, the youth Bardot did represent in the film was the one slice Vadim happened to know best: the *blouson-noir* version of the English Teddy Boys and America's drug-store cowboys; the restless brigade gratuitously flouting every convention minus any replacement philosophy, apart from instinctual self-gratification, self-satisfaction and self-aggrandisement.

And so began the Bardot cult. Not one of youth, as so often said—and by Vadim predominantly—but, as to be later defined in all her other films up until the present dearth, the cult of perpetual immaturity. Avoiding too much religious wrath in Britain, Miracle Films cut the use of God in the most cele-brated title of the year and rephrased it: *And Woman . . . Was Created*. (God came back ten years later in their re-issue.) Their sales-tag told the rest: 'but the devil invented Bardot'. This was Raoul Levy's idea for the original French campaign after the president of the French censorship board exclaimed during the film, 'That's Satan!' Vadim has been known as the devil in person ever since to much of the media and certainly (so he says) to the world's housewives; consequently he called the first section of his auto-biography, *The Devil's Memoirs*.

Fortune. Luxury, of a kind, arrived, and with it...

BRIGITTE BARDOT, comme 9
stars sur 10, emploie le savon de
toilette LUX. Elle aime la douceur
de LUX, sa fraîcheur parfumée

sous feuille d'OR

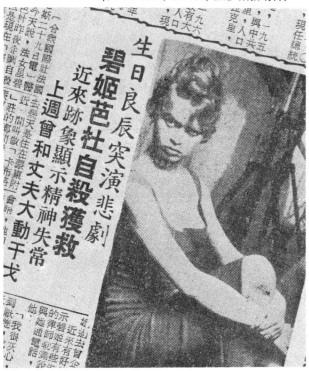

Fame. She became *the* news of the world.

As with all inventions, timing was everything. Whether Vadim's patent was inspired or merely fortuitous is relatively unimportant any more. As he says, all he did was take a piece of gold and show it to the people, saying 'This is gold'. He had not created the sensual, turn-on Bébé doll, but simply developed Brigitte's joyously natural instincts. He was though, without doubt, slap-bang, dead-centre upon the target of his times. Together with Brigitte, he set a new enfranchisement which the entire film world rushed to follow, ridding cinema of its laughable sexual fantasies and symbols (the effusive copulation euphemisms of fireworks, waves crashing onto rocks, coupling railway carriages and even Hitchcock's penile train rushing into a vaginal tunnel). Gradually, directors turned instead to an honesty of purpose in word and deed, action and sound, a truth more appropriate to the times and climes within their characterisation, improvisation, extemporisation, in images and in import. (And in export, too.)

In Great Britain, the new Continental cinema boom had begun slowly in the mid-50s. New distribution companies locked into the often saucy output from Europe, France and Italy in the main; the films, complete with sub-titles, played in London, plus university and other major cities of the realm, in the equivalent of America's art-houses (where, in fact, even the British films were considered foreign). Sub-titles, according to the forever out-of-date movie-row pundits in Wardour Street, would prove too much for the average cinemagoer. No one actually dared say that the average British film fan could not read, but such was heavily implied in the ban on general releases for foreign-language productions. Besides, Europe offered eroticism and, as everyone knew, that simply wasn't British. Hollywood exports survived because any threats they offered to the libido were watered down, not to say completely faked. Anyway, the British, surely, only really went for men's trousers falling down ... Until 1953 and the prize-winner from the very Cannes festival Brigitte had conquered with pin-uppity charm.

The winning item was *Le salaire de la peur/The Wages of Fear,* Clouzot's spine-jangling exercise in sweaty tension, as Yves Montand, Charles Vanel, Peter van Eyck and others drove lorries packed with high-explosive nitroglycerine to an oil refinery fire: one bump and goodbye Charlie! This became the first foreign film to win a general release in Britain, and the gritty suspense obviated any moans about sub-titles. A Swedish documentary followed, Arne Suckdorff's *The Great Adventure,* the 1954 Cannes winner. Then along came Fernandel, already familiar to the art crowd as Don Camillo, playing six rôles in *Le mouton à cinq pattes/The Sheep Has Five Legs*. Martine Carol, the French Esther Williams—except she swam in baths, and always *sans* suit—won wider exposure and the majority of the invidious censor slashes when daring to bare an elbow or some equally unimportant area of flesh. Jules Dassin's *Rififi*, genesis of each and every robbery caper film since, also won general release status—the sub-title argument being ruled out by the robbery being executed in total silence for almost one-third of the riveting film.

Where France and Italy, and to a lesser extent Germany and Scandinavia, prospered abroad, the other 'new' film nations followed. India arrived with Bima Roya Roy's *Two Acres of Land*; Greece entered with *Stella* from Michael Cacoyannis; Japan supplied the unique artistry of Kurosawa in *Rashomon* and *Seven Samurai*. Soon enough, names like Martine Carol, Yves Montand, Gina Lollobrigida, Jean Gabin, Françoise Arnoul, Sophia Loren, Jacques Tati, Melina Mecourey (sic), Vittorio De Sica and Toshiro Mifune were becoming as familiar and as popular as the home stars busily aping their Hollywood opposites so badly.

The influx rolled on, even an expurgated version of *Lady Chatterly's Lover*, a mish-mash mixture of French *élan* (Danielle Darrieux as Lady C), British upper-lip stiffness (Leo Genn as his lordship), Italian perversity (Erno Crisa as Mellors) and censorial obstinacy—the unkindest cuts of all, but this was years before the Lawrence book could even be lawfully sold unabridged in his own country. Gradually, however, the doors of the day's screen strictures were being forced ajar, and the nasty foreign films were gaining respectability and acceptance. By 1956 —Bardot's cinematic birth year—a French short, Albert Lamorisse's award-studded classic, *The Red Balloon*, won selection as supporting feature for the dreadful Pinewood-in-uniform *Battle of the River Plate* at the eleventh Royal Film Performance.

Brigitte was among the stars lined up and presented to HM the Queen at that October première. So was Marilyn Monroe. The only time the two rival sex-symbols ever met, or at least saw each other in the flesh, albeit well gowned. An occasion of some historic significance, felt the *Saturday Evening Post*, as BB met face to face with MM, bowing 'as low as their engineering would permit'. Brigitte never forgot Marilyn. '*C'était unique!* She could not curtsy . . . couldn't move her legs, her dress was so tight. The panic in her eyes!' Sunday-paper columnist Robert Robinson would hardly forget the Balmain-dressed Bardot, either. Asked how she liked Englishmen, she told him: 'To tell you the truth, I haven't tried any!'

Meanwhile in France, the young critics on *Cahiers*

Who is the woman they all talk about?

★ BARDOT

Who is the woman in the news today—and every day?

BARDOT ★

The only newspaper to discover the real Bardot is the News of the World.

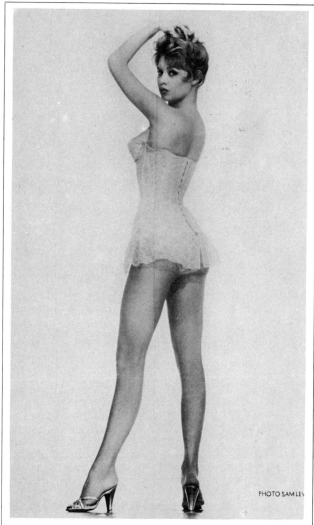

PHOTO SAM LEV

Frame. French photographer Sam Levin's cultish undies-shot became magazine centre-spreads, Paris post-cards (outselling those of the Eiffel Tower) and a life-size cut 'n' stick pin-up in one sell-out issue of Britain's *Reveille* journal.

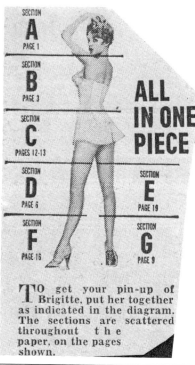

SECTION A PAGE 1
SECTION B PAGE 3
SECTION C PAGES 12-13
SECTION D PAGE 6
SECTION E PAGE 19
SECTION F PAGE 16
SECTION G PAGE 9

ALL IN ONE PIECE

TO get your pin-up of Brigitte, put her together as indicated in the diagram. The sections are scattered throughout the paper, on the pages shown.

du cinéma and other film-addict magazines were beginning to rebel against the kind of Parisian screen product going so well overseas. No class, no content, they contended, these young Turks living, breathing, eating, drinking and digesting movies all around the clock. They preferred the brash American features, even the B-thrillers rarely considered worth review in Britain and America. Something was lacking in French films, they felt—and they were it. The revival of Abel Gance's work at the Cinémathèque pinpointed the lack of originality in French studios; every critic grabbed a hand-held camera and set about creating apace. They required less money on budgets and more artistic licence, and took both where and how they could, often risking savings, small inheritances and family loans on their efforts in a manner their British counterparts would never have dared to consider from the safety of their place in the bar after film previews.

Vadim and Bardot showed them all how with their legendary *Et Dieu créa la femme* in 1956: immediate forerunner of what *L'Express* journalist, France's first female assistant director and lately Cabinet minister Françoise Giroud, was to call 'la nouvelle vague' in 1957. The new-wave began, in the main, with Claude Chabrol's *Le Beau Serge*, although it is true that Jean-Pierre Melville had sown the seeds ten years previously with *Le silence de la mer*, followed by Agnès Varda's *La pointe courte* in 1955. Neither had the insolent flair, mercurial impact and colossal financial success of the Vadim-BB number —French polished eroticism with the James Dean generation firmly in mind. Their triumph, with shoe-string budget and no front-office chains, made everyone else pile in. The *Cahiers* group, François Truffaut, Claude Chabrol, Jacques Rivette, Jean-Luc Godard, Jacques Doniol-Valcroze; the left-bank clique, Alain Resnais, Henri Colpi, Agnès Varda and her husband, Jacques Demy; and the more independent Louis Malle, Alexandre Astruc, Marcel Camus and Jean-Pierre Mocky.

In the 1959–60 period of resuscitated French film activity, no fewer than 67 new directors made their first features; less than half ever made more than three in all. Sadly, Bardot was to work with remarkable few of the survivors of the breakthrough she had helped champion. Truffaut always sang her praises loudly: 'More than an actress, she's a person . . . unique.' But as her fame became too commercial for them, BB was less adored by the new *Cahiers* critics; whereas in May, 1957, in the editorship days of André Bazin, Jacques Doniol-Valcroze and Erich Rohmer, she was given space aplenty to report her admiration for James Dean and *East of Eden*, for Monroe and Loren. The Bette Davis-Joan Crawford school left her cold, and her generation agreed

Majesty. Flanked alphabetically by Dana Andrews and Ian Carmichael, the new queen of France meets Queen Elizabeth II of England at the 1956 Royal Film Performance. The selected film was hardly BB fare—*The Battle of the River Plate*. Marilyn Monroe was there and so was Princess Margaret.

Classic. Brigitte laughs as one of the crew shares the best view of her during the opening shot of *Et Dieu créa la femme*. The camera (alas) stayed on the other side of the sheet.

with her on this point, at least.

Vadim and Bardot were written up the world over as Pygmalion and Galatea, French style. Their producer, the late Raoul Levy, enjoyed his hour of glory too, admitting the entire *Et Dieu* enterprise had been a total gamble from start to finish, and had come exceeding close to never being made at all.

June, 1956, along the Midi, was incandescently hot—as the film shows in more ways than one. Journalistic interest was tepid, not to say cool, the London's *Daily Mirror*'s Donald Zec being about the only English-speaking columnist to turn up on the heady set, and he quit before the sparks began flying. America, unlike Britain, had not yet submitted to the BB overtures, and besides, their own sex-symbol was headline news again—marrying Arthur Miller and filming in London with Olivier. *Paris-Match*, busy on MM patrol, cared little for the BBeat.

As well as the script, Vadim provided his closest *copain*, actor Christian Marquand, to play his wife's lover; and selected a raw-boned newcomer to be her screen husband, Jean-Louis Trintignant (now married to Marquand's director sister, Nadine). But what scant publicity did emanate from St. Tropez, the little fishing village they were all about to put on the world map, along with themselves, centred firmly around Mme. Vadim. On her meeting with Picasso. On Levy rushing her up to Sir Winston Churchill, visiting the Nice studios. 'Allow me, Sir

Winston, to introduce the star of the French cinema, Brigitte Bardot,' said a breathless Levy. Said Churchill: '*Décidément, le cinéma français est charmant.*' (When Churchill's war-time army commander, Viscount Montgomery, was quizzed on his BB views, he replied: 'Never set eyes on her . . . at the cinema or in the newspapers. But I'm meeting Marlène-whatever-her-name-is at lunch tomorrow.')

Soon enough, the location copy became as heated as the weather. The love scenes were being called the most realistic since *Ecstasy*—except Bardot required no stabs with a pin to cue her feigned orgasms as Hedy Lamarr had suffered at de Machaty's hand. The love action was all too real and never stopped when the cameras had to. Vadim's passion had switched from his 'mistress' to his 'wife'—cinema. His cries of encouragement as Brigitte made screen love with Marquand on the beach, more importantly with Trintignant on the marital bed, shocked even his free-minded crew.

Bardot, for reasons best known to herself—'I was trying everything to keep our marriage going'—did all he asked of her. And more. She it was who refused to cease cinematic-copulation when camera magazines had to be reloaded, or when Vadim called a hoarse '*Coupez!*' Evidently, she was testing the mettle of her husband. If he realised it, he never showed it. Levy thought Vadim regarded his relations with Bébé as a game. 'He felt it exciting to let her drift just out of reach and then catch her back at the last moment.' So, he would compliment her work and she would try again and again, pushing herself to the limits of what passed for propriety in the Vadim household, craving for jealousy to manifest itself within Vadim. The plot did not work. Except on the heated screen.

Not that Vadim ever really went as far beyond the bounds as was always suggested. 'The censors cut more out of the film than I ever did. Obviously I cut some material because when you make a film, you have perhaps three hours of movie and you cut to 100 minutes. I didn't have three hours: I shot a short movie. So the only cuts were by censorship. At this time, you could not show a woman naked, if you saw the pubic hair. You really could not show two people making love, if you actually saw the *sexe*. So you had to suggest it all by close-ups and things. So then, there is not so many things to cut . . . because I didn't shoot them! Despite the rumours, the stories, no one has ever made love for real in this or any of my films. I am not against it. I hope it will come about. I don't yet know how to do it without the usual circus-like gymnastic spectacle. Perhaps the way to do it is to train myself to be cameraman, camera *opérateur* as well as director—to do everything myself. And then? What is most important is that you must not cheat. You can pretend you die, you can pretend you are furious, you can pretend to hate—but it is very difficult to pretend an orgasm. That's another kind of death—in French we call it *la petite mort*. So how to capture this crazy moment of a kind of schizophrenia? Very difficult. I don't think you *need* to make love, but you must be in the mood, the atmosphere. Otherwise, even if you are the biggest actor in the world, it will look like the Crazy Horse Saloon!'

Of *l'affaire* Trintignant, Vadim recalls that his wife felt the actor not the type at all—too small, too ugly. Not, however, for long. In his book, the director notes: 'His attitude was not very elegant, but I granted him the excuse of youth. Brigitte was crying and I was sincerely upset by her plight. She was my wife but, in a way, she was also my daughter . . .'

And then, Bardot plainly did not care any more. She would leave the bed-sets with an aggressive smile. Trintignant would follow; eventually, she never returned to the Vadim suite at their hotel. Filming over, Vadim returned to Paris alone and moved into an hotel. He had made his film his way; lost his wife, his 'mistress'—and then fought, tooth and nail, to retain every *millimètre* of the very footage that had lost her for him. 'It was inevitable for me to lose Brigitte,' he was to say. 'I could see they were in love and because I knew it would happen sometime, I allowed it to go its natural path. I knew it wouldn't

last.' It didn't, but the affair was not that brief either, and the Bébé-Vadim marriage, if not their friendship, was over.

For Brigitte, her second lover—she called him Jean-Lou; she was, naturally, Bri-Bri—was the image of James Dean. Trintignant was also married at the time, though separated from his wife, actress Stephane Audran (now Mme. Claude Chabrol). He loved everything about Brigitte except who she was. 'She is too much in the public eye. I'd like her just to be a woman. I can't forget the millions of men who have looked at her in the cinema and who'd like to kiss her, too.' At their first meeting, he thought her conceited, fancying herself as a great star; in the fracture of her marriage, he discovered her sensitivity. 'She appeared to have everything to make her happy and yet she wasn't.'

Bébé adored his strength, his treatment of her and the fact that, unlike Vadim, Trintignant showed jealousy if she even glanced at another man. Such jealousy was vital to Bardot, a tangible proof of love. (In a joint interview with Françoise Sagan, Brigitte could not believe that the writer had never experienced jealousy in her life. It was, she said, impossible.) Eternally feminine, she was to use Jean-Lou's jealous streak as a major cause of their break-up six months later. The truth, said Levy, was that she needed a man devoting his life to her, on call 24 hours a day. Trintignant went absent: he was called up by the army. And she hated uniforms, insisting he visit her in civvies, until, quite simply, she was no longer at home.

Until then, he was ensconced in her plush new flat at 71, avenue Paul Doumer, from where she flexed her new-found independence and watched her film take off—like a leaden balloon. Business in Paris was bad; appalling. Along the Champs Élysées, receipts hardly topped £58,000. In desperation, Raoul Levy almost sold his American rights for a paltry $200,000 in order to recoup something on the £140,000 budget. Vadim retained his faith in the overseas market; and he was right. In Hong Kong, the film took in a single week roughly what Parisians had paid in a year. Box-office riots were reported in West Germany. Attendance records were smashed in London—and a general release was rapidly obtained. Likewise, America was eventually hit for six and could not believe it. One New York cinema owner booked the film for a fortnight—and was still screening it a year later.

Time magazine introduced Bébé to the Americans in 1957: 'from the neck up . . . she looks about 12 years old and bears a striking resemblance to Shirley Temple at that age.' As for *Et Dieu* and the French suggestion that BB would replace MM, the magazine's anonymous film critic opined that Vadim had

sent a girl to do a woman's job. He missed the point: the girl was sent to do a man's job. And did it superbly.

Bébé was, in point of fact, James Dean in bra and panties—more usually without, and hugging bath-towel or well-wrinkled sheets to strategic areas, and thumbing her breasts at Society. Where Colette's *Gigi* had to be taught the rules of sex, Bardot's gamine gave the lessons herself—an irrepressible interlacing of Nabokov's *Lolita*, Southern's *Candy* and Queneau's Zazie, the foul-mouthed brat impatient with adult pretensions and stupidity. (No surprise, therefore, that the director of *Zazie dans le métro*, Louis Malle, would soon work—and well—with BB.)

Jesuit censors in the United States complained about the film's constantly leering, sniggering atmosphere (which must have been news to Vadim); however, they were also uncharacteristically honest enough to add that 'for the truly adult mind', morally objec-

tionable sections in a film did not necessarily invalidate the total moral effect. One priest in Lake Placid, New York, did not agree. Hardly placid himself, he tried to buy off the local cinema, and when the manager refused to cancel his BBooking, Monsignor James T. Lyng put the Palace Theatre out of bounds to his flock. His Episcopalian and Adirondack clergy neighbours followed suit. Philadelphia hit next, living up to W. C. Fields's descriptions of the place, when detectives seized prints from two cinemas. In Memphis, home town of the pelvis-wriggling Elvis Presley, the swivel-hipped Bébé was banned and residents had to cross the Mississippi to West Memphis in Arkansas to catch her act. A Connecticut corset-manufacturer brought out a new line in reinforced girdles to give American girls the BB *derrière*. And in Britain, Leslie Hale, MP, suggested Brigitte be appointed to the House of Lords to 'revive the waning public interest in its debates'.

Quite suddenly, Brigitte Bardot was the hottest female in world movies.

For Americans, she came as a welcome relief from the near asphyxiation of matriarchy. Consequently, she was canonised immediately by the wholly anti-matriarchal *Playboy* magazine, which had started its line of plastically pneumatic Playmate nude pin-ups in 1954 with a star, Marilyn Monroe, and by 1955, was making its Playmates into stars—Stella Stevens for one, Jayne Mansfield for two. If American audiences professed to be shocked by BB, said *Playboy*'s *History of Sex in the Cinema*, they were also intrigued and secretly envious of her emancipated attitudes towards love and life. Women's magazine writers, however, attacked Bardot as being little more than a stupid non-actress. If this were true there would be no BBoom, countered *Life* magazine: 'for what is more commonplace than naked, stupid women who cannot act. The homes of America are full of them every night at 11 o'clock.' America's art-houses, then reputed to be cinemas attracting truck-drivers and murderers only, made fortunes overnight as all the BB produce, made before and after *Et Dieu*, was rapidly imported, drawing vast queues and still more *Playboy* praise. 'She has let slip a towel from a bit of behind in one film, blithely bared a breast or two in another, un-draped an umbilicus in yet another and flashed finely-fashioned, thoroughbred limbs in all.' Un-daunted undress, they termed it; though the magazine also noted she was never seen 'completely jaybirdsville'. (Hugh Hefner's look-but-don't-touch Bunnies followed soon enough, and appeared much inspired by Bardot and Vadim's look-and-see-what's-in-your-mind's-eye imagery.)

France, the country of Bayard and Bossuet, found herself with a new star. Its first big international name since Chevalier, if one forgets the short-lived Leslie Caron (another Vadim discovery, incidentally). Frankly, they did not know what to do about the situation. Intellectual writers turned hacks to explain her success for huge cheques from American magazines. They, Vadim as well, babbled on quite irrationally. Brigitte was, after all, not the first French actress to take her clothes off with such carefree abandon. Even Arletty had done that. And Martine Carol, the sensual comedienne who BB was replacing as No. 1 French star, had made her name doing exactly the same. Although she tried, as Bébé would, to prove she was also a straight actress (a 50s euphemism for keeping clothes on), Martine is best remembered as the woman who bathed to glory, 'the cleanest actress in movies'. Bardot was younger, of course, and typified the rising firmament of youth: 'the fever of loving', as Simone de Beauvoir put it, first in *Esquire*, then in a BB photopacked paper-back (the book sold better), 'the passion for the absolute, the sense of the imminence of death'.

The greater truth outlined by de Beauvoir was that—at this time—the French disliked Brigitte intensely, one reason why the intelligentsia rallied to her defence. Bardot never understood the hatred. 'They say I've no heart, that I'm egotistical and unstable. They say I've destroyed relationships [her own maybe; never another couple's] and that I'm a danger to youth. When I go down the street, I can feel people giggling behind my back. I've the impression that they're undressing me with their eyes. They imagine me as I am in pictures: stretched out all day long, busy with millionaires and prime ministers. That is not true. Anyone can be my friend—if he's nice and amusing.'

As film followed film, triumph chased triumph, dollar followed pound, franc, lire and yen, and inevitably, lover followed lover into her bed, Bardot became to believe in her own legend and lived it to the utmost: no exceptions, no excuses. From 1956 onwards, she

became the biggest national export the French had ever possessed, recognised the world over by her initials alone, like the long-gone B and K of the USSR. Where BB led, the world followed in thrall, until within the self-induced *tristesse* of her too public private life, she began to withdraw and rediscover her true self, and began referring constantly to BB in the third person. 'I'm not like the public conception of BB.' (Any more, she might have added). 'I think I'm a little better than that, anyway.'

The for and against pontifications went on pell-mell, an unsatiated need by global media to turn that which was not quite palatable by mid-50s standards into something less salacious and more respectable; exactly the same kind of scene went on in New York with the arrival of porno-chic in the 70s. No matter which way the magazine writers attempted to cut this particular French mustard, the ungarnished truth remained. The world fell madly in love with BB and for the self-same reason Eve eyed Adam's apple. Sex. Brigitte Bardot was neither as shy nor as overly suggestive about eroticism as, say, the Monroe-Mansfield syndrome; she was certainly more cheerfully natural than the lip-smacking salacity of *Baby Doll* which had—just—preceded her. She was, quite simply, sex. Good, old-fashioned, roll-in-the-hay and to hell with the consequences for to-morrow we die—sex!

This impact began too late, however, for Brigitte to join Vadim in his second movie: *Sait-on jamais*. She could not have joined his Venice locations even if either had wished it, being tied to Paris by a pair of old film contracts, as well as by *l'affaire* Trintignant. Besides, producer Raoul Levy made it quite clear—he did not want her in the film. 'He was kind of upset when *Et Dieu créa la femme* was not an immediate success in Paris,' recalls Vadim. 'Brigitte, at this time, was still not a star. She was a starlet, known because she was in the newspapers often. She was going to be a star. But she was not—yet. The big star at this time [a very smoulderingly erotic actress later to be buried in the BB avalanche] was Françoise Arnoul. Raoul suddenly· decided he needed a name—a star!—for the new film. Brigitte would not bring him the money and so he took Françoise Arnoul. She was all right—that's why I took her, as well. But, of course, I had to change the story because it was not the same.' His scenario was inspired by the novel he wrote in and about his St. Germain-des-Prés days, *The Wise Sophie*, with a heroine greatly resembling the teenage Bardot he had met, marvelled about and married. 'She used to react and talk like Brigitte . . . the character in the book, that is, not as she became in my film.'

In Paris, Bardot began the nebulous *La marriée est*

Love. Vadim shows Bardot how he wants her to make love with Michel Subor in the first film following her suicide-bid, *La bride sur le cou* (1961). Vadim: 'I don't see how I could express myself in the film I want to make, if I were a man incapable of inspiring and experiencing love. I usually work with someone whom I love and who shares my life. Love and work arrive at a synthesis. It's infinitely more agreeable to work with someone whose smallest reactions you know and can provoke with infinite precision.'

Covered. It is arguable if any other star of the screen—or politics, sport, royalty or crime—has won more news-magazine covers around the world than Brigitte Bardot. The 1958 statistic that her image had appeared 29,345 times in the European media can by now be, even conservatively, quadrupled—twice over. Says the mind behind the face and the body: 'The initials BB take all the criticism and I . . . I'm another person who lives just how she wants to. If BB is a sacred monster, it's only because she's an accurate reflection of her and our times. I often read descriptions and commentaries that don't correspond with reality. I think they're talking about a stranger . . .'

trop belle, and hired would-be actor Alain Carré as her confidential secretary—more *Confidential* as he turned out. He later incurred her everlasting wrath by writing a book about life as her 'slave', detailing her frugality in household expenses and excesses in *l'amour*, covering the eventual fall from grace of Trintignant and the following mass of quickly found and even more rapidly discarded lovers: actors Raf Vallone and Gustavo Rojo, tennis player Jean-Noel Grinda, director Marcel Camus, *et al.* 'Without a a man around her,' said Carré's tome, which read like purple publicity prose, 'there could be no happiness for Brigitte.' She needed physical love, he added, 'as flowers need sunshine and some people need pep pills'—and sacked secretaries need to tell tales.

Homo-brigittis are usually dark-haired, medium height and young: as time went on, younger. 'Anyone can be my friend . . .' Anyone over 40 was marked down as RFC, Ready For Chrysanthemums (their funeral). The men usually shared another common point, they were always out for the main chance. As long as they had generous 'unzipped' mouths, good teeth and sincerity, she fell for them over and over again, amassing a total of one lover a year on average for 20 years. This is a conservative estimate, based on her known liaisons only. Not that she hid any. The French Press, however, often covered up some, such as the short fling with married singer Gilbert Bécaud—which led to what has been called Bardot's second suicide attempt.

When filming in Spain, her love for Trintignant overcame her fear of flying, until the location attraction of Spanish actor Gustavo Rojo offered less dangers than weekend jets home to Paris and Jean-Lou. Rojo burned his boats, however, by taking her away for a weekend—after notifying the papers first. Trintignant read about it. She denied the trip. Then denied the denial to Rojo who was busily announcing marriage plans, while Bébé declared she would wed Trintignant, although his separated wife would not hear of divorce. 'It's a mess,' said BB. The first, and least reported, of many. When Trintignant came home on Christmas leave, 1957, he found Bardot more concerned with Bécaud. The singer left for Geneva and BB followed, until he called the Press and said she was annoying him. Brigitte called the resultant 'suicide' bid, food-poisoning: a bad case of mussels.

Either way she was off her next film for two weeks recovering. Co-star Jean Gabin remembers her return to work. 'Very soberly and quietly, she began to act like a professional. It was as if coming close to the edge, she had stepped back and now her work was the only solution . . . It was the first time I saw terror in this child's eyes.' Bardot had visited the

DAILY MIRROR, Saturday, December 7, 1957

DIVORCE FOR 'SEX KITTEN'

—Husband calls her 'capricious'

From PETER STEPHENS, Paris, Friday

THE marriage of Brigitte Bardot, the provocative "sex kitten" of French films, ended in court here today.

A French judge granted divorces to Brigitte and her film director husband, Roger Vadim, on grounds of 'incompatibility"—that they were unable to get along together.

The judge said they were equally to blame for the marriage failing, and that they had both been guilty of "seriously insulting" each other.

Vadim complained that Brigitte was "capricious," sought too much publicity and gave newspaper interviews that were insulting to him.

Came Success...

Brigitte was seventeen when she married Vadim, six years ago. He was twenty-two.

She was an unknown, poorly-paid "cover" girl—eager for fame in the film world.

At first they were considered an ideally-happy couple. Then Brigitte began the climb to screen success.

The higher she got, the less happy her marriage became. Finally the couple separated.

Vadim has said he intends to marry a Danish model, Annette Stroyberg.

Brigitte has said she *wants* to marry French actor Jean-Louis Trintignan, her co-star in several films. But he is already married and his wife refuses to divorce him.

ABOVE — Brigitte Bardot, the "sex-kitten" of the films.

LEFT — Roger Vadim, the man she married six years ago.

RIGHT—Jean-Louis Trintignan, the man she wants to

very jaws of her image's trap: alone, she would be fought over; yet alone was the only way she could achieve some privacy in life, by working. Yet, even now, ambition was hardly paramount with her.

1957 had seen new sides to Bardot's talents, in a second film for Michel Boisrond: *Une Parisienne* put her light-comedienne status firmly on record. Never an actress in the commonest sense, she is happier in comedy than tragedy, able to debunk her own image in a perky, self-deprecating manner—but not just yet. As overseas fame caught up with her, she began to exercise temperament of often dizzying proportions, capricious to a fault. She felt big enough, for instance, to refuse the Cannes festival offer to attend the event which had once helped make her name.

Lover. On film and in life, Jean-Louis Trintignant fell victim to the allure of the scorching Bardot legend. He, among the few, refused to get burned.

She was shooting for Boisrond nearby at Nice, and rejoiced in displaying her vaulted new position by throwing her own BB Party for the Press. Cannes was deserted the day she played hostess, obviously naked under tee-shirt and jeans.

Vadim, meantime, had discovered Danish model Annette Stroyberg, a former London *au pair* and water-skiing instructress at Ruislip Lido. She remained the dutiful wife-figure in the background, until he noted her boredom and prepared to repeat the BB-formula on her. 'She will outshine Bardot,' he claimed. 'Whether she's a success or not, this will have no effect on BB's career.' An obvious remark, since Brigitte was returning to his directoral fold for the misguided and definitely mis-titled *Les bijoutiers*

du clair de lune—in Spain, with the pregnant Stroyberg watching, somewhat enviously, on the set. By the end of the year, Bardot and Vadim were divorced in Paris, the day after Annette gave birth to Vadim's daughter, Nathalie. No longer tied, the couple became better friends and Vadim never really retires from the BB history.

Musing upon their divorce, and his later failed marriages and affairs with other actresses, Vadim relates such ruptures to the modern problem of women attempting to assume their own life and identity. 'For an actress, it is especially difficult to think she belongs to a man, that she participates in the life of the couple. There is always a moment when they want to be themselves, to show they exist

51

by themselves. I imagine that a banker, a doctor, a journalist, even an actor, could eventually live with an actress. Not a director—very difficult! Because a director is the image of the master of the actor. Living with a director, they have the feeling that they are an object. And there is always the moment when they want to escape . . . If I have a chance to be happy with a woman now, it will be because I have decided to follow what Napoleon said, "To win in love is to know how to retreat." ' (Vadim's current wife, armament empire heiress Catherine Schneider, is not a member of the acting profession.)

The sado-masochistic thriller in Spain set Brigitte opposite her first Hollywood leading man, Stephen Boyd. Another adroit move by Vadim and Levy. America had by now latched on to Bébé in such an unheard of manner, that all her previous films, the good, the bad and the downright awful, were playing at almost every corner theatre, coast to coast. They were also flooding into Britain in such a rush that one critic, Derek Monsey, called her grossly unfair competition to other actresses, indeed to other, more important films. 'But it's true. Any week which offers a new picture in which Mlle. Bardot takes off her clothes is inevitably BB week.'

Despite (or because of) all the boyfriends and the divorce, at the end of 1957 Brigitte topped the Belgian *Ciné-Revue* film magazine popularity referendum, easily beating Michèle Morgan and Gina Lollobrigida, while Elizabeth Taylor and Marilyn Monroe trailed far behind in 13th and 14th positions. Bardot films were hurtling around the globe and *Cinémonde* calculated she had accrued one million lines in the French daily papers—two million in the weeklies. Her photograph had, the magazine reported, appeared 29,345 times up to early 1958, and she was the basis of 47 per cent of all French conversation (6 per cent more than politics). Her smuggled pin-ups were selling at 50 roubles each in Moscow; a British husband was divorced because he preferred BB films to sleeping with his wife; a wax effigy of her was stolen in Birmingham, and another one, made for the Cameo Royal cinema foyer in London's West End, was sold for £350.

Even with all that cafe chatter, and ten miles of posterisation in Paris for *Parisienne*, the French had not yet learned what to make of their shock new star. Hypocrisy was rife—as always. One Dominican church journal eulogised her 'animality, sensuality and femininity displays . . . in the introduction of a myth based on eroticism and realism', while a right-wing weekly went far against its usual grain by extolling the Boisrond comedy for its 'audacious documentary record of the natural beauties of Mlle. Bardot, she strips as often and as completely as possible'. In London, the *Daily Mirror*'s Donald Zec

Encounter. Everyone wanted to meet her, know her and indeed write about her. Including Marcel Achard, doyen of l'Académie Française. He worked on one of her (worst) scripts and described her glowingly, flowingly. 'A malicious coquetry, serving an ingenuous perversity; the mystery of

a woman and a child; an irritating gesture, a disarming smile; the only vamp in the world who looks like your childhood sweetheart; the hair of Melisande, the face of Colombe; almost as much poetry as sex-appeal; dynamite touched off by a golden wick.'

presented her recipe for screen success. 'Take a simple film idea, put Brigitte in it, then permutate the following: BB taking a shower; slithering between bed-sheets; walking towards camera; walking away from the camera (that's favourite); teasing, pouting, and partially disrobing. (She can also be soaking—but it's not strictly necessary.) After which, it's merely a question of counting the money.'

In America, she was still being condemned in the *Baby Doll* vilification manner as 'the tramp who keeps mothers of young daughters awake at nights, the diamond eater . . . the monster . . . just the kind of girl to take home to mother if you want to give her a heart attack'. The sex-kitten had truly arrived. And she loved matching the label. 'I purr,' she said. 'I scratch. And sometimes I bite.'

Hollywood was biting as well, with film offers as astronomically high for the period as $250,000 plus a healthy percentage of profits. Brigitte was just not interested. 'When I'd made the taxes and lived the way they would want me to, what would I have left?' Ed Sullivan went as high as $50,000 just for her to say 'Bonjour' on his TV show. Again: *non*. All Bébé wanted to do, said her agent, Olga Horstig-Primus, was to stay in France, have fun and work as little as possible. Even as far back as 1953, she had got cold feet when about to go to Los Angeles and check out a Cannes-proffered Universal contract. Raoul Levy said she took one look at the plane at the airport and went home. The deal was off.

For Levy, deals were always on, simmering and being brought to the boil. He spent up to 14 months of meetings in Rome, London, Monaco and Las Vegas trying to seal his brashest hope: a Vadim venture co-starring Bardot and Sinatra. That Frank Sinatra alone was considered the right type—and age—for the young star said much about why Hollywood lacked gusto in current film fare. True, he was just about holding his own in the Top Ten money-makers, via *High Society* and *Pal Joey*. Youth was on the march, however. France had proved that; Britain was to follow soon enough with its own new-wave. A flock of copy-BBs were at work throughout Europe, and each new Bardot meant a new, young actor getting a co-star break, and often proving of more lasting value than the leading lady with the Bardot hair-style, but never the Bardot flair. Now Brando and Bardot—that would have been more like it. James Dean would have been the only star she would have gone to Hollywood to work with, but he had died in 1955.

Sinatra . . .? His current girl, Humphrey Bogart's widow, Lauren Bacall, was against the idea. And Bardot understood why, thinking the thin singer and she would make great chemistry together. *Playboy* went into paroxysms about the idea. 'What

53

happens when these two volatile substances mingle in the same crucible, when The Voice meets The Broad of Broads? The concept is enough to make an Olympus tremble, the skies darken, the oceans churn, and to knock the whole world on its collective clyde.' Sinatra knocked it out instead, killing the deal—$200,000 and 6 per cent of profits each—when refusing to make what would be called *Paris by Night* in Paris at all. Soured by *The Pride and the Passion* experience in 1957, he complained: 'I've had that location bit. Too many idiots around watching.'

For the record, the projected scenario had him as a dead-beat impresario drinking himself into a Parisian stupor. Dancing girl Brigitte rescues him from the gutter and puts him to bed at home. 'Is not sexy like my other films,' she explained. 'I sleep in the bath. He kills himself in my car.' All this, plus music by Cole Porter, sounded like a re-make of Sinatra's *Young at Heart* with Doris Day (itself a 1954 Warner Brothers re-make of *Four Daughters*). Six months of re-writes could not satisfy The Voice. And he was never that hot for Bardot anyway. For a start, she was not Italian, and he was sure 'people will be sick of the sight of that doll before our picture is made'.

For a while, Levy considered Danny Kaye instead, then the project fizzled out, leaving Bardot in a huff. With Levy—even more so with Sinatra. 'I don't like this impression that I'm mad about Sinatra and would crawl to make a picture with him. I like him—but he's no chicken. Mr. Tony Perkins is more to my own taste.' She got Perkins later, amid the kind of British location mêlée that not even Sinatra could have envisaged. 'I wish,' said BB later, 'I had met Sinatra . . . just once. Once, I think, would have been enough!'

The incident perfectly illustrated Brigitte's distrust of the entire Hollywood system; and the cowardice of name actors to share billing with her. Most male stars steered well clear. Another Italian, Rossano Brazzi, for example, agreed to work with Sophia Loren—not BB. 'Professional suicide,' he opined. 'Leading men in her pictures spend most of the time just looking at her. So does the audience.' (Incidentally, Vadim still chased after Sinatra during his Paramount contract days in Rome, for a film with Stroyberg and Jean-Paul Belmondo. The singer turned it down—Stroyberg was not Italian either—and Vadim eventually produced it as *L'Enfer au paradis* with an unknown cast and himself in the Sinatra role.)

The French finally began taking Bardot seriously enough for Raoul Levy to mount a production featuring Brigitte with Jean Gabin and Edwige Feuillère, the grandaddy and the *grande dame* of

le cinéma français, for her opening 1958 shot: *En cas de malheur*. Gabin had legally to be coerced to fulfil his contract and work with 'that thing that goes around naked', though he was putty in her grasp by the end of shooting. *Malheur* proved a more important picture than either Vadim vehicle; here was an RFC veteran, Claude Autant-Lara (like Clouzot later), depicting the 50s generation gap in matters of sex above all else, and thereby using Bardot for a far more lacerating attack on the parasitical morality which condemned her. BB was the sleep-around girl and Gabin the rich lawyer making her his mistress, though never fully comprehending, nor appreciating, the very personal freedoms of mind

Poetry. And for a while the dance—any dance—became as important a part of any BB film as the bath towel.

or body which had attracted him to her.

After the film, the always healthy actress was ordered to rest by her doctors and went to the Dolomites. On her return, secretary Alain Carré took her to the theatre and she fell instantly for Italian actor Raf Vallone—although he was RFC-rated. Vallone was a short, sweet, sharp episode. He introduced her to Brahms and Beethoven (Trintignant had supplied Bach); the flamenco beat took her over next, during dance rehearsals for *La femme et le pantin,* and renewed her love of the guitar, which in turn led to Sacha Distel. She started holding flamenco parties at her flat; the music, she said, was like making love. The new film, alas, was not. The inspiration of

another veteran film-maker, Julien Duvivier, *La femme* was almost a complete disaster in everything save for some BB sequences and the box-office riches of a world still hungry for her every move and movie. Dietrich had made the original version, and while Bardot was essentially suited to the hoydenish image of the nubile young virgin torturing the man she loved, neither her co-star—unknown Spanish actor Antonio Vilar, unknown before or since—nor her director was in touch with the reality of the day, the age and the entire BB spirit. She had the script re-written 20 times, but Duvivier was the problem. Definitely RFC-rated—in style.

Returning from Spain, she bought her all too famous

hideaway home. La Madrague, in St. Tropez, is nothing super-de-luxe, and therefore fitted her equally well-known frugality. The house is up the end of a dirt road on the bay of Des Caroubiers. But it did boast a secluded beach behind a dense thicket of bamboo fencing—and five bedrooms. The fence was soon enough infiltrated by long-tom cameras, the bedrooms were always filled (Vadim and most of his new lady loves being among the constant stream of visitors). Tourists were sailed around the bay to catch a glimpse, perhaps, of the nude, sunbathing superstar, and more photography of the naked BB sun-worshipping on her own back porch and pier has been published than from all her movie stills put together. Bardot spending most of her summers in St. Tropez has made the town more famous than when chosen for the post D-Day Allied landings in the war. Photographers climb her trees—'The tree are full of fruit,' she would say. And the place was once burgled: she lost one pair of black panties, two pair of stockings, three photographs of herself in bikinis and a pair of old jeans. Some hideaway.

First man invited to the charms of La Madrague was the new lover, guitarist Sacha Distel—'he has brought music into my life. There was always something missing and now I know what it is.' They were introduced by pianist Claude Bolling, although she had seen Distel before in an orchestra recording music for one of her films. He was the nephew of music publisher Ray Ventura, who had been connected with Raoul Levy. BB and Sacha were kindred youthful spirits, the ideal swinging French couple, in jeans and suntan—the first of Europe's beautiful people. He became a singer on the strength of the enormous publicity their affair aroused; Vadim apart, Distel is the only man to have achieved more than passing stardom out of mating Bardot.

She had now made five films since the first Vadim success, and she was big money and hot news the globe around. *Life* magazine examined her in August, 1958, comparing her to a European sports-car, arriving at the exact time when Americans were ready, even hungry, for something racier and more realistic than the familiar domestic product. Writer Paul O'Neill hammered home the auto-metaphor as he assessed the ramifications of the calculated Bardot myth. She had been built, created for a need, everything about her was calculated to seek out and dramatise the failings in the soul of the beholder— 'the uneasy suspicion that he is a wicked old man'. This matched Simone de Beauvoir's summation, but missed Vadim's aim completely. All the same, it must have sold plenty of tickets. Comment enough, though, added to the over-headlined Distel affair, to cool Raoul Levy's ardour and to note the dangers

inherent in running through the gamut of erotica too far, too much and too quickly.

He dropped plans to make *Aphrodite* with her, which is something of a pity—Bardot coming out of the water would have been even more outstandingly memorable than Loren in *Boy on a Dolphin* or Andress in *Dr. No.* Levy decided instead to dress up, literally, an original Vadim notion about army camp followers and turn it into a frothy comedy. 'I've made my last sex film,' he declared. 'You will never see Bardot nude or nearly nude or jumping in and out of bed in any film of mine.' BB would play a bordello maid recruited into the French resistance, trained in London and parachuted into her occupied homeland. 'And there are some things,' said Levy, 'you simply cannot do in a parachute.' Actually, there were plenty of things Vadim, for one, could do with parachutes and other parts of her secret-agent equipment—and Levy had them in one script, before changing his approach in mid-jump.

The new project, *Babette s'en va-t-en guerre*, resurrected the old headache of finding a leading man. David Niven was approached but proved either unavailable or uninterested. Sacha Distel had vociferously turned down the possibility of the rôle—or any in any BB movie. Not that he was ever seriously considered. He was far too busy carving out his singing career and was, consequently, away from Bébé too often for his own good. Alain Carré took her to the theatre once more, to check the potential of a possible co-star: Jacques Charrier. He was starring in *The Diary of Anne Frank* opposite the impeccable young Pascale Audret, then engaged to another trendy *jeune vedette*, Sami Frey. (Not for long, as time and BB's imperturbable sexual pendulum soon showed.)

Together on the set, the newer in-couple worked well, both adept at light comedy. Bardot welcomed the respite from strip 'n' tease, and said she was making *Babette* so that the world's 16-year-olds could finally see one of her films. 'Will clothes spoil BB?' asked *Photoplay*. Jacques Charrier had expected a commercial superstar, and discovered an actress, far from sophisticated, he thought, with her own acting secret: associating talent with spontaneity. She was, said Jacques, 'the most exceptional being I've ever met'.

So it was all Charrier for the moment. Also, it was all Distel. Alain Carré was among the selected few privy to an extraordinary *Jules et Jim* happening of Brigitte running with both men and trying, often with the assistance of her double, Magy Mortini, to prevent one finding out about the other. Carré intimated she could not decide between the two and tested them on capacity for jealousy in her domination game. Neither was an ordinary affair, nor the purpose behind keeping both on fire. Vadim guessed what was afoot. Although, by this time, his second marriage to Stroyberg had folded at the rents, he maintained Bébé was envious of his marriage and his baby. He sensed an imminent marriage—and a child—but whose? Certain sections of the Paris Press nominated Vadim himself as the most likely candidate. Charrier felt it was to be him; so did Distel. Exactly how Bardot wanted them both to feel.

Shortly after returning from a simple, trouble-free location to a British RAF camp (the entire company strength gave up weekend passes to watch BB struggling with her parachute harness), she made up her mind. Alain Carré heard first; she had, according to his book of revelations, phoned him in the middle of the night to say she and Charrier had done it—created a baby. Brigitte later had Carré issue her sole

Press statement about a love affair: 'Mlle. Bardot asks me to announce that she has severed all relations with M. Sacha Distel.'

The date was April 28, 1959; Charrier had wanted the break official before marrying her near the old Bardot summer manse at Louveciennes, on June 18, 1959—the London *Daily Express* having jumped the shotgun and married them off a week earlier. Brigitte wore pink and white and kept her cool as her father lost his amidst the photographic chaos while Mayor Fernand Guillaume did his best to marry them. The scene, said Charrier, was 'nauseating, primeval'. The mayor's office had been bribed to reveal the date, and the young actor, still with but three films to his credit, was staggered by the scant respect for privacy. It was even worse later when the family joined them on their inevitable Madrague honeymoon—or honeyboom as Donald

Wedding. The new co-star—Jacques Charrier in *Babette Goes to War*—became Brigitte's new husband in 1959.

Zec called it that touristy July. 'Not since Lady Godiva stripped to canter through Coventry,' he reported for the *Daily Mirror*, 'has one girl thrown a town into such a tizzy.' Poor Charrier never realised what he had got into. He was in hospital within the week with appendicitis; just the first of his headaches as M. Bardot.

Brigitte went on to finish another lively comedy for Michel Boisrond, *Voulez-vous danser avec moi?* Light, airy, cheery, what used to be called gay—with a touch of what is now called gay. Bright and brittle, save for the double tragedy of two of her co-stars being dead almost before shooting was over. The decade died next, if not the so-called decadence of the screen she had help arouse just three years and eight films earlier. Her sexplosion was merely reverberation elsewhere, as previous unknowns, like ex-newsreel cameraman Russ Meyer and former publicist David Friedman, began the nudie-movie trend in America, as Ingmar Bergman, for once, generated more definitive and psychologically motivated sex in Sweden, as Linda Lovelace became nine years old . . .

Bardot, then, was married, pregnant, happy by turn —and bored. She talked gushingly of her second husband, and put her life and loves into neat and tidy order during various *enceinte* interviews. 'Vadim revealed me to myself, Trintignant seduced me. Rojo fired my passion. Sacha gave me tenderness with every word, every kiss. But Jacques stole my heart. I have not always loved wisely, but I was young . . . Jacques changed my life. There will be no more after this.' Familiar words from any movie queen on any continent. Less familiar was the rest of the flow. 'I'm not really interested in the cinema. When I started . . . I loathed it and to speak truly, I don't enjoy it even now as I suppose I should. I don't wish to be an actress at all costs. I hope to play different rôles in the sort of films I can act in. I've not renounced nudity; if the script says undress, then I undress. It doesn't matter greatly one way or the other. All I want to do, all I can ever hope to do, is to perfect myself playing myself.'

There were those, supposedly in the know, who said she never quite forgave Charrier for making her pregnant—certainly it was the worst nine months, part of the worst year, of her life. As with Trintignant, she lost Jacques to the army, only with more appalling fall-out. Charrier, poor chap, seemed like a day-tripper lost by chance in a harem. He had the best of it, and the worst of it, suffering at home— where his jealousy proved too strong for the jealousy-

Marriage II. Les Charrier at home—even in the kitchen, photographers were gathered.

demanding wife—and when he joined up, facing ridicule in the Press and disgrace upon discharge, due to a heart condition, which had him mistakenly labelled everything from malingerer to mentally unstable.

With a colonel for a father, and three brothers on active service in Algeria, Charrier had high hopes of making officer status, and emulating them all. He could not, however, take the separation from Brigitte, the fears it bred in him—as with all her men—that she would forget him, baby or no baby. He had a complete nervous breakdown after a few days in barracks with the 11th Lancers and was dispatched to the military hospital at Val-de-Grâce for strict—almost barbaric—observation. Sharp instruments were banned and he began to feel like Caryl Chessman: depressed enough to attempt slashing his wrists.

The papers were full of stories about him going berserk on finding BB pin-ups plastered inside every colleague's cupboard, of being taunted repeatedly by the troops about his wife. In fact, he says, he never saw any other soldiers. 'I didn't get past the doctors. I was only in uniform for a total of some two hours.' His depressive state was not lessened by being shot down by leader writers comparing his

lack of fibre with Elvis Presley's exemplary attitude in completing two years as GI—nor in quotes from his wife about never wanting another child. After three months, he was discharged as *inapte à servir*, unsuitable for service. The first major victim maimed by Bardolatry.

During her pregnancy, Bardot was seen only when visiting her husband in hospital. She was hardly forgotten, however. The *Observer* in Britain celebrated her 25th birthday with a rather tame page profile, tying her fame with the speed of communications in the rapidly shrinking world. She also had a legal run-in with the publicity posters for Charrier infants' mineral water: '*Bébé aime Charrier?*'—she was convinced the question-mark referred to a possible break-down of her marriage. The firm covered the questionable query with a baby's head. (Bébé signifies baby in France, as well as being the affectionate nickname for, indeed the pronunciation of, BB.)

As for the real Bébé baby, Brigitte was as brutally frank as ever. 'I never do anything by chance. But I don't find pregnancy much of a joy. I'm certainly frightened of childbirth. But I'm afraid I can't find a way of avoiding it.'

59

Zoo. Animals are rarely far from Bardot or her thoughts. Her much reported love of fauna led to her battling for changes in French slaughterhouse laws, and she has been likened to pets since the very first sex-kitten tag—from 'gorgeous peke' to 'little gazelle'—by fans and critics. Vadim himself said she had the face of a kitten and the ardour of a tigress. *Sunday Dispatch:* a delicious little duckling. *New York Times:* a caged panther. *Daily Herald:* a rather naughty young foal. *Daily Express:* a stroke-worthy kitten. Writer Renaud de Labordière thought her face was that of an amorous cat. Twice co-star Stephen Boyd saw her as a stalking panther. Mary Quant, whose mini-skirt revolution could hardly have been considered without BB in mind, commented: 'She has the best legs in the world and looks like the delicious white horse in the film, *Crin Blanc.*'

The Searing Sixties: Demystification

'Strangely, her ideal body reveals an ideal soul which masks her depravity in innocent stimulation, and its revelation becomes a symbol of virginal temptation rather than depravity. Her image in its mask stimulated the cause of Bardolatry and in the traditions of great goddesses of the screen—Pickford, Bara, Negri, Garbo—she compelled the audience to recognise their right to imitate the gods. But a new struggle of relationships has been born: the worshippers wanted the goddess brought down to earth. They wanted her available, not venerated; they wanted her as a mediator between the real world and the dream world, not as a creator of dreams . . . And the journalists and photographers complied.'
—**Cinema** magazine

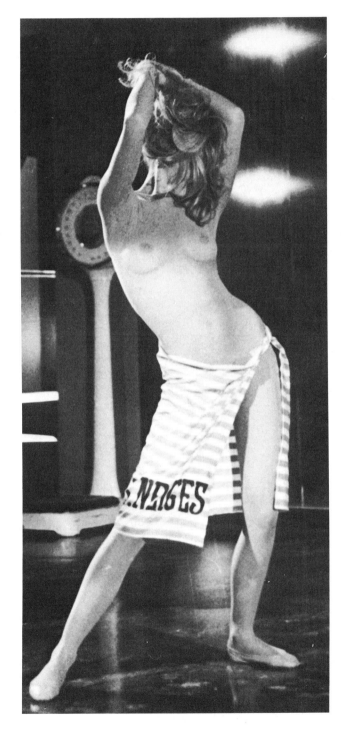

During the halcyon period when *Et Dieu* created them all in St. Tropez, Raoul Levy looked at his pretty promotional asset and told the world she would last 20—no, 30—years. 'Because she has the bone structure.' When her life and myth became hopelessly interchangeable, Levy forgot the Bible and cast the first stone, denouncing the demystification of her (and thereby, his) box-office potential. 'There is no longer any mystery about Bardot,' he carped—as if there ever had been, both he and Vadim had seen to that. 'The public knows too many intimate things about her life. Bardot sells newspapers and magazines but she does not sell tickets.' Not for *Babette*, anyway; the turned-on world preferred her bared body to bare-faced comedy.

Why attack her, asked André Maurois in *Playboy*, ever her stout defender. 'Because her curves were charming and she displayed them willingly? . . . Because she followed her instincts without trying to control them? Because to please, she only needed to appear? Because of her instability, her kaleidoscopic loves? . . . No, in point of fact, she was attacked because she was envied, out of jealousy. Not only was she earning vast sums of money, enriching her producers and filling theatres, she was doing it with such ease, simply by being herself. That was unforgiveable . . .'

French critic Lo Duca joined the defence, calling her

the virtual daughter of the artists Lenor Fini and Modigliani, 'blessed with the ambiguous and para-cynical features of the artful ingénue of our day.' Writer-director Carl Foreman saw her as the young Linda Darnell, the same long legs, the torso, the appearance of great sexual promise, with a Lolita face of carnality, the faces to be seen all over Europe's post-war generation: 'not faces, *masks,* façades of virginity concealing a vast amount of dreadful knowledge'.

IT'S A 3 a.m. BOY FOR BARDOT

Says Father: He Has a Powerful Tenor Voice

The baby's delighted father, actor Jacques Charrier, talks at an impromptu Press confer ence in a small cafe

PARIS, Monday.

THE news rocketed round Paris to-day: "Brigitte's had a son." Miss Bardot's baby, who will be called Nicholas Jacques, was born at 3 a.m. at her 7th-floor flat

Her supporters came higher still. Vivien Leigh had said 'no actress since Garbo had created such a personality and with such humility'; Maurice Chevalier called her the jewel of Paris, 'pretty as a heart'. In London, a Harley Street psychiatrist in need of publicity compared her to Nell Gwynn—'both eternal guttersnipes whom men instinctively want to protect and improve, and so the basic attraction of beauty is strengthened by feelings of chivalry'.

As the 60s shuffled in, soon to be swinging—for almost everyone, save Bébé—La Bardot was still the talking point of the world. In France above all, where The Birth was more eagerly anticipated than Neil Armstrong's giant leap for mankind less than ten years later. The French forgot their Algerian war along with their GNP and the national debt, their big little *bombe atomique* and their fears of the resurgent Germany. Even Charrier's contretemps with the army was forgiven in the country's unified happiness as their Bébé—yes, she was theirs now—was about to attain utter respectability as a mother. A married mother at that. For Charrier, the confinement was reminiscent of the marriage. His wife's doctors were being bribed to photograph the birth or the baby—or both. The chosen clinic was busy auctioning photographic rights and other people were attempting to persuade the good doctors to give Brigitte a Caesarian operation to avoid spoiling the national Bardot treasures. In the end, Charrier drove to his country home area, found 'a simple, honest practitioner' and had him arrange to deliver the baby at the avenue Paul Doumer flat.

No one had to wait long. Nicolas Jacques Charrier arrived early in the morning of January 11, 1960, with 30 or more pressmen camping at his front door awaiting *la belle maman*'s immediate reactions. BB: Is it a boy. Nurse: *Oui!* BB: *Chic alors!* And even the staid, conservative London *Daily Telegraph* headlined it: '7 lb. 4 ozs. boy for Brigitte Bardot.' According to the much less staid *Weekend* magazine, the birth unleashed scenes of national hysteria unparalleled since the Revolution. 'Their national Sex Kitten had provided them with what they had always suspected: she was a woman. She had had a baby. The corks popped. Those who couldn't afford whisky drank champagne. The national hangover lasted three weeks. Then Bardot was at work again.'

She did not even wait that long. Brigitte had obviously made a sustained effort to kill off BB during her marriage to Jacques Charrier. She was determined to start new pages in her life and refused all journalists wanting long interviews with biographies in mind, during her confinement. She would not sanction such books, she would sue if necessary. 'The initials BB take all the criticism and I—I am another person who lives just how she wants to. I often read descriptions and commentaries that don't

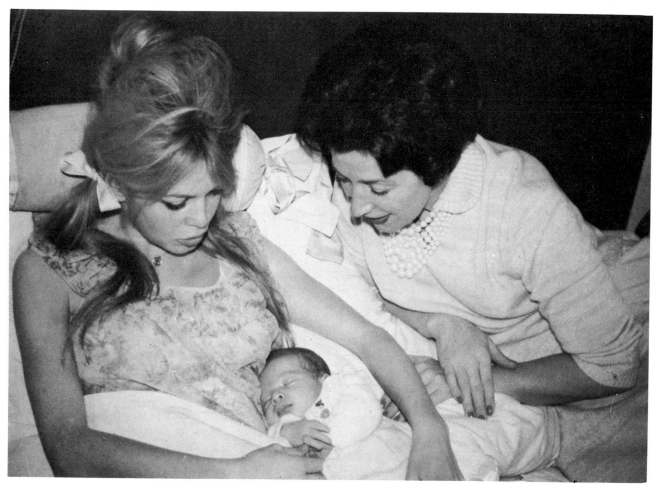

Maman. Paris went mad—so did the inevitable photographers camping on her doorstep—as Brigitte Bardot gave birth to Nicolas Jacques Charrier on January 11, 1960. Among earliest visitors' Bébé's choice of Godmother for her own *bébé*— her producer friend, Christine Gouze-Renal.

correspond with reality. I think they're talking about a stranger.'

What was past was past. As it happened, the future was to be even more chaotic. Any man coming into Bébé's orbit has to sacrifice his identity, totally, and no man of self-respect would agree to that. Not for long. The birth of Nicolas beatified her for the French: Brigitte, however, could not wait to get back to some kind of normalcy, or what had previously seemed like normalcy to her. And that, according to British writer Thomas Wiseman, was her contribution to cinematic art: making promiscuity seem painless, demonstrating her own unique variation on the square dance, changing partners without treading on feelings. In her films, Wiseman noted, 'she flits gaily between bedrooms like a busy chambermaid. And nobody terribly minds. For she is not real. She is merely the embodiment of male fantasy, a dream of conquest without consequence, a Santa Claus of sex.'

But she was real enough . . . Within ten days of the birth she was back at the old grind—testing co-stars galore in a makeshift bed set for her 26th film, *La*

vérité. Another esteemed veteran writer and director, Henri-Georges Clouzot, was given the assignment by Levy and had been working for months during the confinement until almost 'giving back my pen'. He could not locate Levy flitting around Hong Kong, nor Bardot who had suddenly taken not to answering the phone, not even to her mother. (One magazine interviewed her by mailed questionnaire. Q: Who does your hair? A: My right hand.) She was, during the final stages of pregnancy, incommunicado; but that was one little problem she delivered with a vengeance.

Clouzot's story, originally of a girl wanting to star in movies and winding up as a stripper, murdering her lover, became more polished: the sole scenario to attempt to strip Bébé to her soul. A girl of her time (again), beatnicky, a distant cousin of Yvette in *En cas de malheur,* travelling with the bohemian set, working not a jot, and seducing her sister's fiancé, a classical musician, and then killing him in a frenzied *crime passionnel* when he attempts to drop her, to treat her much as she had previously treated him. Much of the affair was akin to Brigitte's life-style; the premise was a matter, as she had said so often of her own men, of a couple being in love with each other, but never at the same time. (In trying to equate the turgid *Don Juan 1973* scenario to the same life-style, Vadim had her say: 'One thing I can't stand is people treating me the way I treat others.')

A new film: the old question. Who would play the lover? A new actor, demanded Clouzot. Hence the lengthy bed screen-tests at the studios, with Bardot in jeans and tee-shirt, romping under blankets with a fast array of possibilities from Belmondo to Laurent Terzieff (both of whom had shared their breakthrough film with Charrier, *Les tricheurs,* 1958). There was little doubt that Brigitte enjoyed the auditions, said Clouzot. 'Dying with fatigue she would still get up once more to do her testing whenever I called—she loves to excite men.' Gérard Blain, Charles Belmont, Jean-Pierre Cassel, Marc Michel, the list went on and on. In hindsight, it could be said Bardot was searching for a replacement for Charrier: the marriage was already slipping out of its euphoria, and indeed when *La vérité* started shooting in May, he attempted his second suicide. If Brigitte recognised the possibility of an ulterior motive in the tests, this would explain her battle to have Jean-Louis Trintignant as her co-star. A man from the past, rather than a brand-new temptation which might kill her marriage for good. She insisted loudly upon Trintignant, but having broken his leg skiing, he never reached the testing site in time. Clouzot had settled his mind upon young Sami Frey.

Come the filming, Clouzot worked her hard, with again no doubt, no excuses necessary either; it was her greatest dramatic opportunity and she was soon engulfed in respect for Clouzot's technique, even more so for young Frey. The ever-present French Press picked up certain vibrations from the extras and crew, and began turning them into largely uncorroborated headlines. Far from the tumultuous reception of Nicolas, Bardot was suddenly receiving the worst pillorying of her life. She had dumped Charrier, it was alleged, she was wildly in love with Clouzot and chasing Frey at the same time. Neither spouse could hit back; Mme. Clouzot happened to be seriously ill in hospital, and soon Charrier was hospitalised anew. 'The papers,' said a furious Bardot, 'had the audacity to imply that all this was arranged in order to leave us—Clouzot and I—free to have an affair together . . . There was, of course, no vestige of truth in this fantastic tale!' The Press, making Hollywood's *Confidential* seem like *Boy Scout News,* remained unimpressed. Bardot was trapped in the journalistic aspic of her myth. 'If I deny anything, they say it must be true—otherwise why bother with a denial? If I remain silent, they say it must be true—otherwise why doesn't she deny it?'

Clouzot obviously denounced the rumours as gutter-rubbish; his sole influence over his leading lady, he said, was purely aesthetic. 'I'm 51. If I'd met her in 1938 without any doubt I'd have had a passion for her.' What he did adore was her large range as an actress—'she can pass easily from comedy to drama to tragedy'—and her beautiful *derrière.*

Bardot simply had to put up with the row as best she could; she knew the Press, had used them often enough since her start. She could not resent being big news, indeed, professionally she welcomed it, although it meant no private life at all—'just loneliness'. What she abhorred was news-invention. If there was nothing genuinely new to say about her every two days or so, the Paris Press made up something and the lie could be repeated throughout the world if it were juicy enough. The headline holocaust never let up, however: too much for anyone to suffer alone and remain on the right side of sanity.

As the filming switched to the BB–Frey love scenes, the papers started a new tack, electing Sami Frey as the lover, and having Charrier 'mad with jealousy' and being officially barred from the set. Columbia's publicity department issued a message from Brigitte, a véritable *cri du cœur:* 'I am a woman just like any other. I have two ears, two eyes, a nose and a mouth. I have feelings and thoughts and I am a wife and a mother above all else. But my life is becoming impossible. My soul is not my own any more. Stardom to me is a monster, like the sorcerer's apprentice. I cannot live like I want to. I merely exist underground. If I want fresh air in my home, I cannot open my window because there's a photographer sitting on the

Jean-Paul Belmondo

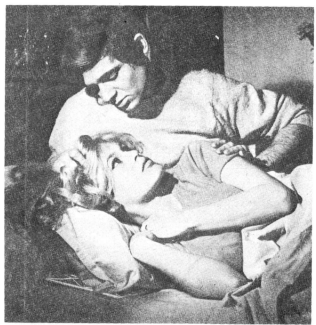

Charles Belmont

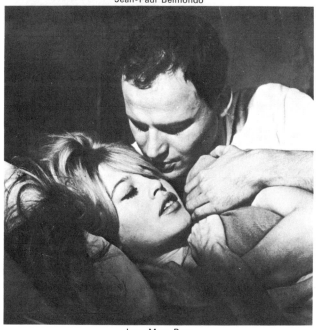

Jean-Marc Bory

Marc Michel

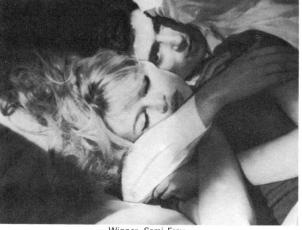

Winner. Sami Frey.

Test Match. One by one they came, all the virile new actors on the Paris new-wave film front. To test with their No. 1. superstar. The prize: to be Bardot's co-star in *La vérité*. The hunt began within ten days of Brigitte becoming a mother and it seemed at times more like Bardot auditioning for a new lover than a new screen partner. She attempted to avoid this particular temptation by insisting upon a former lover, Jean-Louis Trintignant, for the rôle. Director Henri-Georges Clouzot was adamant in his demand for a raw newcomer. So in they trooped, one after another. Clouzot's instructions on the bed-set was the same to them all. 'Go on—*go on!*—promenade a little with your lips on her face. Breathe in her ear ... Murmur something ... Be sexy!' Sami Frey obeyed better than most. He won the part—and the girl.

Calm. Before the storm. For the magazine layouts, everything in the Charrier household is serene. Privacy was scant, however.

roof opposite with a telescopic lens. I would like to give up films if this continues . . .'

That any film was completed in such traumatic circumstances is beyond belief: much less Bardot's one and only genuine acting performance—even if it is one in the old-fashioned tragedienne sense of acting being seen to be done. Once again, though, she was setting the style for everyone else. The following year saw Loren tackle *Two Women* and Monroe make *The Misfits*. If all three performances were on a par of surprising brilliance and insight (from so-called sexpots), the background to Bardot's staging, more retrograde even than Monroe's in Reno, made hers the most creditable.

When looking back on the ruins of his tempestuous marriage, Jacques Charrier denied ever objecting to Brigitte continuing in films. 'And as all her films are love films, love stories, and have love scenes in them, how could I object to her shooting love scenes?' The truth behind *La vérité* hit the worst heights during a *paparazzi*-photographed fist fight between Frey and Charrier over Bardot, when all three met outside the La Rhumière nightspot in St. Germain-des-Prés. The news pictures told too much of everything, although there were also rumours that the entire Charrier-Frey affray was a put-up job for publicity.

(The same was suggested of her post-*Babette* marriage to Charrier, of her affair with Trintignant during and after *Et Dieu,* both of which were also Levy productions and—adding fuel to this theory—were considered chancy enough projects, much in need of a spur at the box-office.) Interviewed on television around this hectic time, Brigitte vehemently declared: 'I must kill the monster that is in me. I must chase away from my halls the intruder who has the name of BB. I want to be able to say: BB is no more. *Vive* Brigitte!'

And that is exactly what she very nearly did.

Filming over, she fled to Cabrolle, near Menton, to hide from the incessant Press barrage and to take stock of her situation. Raoul Levy said she was all systems go for a crack-up. Crack she did—drastically, almost fatally. She stayed with some friends, motor-rallyist Jean-Claude Simon and his wife, Mercédès, a former secretary to Sophia Loren. Three reporters and two photographers from the dreaded *France-Dimanche* Sunday yellow news-sheet followed and kept less than a respectable distance. 'They refused to leave and to me they looked like an ugly black octopus trying to pull me away from my simple life. Something went snap. My mind filled with fears. There seemed no way out. I tried to stop falling away.

Adieu. 'I am in despair . . .' Brigitte's suicide note—as reproduced, inevitably, in the French Press.

It was no good. I couldn't stop myself. I spun in darkness, ran out into the garden in panic. The world had come to an end for Brigitte Bardot.'

And so, very nearly, it had. Death was a hair's breadth away when a neighbour's child, 13-year-old Jean-Louis Bunos, found her face down in the grass. Both wrists were cut and she had swallowed an entire jar of sleeping pills. Inside the house was a note in a hurried, incoherent scrawl. *'Je déborde de cafard je suis désespérée et malheureuse, je pars me changer les idées de toute façon j'ai mal alors autant avoir mal pour quelquechose. A tout à l'heure, B.'* Neither the French nor the translation made very much sense, as if it should: 'I overflow with the blues [or more directly: I've got the hump]. I am in despair and unhappy. I leave to change my feelings, as anyway I'm in pain and I might as well suffer for something. See you later, B.'

The date was September 28, 1960, her 26th birthday. It was a miracle she lived, revealed her agent. 'The doctor said she would have died if she'd been found even 20 minutes later.'

Without the compassion of some 23 months later when Marilyn Monroe died in similar straits, the world's shock quickly transmuted into an ugly continuation of the very kind of insidious headlines which

BARDOT TAKES AN OVERDOSE OF DRUGS

She is found in garden with wrists slashed

From SAM WHITE: Paris, Thursday

Brigitte Bardot, who was found last night with slashed wrists and who had taken a heavy overdose of sleeping tablets, is stated to be "recovering and in reasonably good condition" at the clinic in Nice to which she was rushed after being discovered in a state of collapse.

Her parents were told at midnight. Her husband, Jacques Charrier, from whom she has been living apart for the past two weeks, left the Basque coast by car and is expected in Nice today.

Four weeks ago her Paris doctor was reported in the French Press as having visited her after an emergency call from her husband who discovered her in a state of collapse—also due to an overdose of sleeping tablets.

On a cliff

Miss Bardot who left Paris after a wild scene between her husband and her new leading man, Samy Frey, outside a Paris cafe weeks ago, has been a close friend.

NOW SHE IS OUT OF DANGER

Brigitte Bardot Drugged, In Coma

From FRANK TOLE PARIS, Thursday.

DOCTORS to-day saved the life of Brigitte Bardot. The blonde film star took an overdose of sleeping drugs after a party for her 26th birthday yesterday.

The official French news agency said she took what

had led to her bid to destroy myth and life. Brigitte, of course, made one major media mistake. She did not die. Which is to say, she failed to end her own being and therefore helped to kill off her myth herself (instead of allowing the Press to do it) by giving it a new lease on life and, consequently, on death—natural death in the fullness of time. Had Bardot died, this myth would have been sentimentally perpetuated, à la Valentino, Dean, Monroe and, more lately, Bruce Lee. That she survived was somehow wrong, and led instead to charges of more publicity-stunting. London's *Sunday Graphic* front-paged the wrist-slashing climax from *La vérité* under the accusation: 'Was this a put-up job? It is odd that in her latest film—now being given the publicity treatment—Bardot attempted suicide. The method: by cutting her wrists and taking drugs.' (She 'committed' suicide in the film, but that, of course, would not have read so neatly.) Long-time journalist fans refuted such nonsense; among them Leonard Mosley, the film critic and former war correspondent of the *Daily Express,* who had literally tripped over Bardot at the 1953 Cannes festival and first introduced her to British readers. 'Brigitte Bardot today,' he wrote, 'is a doom-laden Peter Pan trapped in an adult world which she hasn't yet learned to live with.' Or vice-versa.

Clouzot blamed the Parisian journalists; Levy singled out *France-Dimanche* in particular, as well as the more influential *Paris-Match,* for hounding their own star creation. *France-Dimanche* had enough gall to hit back, asking who dared call the kettle black—had not Levy helped in her 'création' as well, had not Clouzot tyrannised the *Vérité* performance out of her?

One French actress, who understandably refused to be named, said with Bardot out of the way, there would be room for proper actresses in French films at last. More cynics, of which there are plenty in Paris, implied it was most certainly publicity, because *La vérité* had cost too much and the backers were scared Bardot's acting ability would not stand up to unsentimentalised criticism. Clouzot jumped on that idea, knowing he had the finest BB performance on emulsion. 'Her force as a film star of talent is just beginning,' he declared.

Leslie Mallory in an otherwise excellent investigative summation for the *News Chronicle* in Britain, was also suspicious: film stars did not kill themselves for receiving too much publicity, said he, rather for too little. Nonsense, replied Bardot's old friend (and baby Nicolas's godmother), producer Christine Gouze-Renal. She told the *Daily Express*: 'Suicides do not happen in 24 hours. They are a culmination of the way we are forced to live. People everywhere in the world have an ambivalent attitude towards Brigitte. They hate her and love her at the same time . . . She felt she was going mad and so she tried to end it. The attempted suicide awakened her to many things, made her more maternal to Nicolas, to responsibilities, to her world, her people. She will never try it again.' Nor has she, managing, tentatively at first, to cope with her own twin personas.

Probably the most decisive comment of the entire episode, of the Bardolatry phenomenon itself, came from the small-town French chemist who had sold Brigitte her suicide ration of sleeping pills. Why had he not recognised the great Bardot in his shop? '*Pouf!* I serve a hundred Bardots every day!'

With the kind of irony that is more French than chauvinism, the incident built renewed respect for the girl. The over-sexy starlet, the blot on her country's image, revered, if, momentarily, as a mother, was finally—in part—understood. As a victim of the rat race, of the *panier de crabes* (crab basket) of her chosen, cannibalistic career.

She left the St. François Clinic at Menton on October 2, accompanied by producer friend Francis Cosne, for whom she was booked for her next film. She carried a long-stemmed blood-red rose, on her wrists were flesh-coloured medical dressings. Pale and slight in sweater and trousers, she made no statement. Some of the crowd, as many public as journalists, shouted *Bonne chance, Brigitte* and she replied with a scarcely audible *merci.* Her family doctor, Gérard Dupouy, explained she had deep problems—'we must bring them out and talk about them with her until she realises they do not matter any more. Then the world

Saviour. Reflecting in the wings, Vadim returns to Bardot's side as she takes up her career anew with *Le bride sur le cou.*

Survivor. Brigitte leaves hospital after her suicide attempt, with bandages on her wrists, a single red rose and the comforting arm of her next producer, Francis Cosne.

will have the real Brigitte Bardot back again.' A few days later she was seen hand-in-hand with Vadim. Both denied re-marriage rumours. 'So stupid,' said Brigitte. 'Vadim is my best friend. In fact, I like him better now than when he was my husband.' She added, in perhaps innocent irony: 'Everything I am, I owe to Vadim.'

And he says he always knew when Brigitte was feeling low enough to consider suicide and attempt it—which is why Vadim does not remember this particular incident any more or less than any other in his and her lives, together and separated. 'Even if I had not seen her for one year, my instinct would tell me when something was about to happen. One time, I remember calling Paris when I was far away—in Spain, or somewhere—to check on her, knowing that something was wrong. And something *was* wrong. I had some instinctive feeling which I cannot fully explain . . . You know, people who are *suicidés,* it is not always for a logical reason; it comes from time to time in a certain period and if you know them, you can have a feeling of what will happen.'

He had once explained that since left alone one evening, aged eight, she felt herself alone in the world and it scared her. She was never to be alone again.

If the self-analysis with her doctor ever did take place —or with Vadim or any other members of her BB retinue—no one ever mentioned it, but there began a definite new and indolent flair about Bardot from 1961 until today. Freedom became absolute. The permissivity of the modern world caught up with her, what had been labelled scandal yesterday became the average for today, mere paragraphical news tomorrow. The pop world took over the headlines, and drugs, less prosaic than sleeping pills, governed stellar lives more than sexual entanglements, heterosexual or otherwise. Bardot began making films again, this time not to create or continue a legend, but to pay for it. Her generosity is less known than her frugality, and her taxes are heavy. She once wrote to De Gaulle threatening to quit, to stop earning vast dollars for France without tax relief: by 1964 one estimate was BB had earned $50,000,000 for France. She began love affairs, always for longer periods than her 50s flings. The men were generally younger, *'j'adore les beaux jeunes hommes',* an odd and increasing mixture of the mediocre in search of the magnificent. They had nothing to lose and everything to gain; two of her mid-60s lovers became male models afterwards, two more acted with her in films, and her current

71

ex-beau was the first lover she had allowed to become her personal photographer.

For her return to the screen after her brush with death, she started afresh, cancelling all previous plans for a second film with Charrier, *Le grand dadais,* and another project with Marcel Camus. She chose Cosne's offer of a comedy, more mild than wild, called *La bride sur le cou—Loose Reins* or somesuch in English. Straight away she showed her new order. Simple compliance was out. BB was calling the shots. Within a few days of rehearsals and shooting, she had the young director, Jean Aurel, sacked—which did not please fellow new-wavers much and had Truffaut, for one, leading a fight for Aurel's reinstatement. Vadim became script and film doctor. Although he praised the venture as (rapidly re-written) American slapstick, French style, it flopped like a custard pie at the box-office—enhanced only by another of his dreamy fantasies of Brigitte dancing, apparently nude, in soft focus. The music was by James Campbell, former member of the Katherine Dunham troupe, creator of her sultry mambo in *Et Dieu créa la femme,* and a participant again in Vadim-BB film games for *Don Juan 1973.* As the stills proved, Brigitte was not naked, but clad in a neck-to-toe cat-suit—transparent enough to have the entire sequence excised by the British censor. This showed the annoying double standards of Swinging London, *circa* 1964, when the film eventually arrived as *Please Not Now* and did not even rate a Press screening.

There followed a sketch in the star-packed *Les amours célèbres,* a reunion with one of her better directors, Boisrond, and the culmination of every French film fan's dream couple: Bardot plus Delon. Their special 'nude' embrace for photographer Sam Levin's *Cinémonde* cover actually contained more excitement than their scenes in the film. The chemistry was totally absent: a case of a leading man being almost as pretty as his leading lady. And neither required the gorilla-like wrestlers employed by the Studios Billancourt to keep cameramen at bay.

Christine Gouze-Renal had the next important idea, announced with some apoplexy by the London *Daily Mail*: Bardot would remake *Private Lives* in the Gertrude Lawrence rôle. The private life everyone wanted to see was Bardot's, and under the slippery control of Louis Malle, the film became *Vie privée/A Very Private Affair,* very much the BB *histoire* via a Swiss miss called Jill, and her fatal inability to cope with her acclaim as a sexy screen legend. Jill's end was accidental instead of suicidal, falling from a roof (in a ridiculous slow-motion freefall) on being startled by a photographic flash-bulb . . . 'there's a photographer sitting on the roof opposite with a telescopic lens'.

More than one sequence in the film came directly from

Swimmer. Brigitte recovers in the sun and the sea...

Brigitte's experience, in particular the quite horrendous happening in a lift which all critics never failed to mention, where a charwoman hysterically upbraids and attacks the screen star. 'Absolutely true,' said Christine Gouze-Renal. 'She visited a friend in hospital and was attacked by one of the women employed there. The woman tried to stab her with a fork, screaming how her son was fighting in Algeria while Brigitte was making millions of francs for stripping and showing off her disgusting body. Brigitte was terrified. She never dreamed she could be so detested. I tried to comfort her, to explain that worship and envy were inseparable.'

Malle's film also exposed much of the Press-baiting at its worst; paradoxically the journalists on location lived up to their reputation, loosening hot rumours about BB and her new partner, Marcello Mastroianni. He loved her! No? Okay then, he hated her! 'What idiocy!' he snorted. 'Can you see me, can you truthfully, telephoning Fellini and complaining . . . "Papa, I can't make a go of it. I've bumped up against a girl with a bust!"' Truth was, the Latin star (who

...of a St. Tropez packed with photographic spies.

later took up with Vadim's BB Mk. III, Catherine Deneuve) was wholly indifferent to Bardot. If anything, he was sorry for the frightened girl with two personalities, one living in fear of the other . . .

'She's not too bright as far as men are concerned,' he told Hugh Hefner's *Show Business Illustrated*. 'She is a victim of the men who fall in love with her . . . all became famous through her . . . Even Roger Vadim, well, he was the only one that wasn't a kid, but even he became famous by using her. They live on her name . . . basically they're the same type. Youngsters, nobodies, who got themselves known and reached an unwholesome conclusion with their nervous breakdowns and their inability to complete military service. It's fortunate she doesn't make too many pictures or France wouldn't have an army.'

For the public, the film explained much behind headlines, and refurbished her new-won respectability; so did another terrifying incident, winning praise from De Gaulle himself: 'This young woman seems to be made of sterling qualities.' Just after the première, the OAS threatened to kidnap Bardot's son

and, as events showed, the police discounted her pleas for help as a publicity stunt. On her own, Brigitte sent Nicolas to Switzerland, hired armed guards and sent the letter demanding 50,000 francs (£3,600) on to *L'Express* magazine—with her answer. She refused to pay one *centime*. 'I won't pay because I have no wish to live in a Nazi country.' The move showed extraordinary courage for a mere sex-pot; and publicity had nothing to do with it. Soon after her stand, French writer Vladimir Posner was injured as a result of an OAS *bombe-plastique* in a similar blackmail attempt.

The divorce from Charrier opened 1962 and it surprised no one when she allowed him custody of Nicolas. 'I don't see him so often. He's all right, I suppose. He's looked after well enough. I never planned to let my baby change my life or stand in the way of my career.' Sami Frey was on hand as Bardot reiterated her new independent philosophy, that she was unconventional, did not care about society, and even if she were not rich, her attitudes would remain the same. 'I love to the limit of myself and my emotions. I love . . . and . . . live . . . right to the end. When the love flies, *pouf!* it is cold, finished.'

Similarly philosophic years later, Jacques Charrier displayed little bitterness and remained a firm admirer of his wife's talent. He always insisted for instance that Vadim was no more Bardot's creator than he was. 'I don't think he released the flower from the weeds. I believe she made Vadim rather than Vadim made her. She has done very well without him.'

Indeed there was little coinage in Vadim claiming 'without me . . . she wouldn't be where she is today'. Since the high of his BB films, reinforced by his own solo achievement of *Les liaisons dangereuses* (1969), his career was floundering due to heavy French censorship at home and little fortune in filming for Paramount dollars in Italy. After Stroyberg, he had begun living with, and likewise changing the personality and image of, Catherine Deneuve—but Bardot refused to co-star with her in *Le vice et la vertu*. 'They may have some physical similarities,' commented Vadim, 'but emotionally they're quite different. Catherine will not be another Bardot—her body is not sensational.'

However, he had another BB project afoot, and Brigitte made *Le repos du guerrier* as a favour to him for rescuing her comedy comeback. The reunion, titled *Love on a Pillow* in the United States, created a furore in Paris, selling tickets like hot *croissants*. It paid few bills elsewhere though and was enough to have Bardot saying yet again that she was quitting—'*Ma décision est ir-ré-vo-ca-ble.*' Not quite. The next offer was perhaps too surprising to refuse: Jean-Luc Godard himself, the doyen of *la nouvelle vague*, found that her reported interest in *Le mépris/Contempt*

Triumph. The come-BBack continues (Vadim's, too) and every Paris box-office record is smashed by *Le repos du guerrier* . . .

resuscitated his project. They seemed the odd couple of the French cinema. Mlle. Commercialité and M. Avant Avant-Garde. Yet they worked extremely well together, despite the picture nearly being ruined by the American backers' insistence upon nude Bébé scenes added after completion.

Throughout the Naples and Rome shooting, Brigitte was surrounded by news cameramen and Jacques Rozier took the opportunity to make a documentary about her battles, *Le paparazzi*. Bardot by now was far more wary of the Press. 'Each time I say a word in front of a journalist, I earn him 500 francs, same for the photographers . . .' She avoided much of this by increasing her retinue to include her own photographer, Jicky Dussart: a smart move which led to some extraordinarily beautiful nude studies which sold mightily around the world—after chauvinistic first exposure in *Lui* magazine, the Paris rival to *Playboy*. (The real *Playboy* printed the photo-spreads as well, just as *Lui* came out with another more beautiful, more daring set.)

In close attendance all this time, instead of pursuing his own career, was Sami Frey: 'the only man who can make me vibrate fully as a woman'. His days

were numbered when she caught sight of South American businessman Bob Zaguri, at the 1963 Cannes festival. 'My heart turned over. He dominates me and I love it. He fills every moment with rich South American laughter. He's a big man. This will last.' Zaguri agreed that they were in love and did not wish to spoil it with marriage. He remained quietly in the background when she arrived in London to make *La ravissante idiote* with her Sinatra-preference Tony Perkins. The film was a comedy. The locations were a farce. Crowds of sightseers and Press got out of hand, and the visit was aborted; stars and crew took the first plane out and the locations were atrociously faked up in a Paris studio. Historically, the film is remembered only for the day Bardot discovered popularity could outweigh envy, though even love *en masse* could prove too much to handle.

She took the visit as a cue for her often repeated desire to quit movies. For good, she thought. All was not peaceful, however. At La Madrague, the cameras still hovered, poking through the fencing, the trees were still full of fruit, and telescopic lenses were trained on her sunbathing from boats in the bay. 'I tried to retire, so that I could be free and at peace, so I'd

... her 30th film and, so she insisted, her last.

not have photographers chasing me day and night, so that I'd be on my own at last. It hasn't happened that way. In some ways, when I work, I have more peace than when I do not. At least in a film studio, I have guards and the other people are professionals like myself. I don't have guards on public streets.'

Another comeback then: and her best. Bob Zaguri was her escort as she picked up her career to greater glory in *Viva Maria* at Cuernavaca, in Mexico. 'When Brigitte is nervous, tired or uncertain,' explained Zaguri, 'she turns to me. Because I'm never nervous, tired or uncertain.' (He soon would be.) Louis Malle's inspired re-vamping of Preston Sturgess's *The Beautiful Blonde from Bashful Bend* cast her opposite another woman for the first time, a star of similar stellar magnitude to the French and the world— Jeanne Moreau. The idea created more screen steam than her recent spate of dullard leading men. 'We lived together like two comrades in the army who have fought a war together,' Brigitte recalls.

The film also led to her first official visit to America, for the New York and Hollywood premières in December, 1965. Earlier, she had appeared in her first Hollywood film, a literal guest appearance in a James

Stewart family number first called *Erasmus with Freckles,* until she agreed to appear, when thereafter: *Dear Brigitte.* In America, she proved her new-found stability with consummate ease for a girl terrified of crowds. Clenching hands with Zaguri, she took on the Press easily: no contest.

She had two major receptions, at Kennedy Airport, December 15, and the next day at the Plaza Hotel (where, as in London, she could not escape her suite for 48 hours). Bernard Varley, in the *UK Press Gazette,* commented: 'In 30 years of journalism I've never seen such a dazzling performance as put up by this thoroughly scared girl on her first visit . . . She made tough American newspapermen and women eat out of her paws.' In the *New York Telegram,* Nina McCain agreed—Bardot gave as good as she got. 'She fended off absurd, sometimes insulting questions with aplomb and wit . . . She drew a number of genuinely appreciative laughs from people who are not easily impressed. There was an inescapable feeling that Miss Bardot and the audience both enjoyed the performance and shared a kind of private joke about the whole thing.'

First question, inevitably, at Kennedy: *How old are you, Brigitte?* / 31 and you? *What do you think about being called a sex-kitten?* / It's all right if you've got the right figure. *Do you feel a sex-symbol?* / I am myself. *Well, who are you?* / Look . . . (and she left the podium and paraded in front of the table like a mannequin).

One extremely persistent woman shouted: *Do you think a woman has to have children in order to be fulfilled?* / You should try anything once. *Yes, but what do you think about free love?* / I don't think when I make love. The same journalist was at the Plaza Hotel conference the next day, and Brigitte recognised her when she asked: *How do you reconcile your ideas on marriage and free love?* / Have you tried it since yesterday? *Yes, I did; but, what do I do now?* / Keep trying!

The New York première was a controlled riot with Julie Christie being mistaken for Bardot, and when the French goddess did arrive, surrounded by six Pinkerton guards, she had eyes hurt by one myriad attack of flashbulbs. She was treated by two doctors—neither of whom would accept payment for attending her.

In Hollywood, the film city was at her feet. President Kennedy's ex-Pressman, Pierre Salinger, looked after her and she was happier with the film's reception ('they are more used here to sub-titles') and once more handled her press reception superbly. 'They found me intelligent and spiritual, as well—all the better.' Stunned at her arrival, the awaiting Press greeted her with a respectful silence, until she encouraged them to begin with a smiling 'Well, what are you doing now?' First Hollywood query: *Who is Brigitte Bardot*

Control. Brigitte handles the Press with consummate ease. In New York, Mexico and London.

—*how do you view her?*/Here she is—disappointed? *What kind of woman are you?* /You want to leave for a week with me to find out? *I'd have to ask my wife.* /But of course, that's exactly what I mean, you and me and your wife!

In more privacy, Bardot saw again Paul Newman, whom she had first met filming in Paris; Robert Wagner and Robert Mitchum; and went out of her way to meet one of her idols, George Chakiris from *West Side Story* (director Michel Deville once hoped to team them in a French musical). In the end she left town quietly, disguised and using one of her aliases, Kathleen Price. Back in Paris, she had to be ordered to bed for four days to recover from the finest public relations exercise of her career. She was to be back in the States within six months—to marry Gunther Sachs.

Now it was Bob Zaguri's days that were numbered, not that he, like Frey or anyone before, ever realised it. Zaguri just never learned. In the autumn of 1965, he had taken Brigitte to the £2-a-drink disco, Castel, on the left bank. At the next table sat independently wealthy dentist Paul Albou, 43, whose clients included ex-Queen Soraya, Lady Docker and BB: he had extracted a wisdom tooth for her. They danced for an hour or more and disappeared for a week. Then

Roaming. Brigitte and third husband, Gunther Sachs, take in Rome night spots with her current co-star, Alain Delon.

early in 1966, Zaguri took her to dinner at a fashionably intimate St. Tropez restaurant. At the next table this time was millionaire playboy Gunther Sachs von Opel in a party headed by Roger Vadim. Vadim made the introductions and three weeks later they were wed. The whirlwind marriage took everyone by surprise, Bardot included. She once said she had married Vadim to find out what it was like, and wed Charrier for reasons she did not remember any more. 'It is not because I married some men, that I liked them more than others. Marriage must be like a stroke of madness!'

'I was married,' she said later, 'James Bond style.' 'Like a fairy story and James Bond film together,' countered Sachs. It was, she recalled, at 4 am on July 8 that Sachs proposed in his fashion: 'I'm going to marry you.' They examined globes to find a suitable place. Vadim suggested Vegas, having wed Jane Fonda there the previous year. Neither knew the place that well. No problem for Sachs. He phoned 'the only man with weight that I knew in the USA': Teddy Kennedy. 'Can you help me get married with Brigitte without anyone knowing—as soon as possible.' From Sachs's Bavarian chalet, they took fast cars to Fréjus, a plane to Nice, another to Paris, travelling as M. Scar and Mme. Bordat. From Orly, his Rolls sped them to their

flats in avenue Paul Doumer and avenue Foch. He called his Lausanne lawyer to join them pronto, with his international marital law books. Then off from Orly to Los Angeles with a party of four: Christian Marquand's brother, Serge, lawyers Peter Notz and Gérard Le Cléry—*les pieds nickelés,* BB called them after her favourite comic characters—and the inevitable photographer, Philippe d'Exéa. At Los Angeles, Kennedy's lawyer had awaiting two small jets—'like flying Ferraris'. In 35 minutes they were in Vegas, met by a pair of black Cadillacs and taken straight to the town hall for the licence at 11.45 pm, July 13. From there to a lawyer's house where the Irish-American judge John Mowbray greeted Brigitte, resplendent in a purple mini, and Sachs, in blue blazer and white flannels, and married them surrounded by enormous lilac bouquets from Teddy Kennedy. By now it was July 14, Bastille Day—a most appropriate date for the day Sachs stormed Bardot.

'I was very frightened,' she said, 'because I had to repeat the words in English. I didn't understand what I was saying. But him the German, and me, the French, both said "Yes".' The judge expressed the presumably Irish-American hope that 'the road rise to meet you and may the wind be ever at your back' and they celebrated with dinner for six at the Tropicana and moved into Bungalow No. 1 at the Beverly Hills Hotel.

Bob Zaguri thought she was shopping in Paris. Vadim commented: 'It's bound to be stormy, but who knows?' and BB received the usual religious castigation in an open letter from Dr Marie-Dominique, 40, in the *Vie Catholique Illustrée,* 'Whether you believe in him or not, dear Brigitte, may God forgive you for the harm you are doing to us. In eight minutes you get married again . . . You no longer belong to M. Vadim, not to M. Charrier, not to M. Zaguri: you belong to M. Sachs. In eight minutes you will swear faithfulness for life. If someone else comes on the scene tomorrow, whom you do not know today, will you get married again? Will M. Sachs in turn use the words uttered by your last boyfriend, M. Zaguri, when he heard about your recent marriage— that it was all a big joke. You will say that your private life belongs to you . . . marriage is a public act.'

So is the breaking up of the same. With Sachs it did not seem to take long. Less than two months later, he was little in evidence when she found it more easy to film once more in London. *A cœur joie* was, ironically, a production Zaguri was connected with. The Anglo-French project suffered abysmally from being shot in French and unhappy Engleesh, an almighty flop. Zaguri left the set if Sachs turned up, but the German preferred golf and it was soon obvious to all on the production that Brigitte was smitten, momentarily at least, with one of the cast, ex-pop singer and director-to-be, Mike Sarne. They simply disappeared from the movie for a short while. Sarne called her totally irresistible: 'one of the all-time great girls'.

'When a man attracts her, Bardot goes straight to him,' Marguerite Duras wrote two years before. 'Nothing stops her. It does not matter if he is in a café, at home or staying with friends. She goes off with him on the spot without a glance at the man she is leaving. In the evening, perhaps, she will come back—or perhaps not. Thus, this woman who has never been forsaken does not understand—among other things—the atrociousness of her behaviour. Although she has left many corpses in her wake, she herself remains unharmed . . . Her will is strong. Nobody has ever broken the toy.'

However, the BB–Sachs union picked up—he called her Mamou, she called him Planti or Saxy. They went to Rome in 1967 for her third Louis Malle project, one of the episodes in an Edgar Allan Poe trilogy, *Les histoires extraordinaires,* using up some of the Poe stories not yet impinged upon by Roger Corman, Vincent Price and American-International Pictures (who naturally distributed the film in the States). Les Sachs stayed at the Solo Beautitudo villa on the

Jane Fonda

Catherine Deneuve

Anna Gael

Sandra Jullien

France Anglade

Bibi Andersson

Ursula Andress

Cybill Shepherd

Ann-Margret

Barbara Bouchet

Sharon Tate

Stella Stevens

Senta Berger

Edy Williams

Ewa Aulin

Elke Sommer

Cheri Caffaro

Ahna Capri

Haydee Politoff

Joey Heatherton

Susanne Benton

Claire Gordon

Julie Christie

Mylène Demongeot

Britt Ekland

Suzy Kendall

Olinka Berova

Margaret-Rose Keil

Marianne Faithfull

Carol White

Anouska Hempel

Veronica Carlson

Justine Lord

Virna Lisi

Marisa Mell

Susan George

Verushka

Margaret Markov

Anita Pallenberg

Doubles. The Bébé image has influenced almost every young actress in movies since 1956. These 33 examples include a Prussian countess, Verushka; an English lady, Anna Gael (Lady Weymouth); five Vadim re-creations; plus Cheri Caffaro, starting her US career in the *Ginger* femme-spy series, after winning a Bardot Lookalike contest in *Life*; Marisa Mell as BB (or FF!) in Ken Russell's *French Dressing* satire, 1963; and Virna Lisi winning a whole new career in George Axelrod's *How To Murder Your Wife*, 1965, after Brigitte refused his Hollywood offer.

Mireille Darc

Edina Ronay

Marilyn Rickard

Sydne Rome

79

Peep. Wherever BB goes, prying eyes gather and gaze.

Peace. Only among friends: like Christine Gouze-Renal.

Appian Way, the Burton's residence during *Taming of the Shrew,* and just an Appian step from the villa taken by les Vadim, working on another sketch in the film. While Bardot worked—again with Delon; a much better result than their first outing—Sachs played film-man himself, working on a script with New York novelist Harry Matthews: *Narcisse dans le mercure,* then *Au fil de la splendeur* and finally known as *Le Pari.* Curiously enough it was the story of a playboy seducing a cover-girl. Sachs wanted his brother-in-law Patrick Bauchau (Mijanou's husband) to play the lead and everyone guessed Bardot would be the girl. She was not so keen, having suffered mightily as a cover-girl yet again in the disastrous *A cœur joie;* she was more 'passionated' with the idea though when Gunther said he would direct. Bondsman Harry Saltzman was rumoured to be interested in a deal, but nothing came of it and the film was never made.

During 1967 *Cinémonde* was reporting *'dans les studios internationaux une obsession: sexe',* although Vadim kept panties on Fonda in the *Playboy-paparazzi* shot scenes with Peter McEnery in his version of Zola's *La curé,* his first major festival entry and one of his best three films. Bardot, however, wouldn't make her mind up about continuing with

the world obsession or not. 'I do my best but I am not an actress. Lady Macbeth doesn't interest me. I am just Brigitte Bardot.' That was enough for Visconti to express interest in her being his Odette Swan in the Proust novel, *A la recherche du temps perdu.* Bardot, herself keen, sought the rights to Sebastien Japrisot's *La dame dans l'auto,* but she spent too long haggling in her frugal mood and the film was made instead with Stéphane Audran, Claude Chabrol's wife and the separated spouse of Trintignant at the time of the 1956 affair. Among other films BB later considered was one about a female James Bond and, because of Vadim's enthusiasm, the Felicien Marceau prize-winning novel, *Creezy,* which was made by Chabrol's company with the American BB of the 70s, Sydne Rome.

More successful—financially if nothing else—were the negotiations for Euan Lloyd's remarkable coup of matching Bardot with Sean Connery. And in a western! 007 + BB = TNT shouted *Cinémonde.* Not quite. Some castings, as BB + Delon, looked better on paper than screen. The setting was enough to turn everyone off movies for life, Almeria; which even the Spanish dislike. This slice of hot, arid scrubland had become the home of the spaghetti Westerns, used by 50 units a year. *Shalako* was reputed to be the 131st Western

Pride. It's in the eyes and the smile of Papa.

Pair. Louis and Anne-Marie Bardot: Pilou and Totty.

made there.

Her entrance had a minor kind of majesty, akin to a royal procession in Fiji or Nepal, not overdone but played to the hilt, reported Jon Bradshaw in the London *Daily Telegraph* magazine. 'The procedure is always the same. Ibe, her tall Negro chauffeur, is the first to alight springing from his seat to open the rear door [of her Rolls; second-hand and since discarded]. Attired in a white suit cut in the Mao Tse-tung military style, he stands solemn, grand, delicately adjusting his shades. Brigitte bought him four of the outfits at Mayfair, Paris' most popular boutique, at a cost of £70 a piece. Born in the Ivory Coast, Ibe is an actor-dancer and has worked for Bardot for two years. When he was hired, Bardot had the Rolls sprayed white. Also in the Rolls is Monique, her personal stand-in, Gloria, her personal secretary, and Mr. Rooney, her personal publicist. Behind the Rolls is usually another car containing Jean-Pierre [Berroyer], her personal hairdresser and one or two of her personal photographers. In Paris, Bardot moves alone. When she is filming, the entourage is in constant attendance, an ascension of larks, flitting confidently in her footsteps.'

Sachs was there too, now and again on the sidelines. Bardot complained about him to *Life* magazine:

'Gunther has certainly not given me what men are supposed to give a woman—tenderness. He took me by storm. I was on a flying carpet—serenaded in Venice, baccarat in Nice, marriage in Las Vegas—but when the carpet landed—bang! He was dry, artificial, obsessed with making an impression—to exhibit me to the Shah of Iran, to some important Swiss businessman. I hate that!'

Five months later, Sachs had gone—so had the summer affair with Italian club-owner Luigi Rizzi, accompanied by the usual nude swimming photos together, off La Madrague. She arrived in London for the *Shalako* première with a new young man, Patrick Gilles, 23, the first of her non-actor lovers to have been used in a film of hers. In *Les femmes,* a tired little number for which BB got 80,000 francs, less than half her old fee, the once sacked director Jean Aurel asked Gilles to play a discarded lover of the Bardot character. Typecasting, soon enough. He was replaced by art publisher Michel Engels, divorced father of two, then Christian Kalt took over and led her into the 70s, towards the final decline in box-office kudos, but the start, at long last, of a certain tranquillity in her existence—and no less an influence on world opinions.

Bob Zaguri

Sacha Distel

Jean-Louis Trintignant

Miroslav Brozeck

Gunther Sachs

Sami Frey

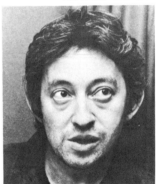

Serge Gainsbourg

BBoyfriends. 'Yes, I've had many lovers in my life . . .' Whether long or short, flirtatious or serious, momentarily torrid or more satisfactorily loving, the affairs gave her collection of *homo-brigittis* a rare kudos in life, and the kind of exclusive, if passing fame in which they either swam or sank. Exploitation or exhaustion. From Vadim to Brozeck, Brigitte has been ever open and frank about her love-life, never hiding an affair, never caring for any comments they produced, and living her rarely private life exactly as she dictated : to the limits of her impulsive emotions. 'I'm not able to exist without passion. When I don't love, I'm bored. I'm not beautiful any more. I'm like . . . dying. When I love, even if I'm unhappy, I'm transformed. The only existence which counts—besides my own—is that of a man. But which man ?' A question with innumerable answers.

Mike Sarne

Jacques Charrier

Laurent Vergez

Christian Kalt

Patrick Gilles

The Sedate Seventies: Rebourgeoisification

'BB is one of the sacred monsters. Into this category go so many of the screen's greatest stars—von Stroheim, Valentino, Garbo, Dietrich, Bette Davis, James Dean and Brando. They are idolised by half the public, execrated by the other half. The spectator finds himself loving and hating them at the same time. When they play villains, they rivet the spectator's attention, the virtuous characters shrink into a pale, vague blob beside them. When they play heroes or heroines, it is with an insolence that takes the spectator's breath away. If they aren't actually psychological freaks they are invariably alleged to be.'
—Raymond Durgnat.

Whatever the Presidential style, the traditional town-hall symbol of the French Republic is the bust of Marianne, the anonymous spirit of the Revolution, first sculpted in 1848. Since 1956, of course, the symbol of France to the outside world which had never heard of Marianne has been Brigitte Bardot. It is, therefore, a fitting tribute to the ever-youthful star's unprecedented position that the latest series of Mariannes to be found dotted around the mayors' offices all over the country is less austere and profoundly more generous in face, mouth and cleavage—BB in fact.

A sculptor named Aslan designed and executed the new busts. André Malraux, one time Minister of Culture, was among the first to buy one. Bardot was given one and had it mounted, by repute, above her bed. Naturally her proud agent, Olga Horstig-Primuz, has one in her office. The radical politician and founder of *L'Express* magazine, Jean-Jacques Servan-Schreiber, has another. 'We should be proud of her,' he once told *Time* magazine, 'of Roquefort cheese and of Bordeaux wine. They are the products that bring us the most profit.' And satisfaction. The French tourist authorities were soon in total *concorde* with J-J S-S. Faced with a 10 per cent drop in American tourists in 1974, they invited Bébé to make a 30-second commercial for use on Stateside television. Brigitte extolled all the virtues of la belle France, adding coyly,

'After all, I am still a child of France.' None finer . . .
Even in the blight of her final movie output, Bardot remains a total star to the French—who comprise, probably, the greatest nation of filmgoers and film-lovers in the Western world. They have, by turn, adored, crucified, forgiven and rediscovered their Bébé doll many times over, never ceasing to be amazed by her everlasting impact on the world and on themselves. When gathering information in Paris for this book, one publicity woman shrugged her shoulders and said, surely, BB was *passé* now. She then discussed Bardot, unrequested, for 30 minutes. Bardot can never be *passé*. She still has too much to offer—if she feels like it.

For a nation so devoted to cinema, it was no surprise to find a French magazine recently asking 16 international directors how they would feature Bardot if given the opportunity. Jean Renoir saw her as one of his father's canvases come to vibrant life. Antonioni suggested a Renaissance character, 'there's something unreal about her features, something rather poignant'. De Sica said she could pass for English, American, German—even Napolitan or Sicilian—every bit as much as French: 'she's purely and simply woman'. Hitchcock thought a film about blue-bloods would suit her best, he would cast her as a 'jokey' princess. Billy Wilder maintained the most important aspect of Brigitte was the way she glowed.

Fellini replied: 'If she didn't exist, we'd have to invent her. Her figure aside, the most striking thing about her is her range of facial expressions. She could play ten different characters in the same film.' Or the lead in any ten movies, considered Otto Preminger. 'She's extraordinary! I'd be happy to give her the lead in any film I might make, provided only that the character be a woman in love—and in love with life.'

That has been BB's most basic image, beyond all argument, throughout her 23 years in films. She is a greater star of life than of any electronic media—and she has starred in them all, except radio. Her voice alone, as distinctive and splendidly evocative as it is, is not enough: seeing BB in motion is essential. A feast for the eye, the brain, the imagination, above all the libido. Her films have disappointed in recent years as she has quietly aged and begun a move back rather than continuing forward in her former insolent, rebellious manner. Indolence has won over insolence. Today, in her sudden, though rather inevitable, time-pressured rebourgeoisification, she has begun to equate eroticism with pornography. The commercial exploitation of sex—'the gestures of love'—disgust her. While she is readily amused by all the erotic books, she will never bother to see the film versions. She refused, for example, to attend any screening of *La grande bouffe* or *Le dernier tango à Paris*. 'If I started it with *Et Dieu créa la femme*,' she has

Sister. Bébé the nun in *Les novices*, 1970. Not so much shock casting as the eventual, almost traditional habit for sex sirens in movies.

stated, 'it was in the air at the time and Vadim felt it. Have you seen it recently? It's simply the story of a liberated girl, free—really nothing unhealthy. My films were never pornographic. Nudity, you know, is not necessarily indecent. The dirtiness is in the minds of the people who see it that way. I never made a film in tucked-up skirt, suspenders and black-stockings—that's hypocrisy. Now quite obviously, I've become imprisoned in an image. Even if I were to play a nun, you know what the posters would be like.' In fact, she did play a nun in *Les novices* and the posters were very much as one might have thought, mainly because in the opening scenes BB's nun kicked the habit, stripped naked on a beach—and posed for cameramen in wimple alone. The rest of the comedy had her novice going on the run, turning would-be prostitute and swimming around in a see-through bikini . . .

One would hardly think of accusing Brigitte Bardot of hypocrisy, she has fought and flouted it too consistently since 1952, with poses akin to a revitalised Statue of Liberty. It is, though, difficult to reconcile some of her remarks upon reaching 40 and a seemingly semi-retired respectability, with the sex-sequences directed by Vadim in her penultimate film, *Don Juan 1973*. Among other episodes, BB seduces a cousin who happens to be a priest, and goes to bed with a woman—British actress Jane Birkin, in a scene, admittedly, of innate ridiculousness. Sole pornography in this venture proved to be the risible script, Vadim's bored (and boring) direction, and the abortive manner in which the production was dubbed from French into some (more) asinine mid-Atlantic English.

A major disappointment, then. Particularly as it had

been such a constant theme of Vadim to classify BB as a female Casanova or Don Juan over the years. As far back as 1967, he was remarking how a man with mistresses galore is regarded by his peers as a Don Juan, while a woman with similar appetites is deprecated as little more than a whore. Obviously, the premise for the film was a long time fermenting in his mind. Too long. The dish was somewhat overdone when it finally came to the table.

Hope had also been high for the film because the script came from Prix Goncourt winning novelist and journalist, Jean Cau. In one *L'Express* meeting with Brigitte in 1963, Cau was the first Press interrogator to understand her, to capture Bardot for what she was, is, that which Vadim had seen ten years before and tried, intermittently, to encompass in his screenplays. 'If I were dealing with a child,' wrote Cau, 'I should say I had before me a headstrong little boy. At half-time in our interview, Brigitte Bardot is a boy-woman.'

Vadim knew all this backwards and had exemplified, rather than inaugurated, her androgynous, polymorphous and perverse qualities. 'The distillation,' as Pauline Kael later submitted, 'of all those irresponsible petulant teenagers who may never know that human experience has depth and expressiveness and potentialities beyond their immediate range of impulses'.

The truth remains, or so Vadim continually impresses upon us over the decades, that the root-cause of Bardot's lasting success is her physio-mental make-up: half-man and half-girl. 'She has the bottom of a young adolescent. She has something in the way she talks, in the way she is built—apart from the bust—which is very close to a man. And yet she is still very, very, feminine.' Psychologically she is sentimental, the way women are, and vulnerable, in the way women are, yet mentally, in her attitude towards sex above all other matters, she is completely masculine. 'All I did was to bring out this aspect of sex which existed but was not understood—the overlapping of what is masculine in woman and what's feminine in man. Bardot was a woman who could be loved by other women, or hated by other women, but not in the manner of the accepted "sexy girl" of . . . years ago. Not like Jane Russell, who was the perfect American sex image at that time—enormous breasts, huge behind, well built, just a pin-up. And not like Sophia Loren . . .'

Whatever one made of all these portraits of Bardot the boy-chick, one was not, apparently, meant to make the obvious. Not when faced with the surprise Sapphic gambolling of Brigitte with Jane Birkin, nude yes, but more on than in bed, during *Don Juan 1973*. Not when recalling this was a sequence which Vadim had quite openly sought to arrange in one form or another in plenty of his previous BB plans, to the point of wanting to cast her in *Le vice et la virtu* (1962) oppo-

Sisters. Under the skin. Brigitte romps with her Paris successor of the 70s—British beauty Jane Birkin—in Bardot's final Vadim film, *Don Juan 1973*.

site his own choice of her successors in his films and beds, Annette Stroyberg or Catherine Deneuve. And not even when faced, as I have been, with women claiming to have had sexual affairs with Bardot. Brigitte has yet to give any hint of public credence to such tales, unlike, for example, the more wholly liberated Maria Schneider. And Vadim will defend Bardot's heterosexuality with a euphemistic, if quite explosive, hand upon heart.

'If one woman in the world is not bi-sexual, it is Brigitte,' he answered point-blank to my likewise, and I judged, necessary question in Paris. 'She never could stand that. Beside the fact that she needs to have a lot of girls around her—to protect her—she was, on the sexual level, absolutely not homosexual. Ever. Well, she may have had, like any girl when very young, a kind of experience—to see what will happen . . . That's not impossible. But that was not with her all the time. Really, basically, she is not at all homosexual, not at all sexually interested in girls.'

The question had not necessarily suggested that she was; rather that Vadim obviously was, and through him, Bardot may have developed such an interest. He looked amused at the very thought. Paradoxically, the BB girlfriend has been an essential rôle in most Bébé vehicles from Vadim's very first script for her—which provided a *copine* in Isabelle Pia, in *Futures Vedettes*. Then on through Isabelle Corey in *Et Dieu créa la femme*; Alida Valli, *Les bijoutiers du clair de lune*; Macha Meril, *Le repos du guerrier*. Other directors followed his lead, hence Nicole Berger as the BB-corrupted maid in *En cas de malheur*; Barbara Sohmers as the very dikey Daisy in *La vérité*; Ursula Kubler, *Vie privée*; to say nothing untoward of the bigger

Model. Brigitte Bardot started professional life as a model and has remained the quarry of nearly every major photographer in Europe, if not the world, mirroring their fantasies . . .

co-starring ventures with Moreau, Giradot and Cardinale.

The *copine,* Vadim maintained, was just that. A friend. A leasing of the theatrical tradition of the leading lady's *confidente.* 'Through her, you can show another part of the main girl's character. She will not give herself away with a man in the same manner as she will with a girl friend. This is why I sometimes use another girl—to have some reaction. There is nothing private in it at all. You see, my life is never, never involved with my movies, no matter what the papers say. Sometimes I do work with an actress who is the woman I am living with. She is part of my private life and of my work—but never do I mix the two on a sentimental or sexual level. Not for any moral reason, you understand. Simply because it's too complicated—and I'm too lazy for that.'

Hardly. Bardot and Birkin in the buff then was the culmination of the *copine,* and a total let-down erotically compared, say, with the fashion in which Vadim had provided Lesbian set-pieces for his later wives: Annette Stroyberg (*Et mourir de plaisir,* 1960); Jane Fonda (*Barbarella*; *Histoires extraordinaires,* 1968). This final (thus far) teaming of Bardot and Vadim proved, if nothing else, how far the cinema had grown up since *Et Dieu créa la femme*—and how little Bardot would attempt similarly to mature and thereby widen her screen persona. The sexual revolution both had bred in the cinema had long since left them behind (although Vadim was to recover brilliantly with *La jeune fille assassinée,* 1974/5). Flop or not, *Don Juan* proved also to be the fourth venture in which Brigitte's most memorable co-star has been another woman. None of them will impart, nor hear anything that is critical of her. Nor vice versa. 'Jeanne Moreau taught me how to be more sure of myself—though I still never managed to dominate myself, it's beyond my strength. Claudia Cardinale (in *Les pétroleuses*) is the opposite of me, full of courage, not lazy, not afraid of anything, a worker, punctual—everything I'm not. Annie Giradot and I got on okay. We were playing crosswords and Scrabble together through *Les Novices.* I think our grandmothers would not have done anything different—we were super-good!'

If leading male stars still avoided her like the plague, so alas did the leading directors in France. Considering her part in the creation of *la nouvelle vague,* it is a great waste that BB worked with so few of the new-wave. Of the main quartet, Godard, Chabrol, Truffaut and Resnais, she filmed with Godard alone.

Resnais rarely goes in for stars, or indeed for films; Chabrol's company hired her for one feature, not made by Chabrol himself, although she seems headed, bourgeoisie-wise, into his favourite premise area of late. She never fitted any of Truffaut's scenarios, though he was munificent in singing her praises: 'More than an actress, she is a person. She symbolises the period in which we live, identifying herself with a rare realism with all the people with whom she comes into contact. For these reasons, I consider her to be unique.'

Of the newer-wavers, Bardot chose, abysmally, Serge Bourguignon for *A cœur joie,* having better fortune in $2\frac{1}{3}$ films with Louis Malle, better still in the hands of Roberto Enrico (creator of a superlative short, *La rivière du hibou/Incident At Owl Creek*); and yet, less well with Michel Deville, although (or because) he had shown a fine understanding of female psychology in *Adorable menteuse.* Unfortunately, she never made a film for Alain Robbe-Grillet, the *nouveau roman* novelist and originally Resnais' screenwriter, and probably the most intellectually erotic of French directors, if more to the sado-masochistic right of Vadim's increasingly bedizened spectaculars.

Upon reflection, perhaps she knew best. Bardot has, to be sure, always understood her image. She could hardly do otherwise as her screen persona is closer to her true self than it is in most other stellar careers. By 1970, she had begun playing down her entire myth. Her affairs grew longer, more successfully attuned and less salacious to her country's Press, and she felt ready to satirise herself even in something as decorous and singularly inappropriate as her nun rôle. Much better was her rich jet-setter type chasing a miscast Jean-Pierre Cassel in Deville's *L'Ours et la poupée* (her most successful film since *Viva Maria*), or her simply glorious parody of a 20s movie siren in Enrico's *Boulevard du Rhum,* one of her finest if largely unsung (and unseen, abroad) performances of the sluggish 70s decade. Gone for ever, though, were the days when a dozen or more BB epics were running simultaneously around Manhattan's art and skin-flick houses. Yet the sex-symbol is not yet dead, and she seems able to project and protect the same sexuality for another decade at least without becoming a travesty of herself, a miniature Mae West.

The retirement stories abound. After the Vadim piece, yet again she said she would quit. But she made one more, for a woman director: Nina Companeez, writer of her last comedy, *L'Ours et la poupée.* The film is *Colinot,* and she has mainly a guest, if top-starring, rôle, as a medieval representation of her everlasting persona. In Britain, however, the film which should have been distributed by the amalgam of Columbia-Warner was turned down for release. While making it, Bardot announced quite categorically that she had quit. Immediately she intimated she could—perhaps

... and their japes. Incandescent she remains.

—change her mind.

Having always been ahead of the game, she knows best when to pull out. The screen today is full still of copy-Bardots from every film-making land on the globe. The freedoms she helped accomplish have been taken to both logical and illogical ends and, in America, Scandinavia, and, by 1975 in France, to the pornographical. Bardot feels that she does not want to compete in that area. Hence the disappointing *Don Juan* exercise, distinctly tepid when seen alongside Maria Schneider's fireworks in *Le dernier tango à Paris,* or the heated *érotisme* of Vadim's latest find, Finnish model Sirpa Lane, in *La jeune fille assassinée.* Screen offers for BB still swarmed in aplenty to her agent, all the same. Until she decided to turn into a TV documentary producer, Brigitte actually deigned to read some proferred scripts. 'If it is *genial,* I say yes. But as they're only proposing *merdiques,* then I have to give myself pain for a result which does not satisfy me in the end.' The agent, Olga Horstig-Primuz, busy enough helping guide the careers of almost every other top-flight *vedette française* from Michèle Morgan to Jane Birkin, says that handling Bardot in the 70s is her easiest task per week. 'I just have to say no.'

And what if Fellini wanted her, say, for an ugly mother rôle in ten years time? What then? Wait ten years and find out, is Bardot's reply. The one director she would unhesitatingly run to work with (like Loren and countless other woman stars) is Ingmar Bergman. 'I've wanted to work with him for a long time. I wrote to him and he replied. But he usually works in this country and in English [sic] . . . I cannot speak it enough. My language is French. I am French. Typically French. One must do things which one is capable of doing. Me, in a scene, I never say the text that is given to me. I improvise. How do you expect me to do this in English? Then again, I would really have to *want* to do it.'

One witness to the Bardot line in chauvinism is George Axelrod, the Hollywood writer, producer and director (*The Seven Year Itch, Bus Stop, The Manchurian Candidate, Lord Love a Duck, The Secret Life of an American Wife,* etc.). He insists it was because Brigitte turned one of his scripts down, that Virna Lisi was born, or re-born as a Hollywood blonde in Axelrod's Monroe/Mansfield fashion. The film he offered Bardot: *How to Murder Your Wife,* 1965, starring Jack Lemmon and Terry-Thomas. Brigitte was the obvious perfect casting: a foreign girl, terribly, terribly attractive, outlined the witty scenario. Axelrod wanted her played by an actress audiences did not associate with speaking English. In short, he wanted BB.

He flew to Paris to get her and waited and waited for a meeting. 'When the audience was ultimately granted and I kissed the ring and everything, she was terribly charming and very, very, very aloof of the whole matter. And to my great chagrin she had never heard of me—that's what blew it! She had read part of the script, noticed immediately that the man's part was bigger and explained she would be available to do the picture in September. We were due to shoot in June. I said: "What's your schedule?" And she said: "My current lover and I will be through in September and I will then be available for a film." This is absolutely real!'

Whatever the excuses Brigitte came up with, it was

plain the major problem was Hollywood. She did not wish to work there. Among the various actresses nominated by the talent agencies in Paris was the fledgling Italian Virna Lisi. She looked the complete opposite of Bardot, or the rôle—'very much the dignified lady, the Italian heiress,' commented Axelrod. 'For a week my wife and I absolutely tortured her in Hollywood, giving her blonde hair and everything for a screen test that was classic. Brigitte would never have permitted herself to be put through that kind of ordeal—and we had to do it in order to get the match right with Lemmon. I understood her position perfectly. Brigitte clearly did not want to work in America at all. Virna did.'

Ambition had never been Bardot's strongest point. The career came to her, not vice versa. And she forever claims she never cared for the fame thrust upon her. The only occasions she has enjoyed being Bardot—or 'someone' as she put it—was in 1961 when she proved she was indeed someone by saying *non* to the pimps of the OAS; and later when her well-chronicled love for animals led her to expose the savagery of the French *abattoirs*. She campaigned for changes in the law about slaughter of animals. A special stun-pistol is used today instead of club or hammer and in France the changes are known as the BB law.

She has aged well, cleverly in fact, with typical French flair. According to London's authoritative *Sunday Times,* Bardot's figure has not changed one centimetre since 1956: 35-23-35 inches. 'Her fans have multiplied and stayed with her,' Meriel McCooey commented, 'and to many men of all ages, she is a goddess, not one of the unattainable sort like Garbo, but a sexual object who appears, nevertheless, to be independent and free; not just the girl most likely to, but the girl who most certainly would if it suited her.' And her latest batch of nude studies, taken by her now ex-beau, Laurent Vergez, show her as one of the finest-shaped 40-year-olds in the world. She puts it down to a healthy life, skiing in the winter, water skiing by summer, and taking lengthy walks at weekends. Then like all French, she eats well, and wisely. Her love of animals does not exactly hinder her appetite, she is no vegetarian.

Fashion experts say she has gained chic, dignity even, in her rarely faulted dress-sense (she shops at Dior, but finds delving into mini boutiques more amusing; Marc Bohan is a *copain* as well). Throwing out lipstick, she has become less obvious in make-up, hair and clothes. Make-up, she says, takes five minutes, which certainly makes her the perfect dream woman. 'Three strokes with the pencil, *pif, paf, c'est fini!* It takes longer for films where the most important work is my eyes. But understand me well, I don't do anything special, I just like to be clean and tidy.' Her once blonde tresses, which helped push the sales of peroxide around the world, have reverted to the natural, normal colour of *Manina, fille sans voile*: brown and reaching down to her waist. 'I don't do anything with it. No more hairdressers. No more dye. No more *care*! It is since I have decided to have my natural colour back that my hair has grown again and become brilliant. I wash it myself as little as possible——maybe twice a month, maximum. Hair is a natural element when you don't disturb it.'

'When she opens her eyes one would swear one is looking at the face of a baby,' said one of BB's ex-lovers, Christian Kalt. 'She is particularly beautiful without make-up. A freshness I've never seen before in any grown woman's face.' Kalt had entered her love-life after meeting Brigitte at a Méribel *après-ski* bar. He was the barman, caught her eye—and vice versa, obviously. They danced together and he accompanied her on yet another location trek to Spain for *Les pétroleuses* with Cardinale, a distinctly lukewarm attempt to revive the *Viva Maria* bravura. He refused to act in the film, but like the long deposed secretary, Kalt was to recover something from the affair two years later by writing all for the newspapers. Unlike Alain Carré, he did not, however, come to bury Bébé, only to praise her, without stint. 'But to love a woman like Bardot is not just an adventure. It is both easy and difficult. For when Brigitte is in love, she gives herself completely. Yet she is very demanding of the man she loves. He has to be with her 24 hours out of 24.'

And he has to pay the price, the one she has always insisted upon: jealousy. Kalt said the major pain of his 18 months with her—in which time she took to adding false freckles to her face to match his—was the constant worry of losing her, a fear well understood by predecessors, except perhaps Sachs who filed for divorce accusing her of 'an abusive conception of marriage and premeditated abandonment of the household'.

Incredibly, the Bardot face and figure remain largely untouched by her richly free life. Nature, suggested Marguerite Duras, happily endowed her with a delicious talent for idleness. But this was never enough to kill time. She would invent childish games to shake off boredom, receive few visitors and live alone with her lover so long as she loved him. 'I am certain that she has never known the end of a love affair, the heartbreaking depression of loneliness and liberty. But she knows the other tragedy of starting afresh, right away. Has she ever paused between two romances—got her second wind—has she ever done this? I don't think so . . . Her men perhaps have loved her too much. Said one: "She is so utterly beautiful, so extraordinarily desirable at every moment, life with her became an inferno of desire . . . One cannot hesitate to approach her, to pester her, to live in terror of losing

her. I think men have exhausted her patience . . . it's enough to drive a man mad. I was *mad* throughout the period we lived together."

'It seems strange,' continued the Duras dossier, 'She wants to be alone and independent. But alone in a bed she is prey to such great anguish that she cannot sleep. She needs somebody to lull her to sleep. Our adorable little girl is a child even in her elementary notion of solitude . . . Each of her lovers is in some degree a night-duty man, the person who will enable her to avoid sleeping alone. The curious thing, nevertheless, is that although all have been warned of the danger of loving her, nobody has yet recoiled.' Of course not!

Living for the moment, with some measure of idyllic tranquillity at last with Laurent Vergez—yet another *beau jeune homme*; and yet another lover introduced to her by Vadim—Bardot's life-style continued at La Madrague, where still the photographic fruit is in the trees. (Her latest nude sunbathing news-photos were more unusual, though: her partner in most of them was her 14-year-old son, Nicolas.) She is searching for a larger home, 'a farmhouse, an enormous place, rustic', with grounds enough for her *ménagerie*; 23 cats, one mouse and a vixen among the latest head-count. When she started in the cinema, 'it was only to get enough money to buy a farm', she would have us believe. Whether in St. Tropez, Meribel or Paris, it's a guarded life, hidden, similar to that of Jeanne Moreau. 'Everything that is not healthy repulses me,' says Brigitte. 'I like a life in a protected universe that I've built for myself because everything that I see outside makes me ill.' In *Don Juan 1973,* Vadim took this utopia to the perhaps illogical ends of her living in a submarine affair beneath the Seine.

And so, where lies her future? To be or not to BB? Vadim for one—and he is, perhaps, in France still the one with the greatest interest in her well-being on and off screen—hopes she has quit movies. Because, quite simply, she is *passé*. She is not what she was any more and should stop trying to act it. To be frank, Vadim is not even that keen to discuss her these days. 'The first reaction of writers is to ask me about Bardot, at best about Jane Fonda, and it starts to be a little difficult for me because Brigitte is really attached to a certain period. She is the Brigitte Bardot of the last two decades. She belongs to the past.'

Indeed, according to Vadim, she is still living pretty much in the past, with nary a hint of my suggested rebourgeoisification status. 'Hardly,' he comments. 'She is always living with young boys. She's always between two love affairs—scared she will lose one and not have another to take his place. She continues to go from one to another like a little girl . . . And it was sort of charming when she was young, this way to be frightened by people, to need slaves around her, to live in a certain way, to refuse to quit the childish universe she was in—and I understood the reason she was like that. But now—I mean it is different when you are 35 years old, 38 years old, 40 years old, than when you were 30. It is very different. Little by little, she becomes *sclérosée*—it's a way to become petrified, the way wood becomes stone . . . *The Petrified Forest, non?* She becomes *sclérosée* in this attitude. She lives with her animals in her little house, hiding away with the same people around. She has not a social life, or very little. It is all a little *malsain*. Unhealthy. For this reason—I still like her a lot; I don't see her any more—it is difficult for me to relate to her today.'

Young lover, sometime actor and, more lately, her personal photographer of all BB nude studies, Laurent Vergez, 29, met the same problem early in 1975. He went the way of all his predecessors—dropped as Bébé encountered her latest man: blond, sometime actor and, more lately, successful sculptor, Miroslav Brozeck, 30. Marriage and hints about motherhood, via adoption, were in the Paris gossip columns as this volume went to press.

With her continually alleged frugality, to say little of various excellent investments in property, she has no need to work, of course. She was, for instance, always more wise with her income than Vadim; then again, making more movies in a year than he ever could direct, she had more money to be wise about. Including a tiny percentage of *Et Dieu créa la femme*, which eventually grossed around $25,000,000 around the globe. (Vadim, on the other hand, did not get one cent of his 3 per cent of the film's profits—'a long story concerning the ending of my contract with Raoul Levy, when he suddenly sent me bills for all the location-searching and other business travelling we had done together over six years! I had to pay him back all the money I got from *God Created Woman*. Brigitte was okay, she was able to put some money away. I was not clever with contracts like her.')

Although she has, very successfully, become a producer of social documentaries for television, Bardot tends not to think very far ahead: it frightens her. 'It's sad to grow old—but nice to ripen,' she comments. 'When Hélène Lazareff asked me to pose for *Elle*, I was 14 and full of complexes. After *Et Dieu créa la femme*, I was very famous. I couldn't go out in the street any more. The women, they detested me. I lived cloistered for ten years. I've always liked the natural life—maybe I should've been a farmer. Vadim was my first love. He took me out of my bourgeois prison. Now he's an old friend . . . although the saddest present you can give to an ex-lover is to be his friend. Sometimes he sends me little notes signed: "Your old Russian who loves you."

'The public will be my mirror. When I feel it is finished, I will stop. The Bardot myth is going away. I want to sing, rest, live simply. I've sold my Rolls and I don't go to parties any more. As long as I feel the same, I will keep my style . . . When I have money—I live. When I've no more left—I make another film. A movie is quite another affair. Like a pregnancy. Except that instead of nine months, it usually lasts only three. In both cases, though, that's the end of all freedom. The future then for me . . . is only more films to do. Some good ones to forget the bad ones.'

She will be fondly remembered, revered, for all of them, for her exquisite, full-bodied attacks on cinema and society—for the courageous changes she has wrought: the good, the bad and the sensually beautiful.

Joker. For all her abundant sex-appeal, Bébé is a joyful comedienne. On and off the *(Viva Maria)* set.

FILMOGRAPHY

Le trou Normand

1952

Rising. Bourvil gives the novice a lift.

The *Norman Hole*. French. Cité-Film production, 85 minutes. UK release: none. US: *Crazy For Love*. (aka. *Ti Ta To*). Ellis distribution, 1960; 80 minutes. Monochrome.
Director: Jean Boyer. *Producer:* Jacques Bar. *Script:* Arlette de Pitray. *Photography:* Charles Suin. *Editor:* Franchette Mazin. *Music:* Paul Misraki; *lyrics*, Jean Boyer. *Sound:* William Sivel. *Art Director:* Robert Giordani. *Assistant Directors:* Jean Bastia, Gilbert Guez. *Shooting:* from May 12, 1952, on location at Conches.

CAST

Bourvil . . . . *Hypolite*
Jeanne Marken . . . . *Augustine Lemoine*
Brigitte Bardot . . . . *Javotte Lemoine*
Nadine Basile . . . . *Madeleine*
Jeanne Fusier-Gir. . . . . *Maria*
Noël Roquevert . . . . *Mayor*
Georges Baconnet . . . . *Pichet*
Pierre Larquey, Roger Pierre and Florence Michael.

STORY

Village idiot Hypolite inherits the local tavern, Le Trou Normand—*if* he can attain his school diploma within a year. If not, the business passes to his ambitious sister-in-law, Augustine, and her pretty, if conceited, daughter, Javotte. Fate, in the shy, maidenish shape of schoolteacher Madeleine, spins an intriguing web for those who would plot against the simple-minded. At 32, Hypolite goes back to his studies, Augustine gets her come-uppance, Javotte leaves for the city and, maybe, an acting career, as the bovine teacher inspires Hypolite to success in school and *l'amour*.

NOTES

BB: 'My first film—it was terrible! I wanted so much to succeed, not only for myself but for Vadim who had such faith in me. But as it was, people knew I was around and began to see me as Vadim did.'
Nothing came of Marc Allegret's plans for *Les lauriers sont coupés,* with or without the young cover-girl who had caught his eye and his assistant's imagination. Vadim began a solo offensive—touting

his girl's assets around every producer with a property and budget. His agenting and another splendid cover of Brigitte called Jean Boyer's attention. He viewed Allegret's test. 'A lot,' Boyer declared, 'could be done with that girl.' He did not do it. However, he earned a place in screen history for creating the début of the 18-year-old looker (more mouse than kitten) who was to become France's biggest, and only truly international, star.

Shooting began at Conches, and long before the end the young Bardot was in despair. Vadim, it seemed, had told her everything about films and nothing about filming . . . 'I knew so much about my new profession that I really believed a film was made from the beginning to the end, smoothly, and not in disconnected little bits. I had thought that on the set I would be able to forget myself and my surroundings and give of my best. But it was nothing like that at all. I did not like my part from the start—a little witch of a girl, somewhat vulgar, a little boorish and very sensual—but that, it seemed, was the star rôle of the picture and I was told by everybody that this was my big break.

'We started shooting without any hitches. Everyone was kind enough to me, helping me over many difficulties and making what I did not like more agreeable. As time went on I felt I was acting more and more badly—fantastically badly! Film-making wasn't at all what I had expected. I felt let down. Was it always to be like this? So mechanical, so insipid, so exhausting. I had my dream shattered.'

French critics were less harsh about the routine slice of parochial comedy, which earned a surprise profit, in dollars, as the last of the early Bardot films to gain an ineptly dubbed exploitative run in America— eight years later. And then at the World Theatre in New York, more recently famed as the first-run home of *Deep Throat.*

Eugene Archer, *New York Times,* gave it a cursory 51 lines, quickly noting its age, 'made well before *And God Created* Bardot'. He also had the colossal nerve to compare the excellent Bourvil with George Gobel in appearance and Jerry Lewis in style! '. . . this mediocre farce offers only one consolation. After three years of theatres saturated with early glimpses of the petulant young star, surely the bottom of the barrel has been reached at last.'

Trade-paper response was warmer. Allen M. Widem, *Motion Picture Herald*: 'Modest bit of wry Gallic comedy . . . with admirable attention to the BB profile and countenance. It figures to play as profitably as the several other BB imports that have graced situations across the U.S. Surprisingly there are long, pleasurable moments of tender poignancy, a factor inadvertently lacking from past Brigitte Bardot efforts.'

In four of those efforts, Noël Roquevert continued to support Bardot with his particular brand of comedy; and her first screen *maman*, Jeanne Marken, became her harridan guardian in *Et Dieu créa la femme.* Sound-recordist William Sivel, already a veteran of the original *Mayerling* in 1936, Clouzot's *Manon* and *Le salaire de la peur/The Wages of Fear,* went on to divide his recording time between the dulcet tones of Loren and Bardot on such features as *Lady L* and *Vie privée*; while assistant director Gilbert Guez was to cover the incredible rise of Bardolatry as a journalist for *Cinémonde.*

At the time more had been expected of the girl playing the schoolteacher than of Bardot: Nadine Basile, the 1952 Suzanne Blanchette Prize winner. However, this discovery of the year was soon swept aside in the BB–Vadim avalanche. The couple married just over a month after *Le trou normand* opened on November 7, 1952, in Paris. Before beginning the rôle of Mme. Vadim, Brigitte made one more film, a real taste of things to come—enough to send her outraged father scurrying to court.

Cluck. The animals were there from the star's star.

Click. So were photographers—and Roger Pierre.

Manina, la fille sans voile

1952

Manina, Girl Without Veil. French. Sport Films; 86 minutes. UK: *The Lighthouse Keeper's Daughter*, Gala Films, 1959; 57 minutes. US: *The Girl in the Bikini*, Atlantic Films, 1958; 76 minutes. Monochrome.

Director-Producer: Willy Rozier. *Script:* Xavier Vallier; *adaptation, dialogue*, Willy Rozier. *Photography:* Michel Rocca. *Editor:* Suzanne Baron. *Music:* Jean Yatove; *lyrics*, Xavier Vallier. *Sound:* André Le Baut. *Production Manager:* René Jaspard. *Assistant Director:* Louis Pascal. *Shooting:* from June 30, 1952, at Cannes, Nice, Golfe Juan, Île de Lavesi, Tangiers and Paris.

CAST

Brigitte Bardot . . . . *Manina*
Jean-François Calvé . . . . *Gérard*
Howard Vernon . . . . *Eric*
Españita Cortez . . . . *Franchucha*
Raymond Cordy . . . . *Francis*
and Robert Arnoux.

Bikini. Too small, roared Papa. Not so, co-star Calvé.

STORY

A Phoenician treasure-trove ship is located off the Corsican coast by the odd partnership of Gérard, a law student, and Eric, a veteran smuggler. They plan to raise the trove for themselves. Gérard, though, is more interested in the local lighthouse-keeper's treasure: the sprightly Manina. And it is this belle of the rocky coastline who saves the student from Eric's double-cross. The smuggler sails off with the trove, and Gérard nearly drowns when giving chase. Manina rescues him and together they watch smuggler, boat and treasure sink beneath the waves.

NOTES

BB: 'I took the part of a wild little girl unclothed and as lacking in experience as the one in the first film. My acting seemed even worse—later I used to blush with shame at what I used to call my setbacks. I had made a bad start—a cheap little starlet hardly acting at all in a very mediocre film. A starlet who would play in anything.'

And Papa Bardot was furious. He had permitted his daughter, still 18 and unmarried though smitten with Vadim, to make the film provided the work and costume were within the realms of decency. When he heard about a tiny nude scene, and saw publicity stills of the skimpy bikini his Bri-Bri wore for most of the film, he rushed to his lawyer, arranged a private screening of the film and insisted on several cuts. Vadim obviously played up this news with his journalist *copains* and the publicity which helped create BB began to roll. The row, both domestic and journalistic, only further upset the girl's dreams of a film career. 'I felt it would be dreadful to add to the heap of pretty little girls looking for just about anything, playing in any old films that came along. So I decided to get out of films. What had I got that no one else had got? Why should I succeed? Millions of girls far better than me have failed?

'Vadim changed my mind. Vadim was the only man who was certain I had something special to offer on the screen. I marvelled at his confidence and laughed at his conceit. It was difficult not to listen to his arguments. "As long as I am here, you need never

be afraid of people or of life. I shall guide you to success. I love you and will make you succeed.'' His trust gave me fresh hope. I would do whatever he told me. He was both my teacher and master as well as my fiancé. I placed myself entirely in his hands. We went back to the beginning and he taught me how to speak, how to remember my lines and tried to show me how to act. Love was the driving force. The experience improved and rewarded me.'

Six years later, the second venture arrived in an America starving for every possible Bardolatry item —with a more straightforward title than its limerick-ish handle in Britain the following year. The Americans received more of BB's *Manina*—19 minutes more.

Richard W. Nason, *New York Times*: 'Now that the plain and unadored film has been lifted off the shelf to capitalise on the renown of the actress, it has an incidental charm as a curiosity piece. If nothing else, it will inform you of a fetching winsomeness and innocence that Mlle. Bardot possessed in those days. And if it were not known that Mlle. Bardot might mount a crag at any moment for another plunge into the sea, the story about the sunken treasure and its trite dénouement would hardly be worth the showing so far from France . . . pointless stuff if it were not for the pictures of Mlle. Bardot when she was younger, fresher and allowed to project some natural human warmth.'

Les dents longues

1952

The Long Teeth. French. Roitfeld Productions. UK/US release: none on record. Monochrome.
Director: Daniel Gélin. *Producer:* Jacques Roitfeld. *Script:* Michel Audiard, Marcel Camus, Daniel Gélin, Jacques Robert, *from the novel by* Jacques Robert. *Dialogue:* Michel Audiard. *Photography:* Robert Juillard. *Conseiller Technique:* Marcel Camus. *Music:* Paul Misraki. *Art Director:* Robert Clavel. *Production Manager:* Georges Roitfeld.

CAST

Danièle Delorme . . . . *Eva*
Daniel Gélin . . . . *Louis*
Jean Chevrier . . . . *Walter*
Louis Seigner . . . . *Josserand*
Jean Debucourt . . . . *Goudal*
Olivier Hussenot . . . . *Maurienne*
Gaby Bruyère . . . . *Maud*
Collete Mars, Bugette, Brigitte Bardot and Roger Vadim.

STORY/NOTES

The opening—'unknown'—stanza of any actor's career requires plodding detection to piece together. There are, for instance, several apparently well-informed filmographies of Brigitte Bardot which falsely claim she appeared in Kirk Douglas's *Ulysses* in Italy, right after her truncated rôle in his Paris film, *Act of Love*. Other lists continue the muddle around this 1954 period with unsubstantiated claims that Brigitte was among the *Frou-Frou* line-up with Dany Robin. Still more insist she—and indeed Vadim—were high in the celebrity-riddled guest-star list of Jean Cocteau's *Le testament d'Orphée* in 1959; both agreed to take part in a car journey during the film. According to Vadim, they did not refuse, they were unable to be in Antibes on the right day. 'Various people knew which scene we were to be in and, as you cannot see very well the people in the car, they presumed it was us.' The Cocteau film was listed (and *La bride sur le cou* was not) in a recently published British biography's filmography of BB, which also went to some pains to deny Italian reports of Brigitte in a film called *Les dents longues*. Any evidence that she ever made such

Stars. Daniel Gélin and his wife Danielle Delorme.

a film, noted the book in question, was very slight and remained uncorroborated by French sources, including production information in the trade press.

The news that not only Brigitte—but Vadim also—*did* appear in the film is hardly new to the French, who have seen this photograph in numerous magazine life-story accounts of Bardot; and the evidence is presented herewith, apparently for the first time, to British and American filmgoers.

The film, part-written, directed by and starring Vadim's actor friend Daniel Gélin, counts as Bardot's third appearance on the screen in her début year. It also proved to be the first of several guest and/or walk-ons for friends' projects during her career, all of which are listed in this filmography section; the most notable of which is her solo appearance in a Hollywood production, which because of her guest-shot became named after her: *Dear Brigitte*, 1966.

For Bardot and Vadim, their few minutes' work as witnesses to the *Mairie*-office marriage of Daniel Gélin and Danièle Delorme showed them the ropes for their own wedding soon after—at which les

Marriage. The fledgling Bardot and Vadim walk-on as the witnesses to their star friends' screen marriage. Les Gélin later had a son named Xavier—who would grow up to take the rôle of Brigitte's boyfriend in a 1970 comedy.

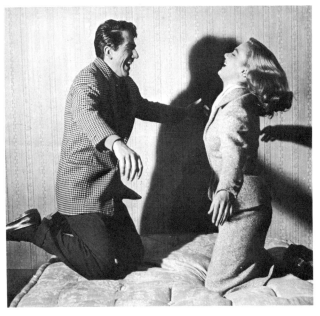

Gélin were their witnesses. Ironically, 18 years and 40 films later, the Gélins' film-minded son, Xavier, then 24, played Brigitte's fiancé in *L'ours et la poupée*.

The marriage sequence is silent on the screen, a flash-cut affair in the saga of Gélin as an ambitious provincial journalist making good in the Paris big time, where his *dents longues* bite hungrily into each and every unscrupulous chance to reach the top.

Four years later, Bardot filmed once more with Gélin, this time as his leading lady, in *En effeuillant la marguerite*, better remembered as *Mam'selle Striptease*. Her rise, when it began, was rapid indeed.

Le portrait de son père

1953

The Image of his Father. French. Bertho Films/Orsay Films; 90 minutes. UK/US release: none on record. Monochrome.
Director: André Berthomieu. *Script:* Berthomieu, Roger Pierre. *Photography:* Georges Million. *Editor:* C. Natot. *Music:* Henri Betti. *Sound:* L. Lacharmoise. *Art Director:* Raymond Negre. *Production Manager:* G. Cohen-Beat.

CAST

Jean Richard . . . . *Paul*
Michèle Philippe . . . . *Marie*
Brigitte Bardot . . . . *Domino*
Mona Goya . . . . *Mother*
Duvalles . . . . *Director*
M. Nasil, P. Faivre, Charles Bouillaud, Maurice Biraud, Philippe Mareuil, A. Tanguy.

STORY

Young farmer Paul gains wealth beyond his dreams as the major beneficiary of a rich departmental store owner: Papa had not forgotten his bastard son in his will. In Paris, Paul surprises himself—step-mother, and step-sister Domino, also—with his high-powered business acumen. It is, though, not the life he craves, and after an initial spree he decides to return to farm and sweetheart.

NOTES

Inverted version of *Le trou normand,* with Bardot fundamentally in the same rôle. In her début film, her village beauty lost a rich peasant to another and left him for Paris; here, the rich farmer leaves Brigitte's *jolie Parisienne* for another and returns to his village.
Good parochial farce, therefore; unique only in that it was one of the two early Bardot films never taken up by British or American distributors in their haste to obtain every Bardot vehicle in sight. This was presumably due to the fact that (*a*) she didn't strip and (*b*) no one could really believe in a hero turning her down for another girl. But then she was his step-sister . . . and the screen had not grown up that much. Not just yet.
A later assistant to the film's director, Berthomieu, was Edouard Molinaro, who graduated high enough to direct Bardot as *Une ravissante idiote* in 1963.

Act of Love

1953

American-French. Benagos Production. United Artists release; 108 minutes. French release title: *Quelque part dans le monde*. Monochrome.
Director-Producer: Anatole Litvak. *Script:* Irwin Shaw, Joseph Kessel, *from the novel, 'The Girl in the Via Flaminia'*, by Alfred Hayes. *Photography:* Armand Thirard. *Editor:* Léonide Azar. *Music:* Michel Emer, Joe Hajos. *Songs:* Michel Emer. *Art Director:* Alexandre Trauner. *Sound:* Jean de Bretagne. *Production Manager:* Pierre Laurent. *Associate Producer:* Georges Maurer. *Assistant Director:* Michel Boisrond, Serge Vallin. *Shooting:* January 5–May 7, Studios Joinville (for Bardot's scenes).

CAST

Kirk Douglas . . . . *Robert Teller*
Dany Robin . . . . *Lisa*
Barbara Laage . . . . *Nina*
Robert Strauss . . . . *Blackwood*
Gabrielle Dorzia . . . . *Adèle*
Grégoire Aslan . . . . *Commissaire*
Marthe Mercadier . . . . *Young Woman*
Fernand Ledoux . . . . *Fernand*
Serge Reggiani . . . . *Claude*
Brigitte Bardot . . . . *Mimi*
Gilberte Géniat . . . . *Mrs. Henderson*
George Matthews . . . . *Henderson*
Leslie Dwyer . . . . *English Sergeant*
Richard Benedict . . . . *Pete*

STORY

Paris, 1944. G.I. Robert Teller shares his hotel room with a hungry, homeless refugee, Lisa. Gradually the couple fall in love. Teller's official request to marry the girl is met with a blunt refusal and immediate transfer to another area. Returning to Paris to locate Lisa, Teller is arrested by the Military Police. Assuming her lover has deserted her, Lisa commits suicide.

NOTES

BB: 'I was nervous when I met Kirk Douglas on the set. "Take it easy," Kirk said to me. "You'll make it. You'll get up there all right."'

Tiny. Brigitte's rôle—tending Dany Robin—was so small, her mother had to see the film twice to notice her...

Not with this film. Her rôle of the maid in the hotel used by Douglas and Dany Robin was small to begin with. Smaller still on-screen; two-thirds of her scenes wound up as wall-to-wall carpeting on the celebrated cutting-room floor.

Both credible and moving, the love story, which began shooting under the title *Somewhere in the World*, contained all the realism of Litvak's earlier post-war item, *Decision Before Dawn*, although its suicidal climax was hard to take by non-European audiences, unused to the rigours and truths of war. The film opened in New York a few weeks after a stage version of the novel had played at the Circle in the Square Theatre.

Si Versailles m'était conté

1953

If Versailles Could Talk. 165 minutes. UK: Mondial Films, 1960, *Versailles;* 158 minutes. Eastman Color.

Director/Script: Sacha Guitry. *Photography:* Pierre Montazel. *Editor:* Raymond Lamy. *Music:* Jean Françaix. *Sound:* Jo de Bretagne. *Art Director:* René Renoux. *Costumes:* Monique Dumas. *Production Manager:* Clément Duhour. *Assistant Director:* François Gir. *Shooting:* from July 6, 1953.

CAST

Sacha Guitry . . . . *Louis XIV*
Georges Marchal . . . . *Young Louis XIV*
Jean Marais . . . . *Louis XV*
Claudette Colbert . . . . . . *Madame de Montespan*
Micheline Presle . . . . . . *Madame de Pompadour*
Lana Marconi . . . . *Marie-Antoinette*
and Giselle Pascal, Fernand Gravey, Jean Desailly, Bernard Dhéran, Jean-Claude Pascal, Orson Welles (*Benjamin Franklin*), Charles Vanel, Gaby Morlay, Gino Cervi, Jean-Jacques Delbo, Jean-Pierre Aumont, Gérard Philipe (*D'Artagnan*), Jean-Louis Barrault, Maurice Teynac, Edith Piaf (*une tricoteuse*), Yves Deniaud, Jean Tissier, Pierre Larquey, Bourvil, Gaston Rey, Louis Arbessier, Jean-Louis Alibert, Pierre Lord, Nicole Maurey, Mary Marquet, Liliane Bert, Georges Chamarat, Samson Fainsilber, Jeanne Boitel, Olivier Mathot, Jacques Varennes, Gilbert Gil, Lucien Nat, Gilbert Boka, Jacques Berthier, Louis Seigner, René Worms, Jacques Morel, Danièle Delorme, Philippe Richard, Michel Auclair, Brigitte Bardot (*Mlle. de Rosille*), Pauline Carton, Jean Chevrier, Aimé Clariond, Nicole Courcel, Daniel Gélin, Jean Murat, Jean Richard, Tino Rossi, Germain Rouer, Raymond Souplex, Renée Devillers, Claude Nollier, Paul Colline, Annie Cordy, Duvaleix, Tania Fedor, Jacques François, Jeanne Fusier-Gir, Constant Rémy, Howard Vernon, Emile Drain, Gilles Queant.

STORY

Simply the story—a grandiloquent, witty history—of the life and times of Versailles, from erection by Louis XIV to 1954 museum life with Bourvil among the guides. Guitry, the Master Playwright, a legend in modern theatrical history, encompassed three generations of history, and mustered almost the

entire stellar population of the French film industry among his players. He opened the film with a patriotic parade down the main staircase with the stars as France's greatest names: Jean Marais as Louis XV, Claudette Colbert as Madame de Pompadour, Gérard Philipe as d'Artagnan, even Edith Piaf as a *tricoteuse* from the guillotine. Plus Orson Welles as a bulky Ben Franklin.

Bardot played a courtesan, a short and sweet rôle, blink twice and you miss her. Also in the cast were six of her previous co-stars (Bourvil, Jeanne Fusier-Gir, Howard Vernon, Daniel Gélin, Jean Richard, Danièle Delorme) and eight from her future. Not bad going for a sixth film!

Filming took more than 12 months. Bardot completed her scenes in 1953, before going on to make her immense impact at Cannes. The result of the incessant photographic survey of her geography there meant an instant invitation from Italy.

Tradita

1954

Treachery. Italian. Flora Films production; 98 minutes. French release title: *Haine, amour et trahison/Hate, Love and Treachery*. UK: no release. US: *Night of Love*, 1960, Howco-International distribution; 93 minutes. Monochrome.
Director: Mario Bonnard. *Producer:* Gaston Hakim. *Script:* Jules Daccar. *Photography:* Tonino Delli Colli. *Music:* Jules Daccar. *Art Director:* Piero Filippone. *Production Manager:* Folco Laudati.

CAST
Brigitte Bardot . . . . *Anna*
Pierre Cressoy . . . . *Pierre*
Lucia Bose. *Elisabeth*
Giorgio Albertazzi . . . . *Enrico*

STORY
Rovererto, Italy, 1915, is occupied by Austrians—a fact dividing Countess Alberti's sons as much as their joint love with town beauty, Anna. She prefers Franco and secretly weds him. The pro-Austrian Enrico, and his brother's cast-off fiancée, Elisabeth, denounce Franco's work with the resistance, a job assisted by his touring Italy as a concert pianist. Franco leaves town, joins up, is taken prisoner, escapes back home to hospital—and Enrico turns him in once more. Suddenly repentant, he takes Franco's place at the execution. After Italy's victory, Franco comes out of hiding and joins Anna and their baby.

NOTES
No apologies to Americans who may have seen the movie, but that is the *real* story of the film—and not the dubbed-up version which went across the United States six years later, five minutes shorter and somehow transplanted 28 years ahead of its original scenario, re-set in World War II with Enrico coming on nasty as a Nazi sympathiser. (Actor Giorgio Albertazzi became used to such screenic puzzles; he was 'X' in Resnais' *Last Year in Marienbad*.) As the entire project was based on a musical comedy, anyway, one supposed the great change did not really make that much difference to this mini-BB-vehicle.
Allen W. Widen, *Motion Picture Herald*: 'There is much here that reminds the casual observer of soap-opera overtones, but the general audience appeal will compensate for such minor matters.'

Whichever war it was, and however small the movie's success, this seventh Bardot film marked her Italian début. She stayed on in Rome for the Hollywood-on-the Tiber version of *Helen of Troy*, sharing an impecunious life-style with another aspiring young beauty of the St. Germain-des-Prés Sartre-Gréco-Buffet-Vian-Vadim-Gélin set: Ursula Andress. For a short time, both had their men on hand: Vadim assisting Allegret on *Femina*, Daniel Gélin making *Woman of Rome*. Then both girls were left to fend for themselves in the hunt for glory. Sophia Loren was way ahead of both at this time, with 25 films under her hungry belt and *Gold of Naples* about to make her a star; Gina Lollobrigida was already a name, into her 26th film—the one with Gélin. Bardot's struggling little career, drying up in Paris, was about to be rescued by the British at Pinewood Studios; exactly the same fate awaited Ursula, though it was eight years later when she said yes to *Dr. No*.

In view of their friendship, it seems remiss of some enterprising producer not to have followed the late-60s and 70s trend of co-starring Bardot with similarly stellar women—and matching Bardot and Andress. Brigitte would not have opposed such a notion. She has described Ursula as a bouquet of flowers. 'Beautiful! Extraordinary! "The most beautiful girl in the world"—*C'est vrai, elle est très belle!* We first met in Rome. We were unknown and we shared a room in a seedy hotel. We did our own cooking—spaghetti on a spirit stove. We borrowed each other's dresses and make-up . . . I have changed since. Ursula has not. Still she is very beautiful, much more beautiful than I.'

Helen of Troy

1954

American. Warner Brothers production and distribution; 118 minutes; UK: 114. Warner Color. *Director:* Robert Wise. *Script:* John Twist, Hugh Gray, N. Richard Nash. *Photography:* Harry Stradling. *Editor:* Thomas Reailly. *Music:* Max Steiner. *Sound:* Charles B. Lang. *Art Director:* Edward Carrere. *Shooting:* from spring 1954.

CAST

Rosanna Podesta . . . . *Helen*
Jacques Sernas . . . . *Paris*
Sir Cedric Hardwicke . . . . *Priam*
Stanley Baker . . . . *Achilles*
Niall MacGinnis . . . . *Menelaus*
Robert Douglas . . . . *Agamemnon*
Torin Thatcher . . . . *Ulysses*
Harry Andrews . . . . *Hector*
Jannette Scott . . . . *Cassandra*
Ronald Lewis . . . . *Aeneas*
Brigitte Bardot . . . . *Andraste*
Eduardo Ciannelli . . . . *Andros*
Marc Lawrence . . . . *Diomedes*
Maxwell Reed . . . . *Ajax*
Barbara Cavan . . . . *Cora*
Terence Longdon . . . . *Patroclus*
Patricia Marmont . . . . *Andromache*
Guido Notari . . . . *Nestor*
Tonino Selwart . . . . *Alephous*
Georges Zavitch . . . . *Dancer*
Esmond Knight . . . . *High Priest*

STORY

Hollywood style close-up of the mighty wars betwixt Troy and Greece and the historic/hysteric love affair between Helen, wife of the Spartan King Menelaus, and Paris, offspring of Troy's King Priam, plus— of course—the subsequent siege and wooden Horse of Troy . . .

NOTES

. . . to say nothing of the war betwixt a forerunner of the international epic's Tower of Babel casts to come, and a literal wooden horse script. *Helen:* It can't be lost, Paris, can it? What has been won and shared can never be lost! *Paris:* Never, Helen! We will

Historical? Somewhere in between the face that launched the armada and Jacques Sernas' moody Paris, glowed Brigitte—far more relaxed than Rossana Podesta's blonde-wigged Helen.

always be together. . . . And it took three scribes to hack that out.

Reputed to have cost $6,000,000 and taken three years to set up and make, providing employment for roughly three-quarters of the population of Rome, the second of the post-war epics set the spectacular trend for the future: i.e. it was spectacular in action only, never in the pedestrian, flagging interpretation of the more intimate side of all the emotional grandeur. Britain's *Monthly Film Bulletin* complained that the lovers were absurdly whitewashed and the film was 'infantile in conception'; although Fred Majdalany, *Time and Tide*, found it a colossal spectacle of bodies, battles and bloodshed, bearing 'more than a superficial resemblance to the Homeric goings-on which inspired it'.

Bardot was basically signed on as a kind of first reserve for the title star, blonde-wigged Italian newcomer Rosanna Podesta. Director Robert Wise seemed pleased enough with his first choice, however, and Bardot had to make what she could of a smaller rôle: one step up from walk-on as Helen's slave-girl maid and confidante. . . . More to rush, than write, home to Vadim about. At least she survived with fledgling reputation and name intact. French actor Jacques Sernas was billed in the United States as Jack. Fortunately Bridget Bardot just did not ring true—even if Americans called her Bardotte.

Le fils de Caroline Chérie

1954

The Son of Caroline Chérie. French. Cinephone/ SNEG (Gaumont) production; 105 minutes. US/UK release: none on record. Technicolor.
Director: Jean Devaivre. *Producer:* François Chavane. *Script:* Jean Devaivre, *from the novel by* Cécil Saint-Laurent. *Photography:* Maurice Berry. *Editor:* Germaine Artus. *Music:* Georges Van Parys. *Sound:* Jean Rieul. *Art Director:* Jacques Krauss. *Production Manager:* Robert Sussfeld. *Shooting:* June 24– September 5, 1954, Studios Saint-Maurice, locations at Roussillon.

CAST

Jean-Claude Pascal	*Juan d'Arandra*
Jacques Dacqmine	*Sallanches*
Brigitte Bardot	*Pilar*
Magali Noël	*Térèsa*
Micheline Gary	*Conchita*

Sophie Desmarets, Alfred Adam, Georges Descrières, Bernard Lajarrige, Daniel Ceccaldi, Maurice Escande, Marcel Pérès, Michel Etcheverry, Dinan, Robert Manuel, Robert Le Béal, Robert Dalban, André Dumas, David Maxwell.

STORY

Breezy recital of the adventures under the flag, and sheets, of Caroline Chérie's like-mother-like-son offspring, Juan D'Arandra—a handsome officer in the army of the First Empire occupying Spain, and forever swashing the buckle with great gusto.

NOTES

The further adventures of . . . so to speak. Of the son, not the dishy lady herself, popular from the Cécil Saint-Laurent books and two successively successful Martine Carol films, remembered best for her beauty and bathtime rituals.
Bardot had to share the favours of leading-man Jean-Claude Pascal with Magali Noël and Sophie Desmarets, to single out but two of his conquests; and she did so with enough élan, and experience by now, for French critics repeatedly to agree that this eighth film was the first to show off the potential that Vadim had been going on about for two years or more.

Hysterical. Martine Carole had made *Caroline Chérie* scandalous—top movie with the Paris tourists. Now, Bardot edged into her sequel—and her limelight.

Variety's man in Paris, Gene Moskowitz, however, could not bring himself to mention her in his short review; indeed he has never been even a coolly ardent fan as time and later pages will show. His main comment: 'Shadow of Martine Carol, the previous Caroline, hangs over this and is sorely missed.' Bardot was soon to remove Martine from the upper shelf of French goodies for good and all.

Futures vedettes

1955

Future Stars. French. Régie du Film/Del Duca production; 96 minutes. UK: *Sweet Sixteen*, Gala Films distribution, 1958; 96 minutes. Monochrome.
Director: Marc Allégret. *Producer:* none on record.
Script: Roger Vadim, Marc Allégret, *from a novel by* Vicki Baum. *Dialogue:* Roger Vadim, France Roche.
Photography: Robert Juillard. *Editor:* Suzanne de Troye. *Music:* Jean Wiener. *Sound:* Robert Biart.
Art Director: Raymond Nègre. *Choreography:* Georges Reich. *Production Manager:* Claude Ganz.
Assistant Director: P. Boursaus. *Shooting:* started December 10, 1954, Studios Saint-Maurice.

CAST

Jean Marais	*Eric Walter*
Brigitte Bardot	*Sophie*
Denise Noël	*Marie*
Mischa Auer	*Berger*
Isabelle Pia	*Elisa*
Yves Robert	*Clément*

STORY

Operatic star Eric Walter has the time of his life teaching at the Vienna Conservatoire of Music. The girl students revere him like a pop idol; and while separated from the wife he loves—another singer, Marie—he is nonchalantly fancy-free in his pick of the nubile student body. His prime selections are close friends, though never realising each is smitten with him. Sophie is very young, very provocative, very sure of herself, very ambitious and very, very sensual; Elisa is more shy and reserved, though no less passionate. His wife's return ends both affairs abruptly and the girls console themselves with the theory that bruised hearts improve artistry.

NOTES

Marc Allégret finally gives in to his persuasive assistant and uses the girl who seemed to talk with her mother's dental plate! Obviously Vadim had not let up in pushing his continually improving young wife to all and sundry in film circles. And neither had he left out his patron from his sales-talk. This was Vadim's fifth film venture with Allégret since their original 1947 teaming in Britain, *Blanche Fury*;

Aria. Jean Marais is an opera star beset by groupies— as Bardot finally works for the men who discovered her, director Marc Allégret and scripter Vadim.

the veteran director had come to appreciate the young man's talents—and those, more abundantly clear, of his wife. (All three had been in Italy the year before on separate projects.)

Vadim suggested the Vicki Baum story, and worked on the script with Allégret; it fitted Bardot perfectly— a conservatoire musical student falling in love with an older man. Her story, exactly, of the early 50s—and as became usual with a Vadim script, she helped more in the writing than most people knew. 'She spoke and I wrote,' admits Vadim. 'The words in those first films, as in most of our films together, are really hers. They are written for her, because she more or less wrote them.' What he added, ever keen to extend her talents, provided her first deep affair with a man in a film . . . plus his own inescapable need to show her off as fully as possible in a nude scene. He had her taking a bath in the tenor's flat—in a pool of Chinese fish! Even so, she did not have things all her own way. *The Monthly Film Bulletin* felt that Isabelle Pia claimed more attention than the slight and still brunette Bardot.

Doctor at sea

1955

British. Group Film Production. J. Arthur Rank distribution; 93 minutes. French release title: *Rendez-vous à Rio.* US: Republic Pictures, 1956. Vistavision and Technicolor.
Director: Ralph Thomas, *Producer:* Betty Box. *Executive Producer:* Earl St. John. *Script:* Nicholas Phipps, Jack Davies; *adapted from his novel by* Richard Gordon. *Photography:* Ernest Steward. *Editor:* Frederick Wilson. *Music:* Bruce Montgomery. *Song:* 'Je ne sais pas', Hubert Gregg. *Conductor:* Muir Mathieson. *Sound:* John W. Mitchell, Gordon K. McCallum. *Art Director:* Carmen Dillon. *Costumes:* Joan Ellacott. *Make-up:* Geoffrey Rodway. *Technicolor Consultant:* Joan Bridge. *Assistant Director:* David Orton. *Shooting:* at Pinewood Studios.

CAST

Dirk Bogarde	*Dr. Simon Sparrow*
Brigitte Bardot	*Hélène Colbert*
Brenda de Banzie	*Muriel Mallet*
James Robertson Justice	*Captain Hogg*
Maurice Denham	*Easter*
Michael Medwin	*Trail*
Hubert Gregg	*Archer*
James Kenney	*Fellowes*
Raymond Huntley	*Captain Beamish*

Geoffrey Keen, George Coulouris, Noël Purcell, Jill Adams, Joan Sims, Cyril Chamberlain, Abe Barker, Toke Townley, Thomas Heathcote, Frederick Piper, Michael Shepley, Felix Felton, Joan Hickson, Eugene Deckers, Mary Laura Wood, Ekali Sokou, Martin Benson, Harold Kasket, Stuart Sanders.

STORY

Bored with the vicissitudes of general practice, newly qualified medico Simon Sparrow signs on as ship's doctor on the cargo-steamer *Lotus, en route* for South America. To his surprise, skipper Hogg's fury and the crew's delight, two ·women are added to the manifest for the return trip. Muriel, daughter of the shipping line's chairman, is soon acting very maternally towards the captain, while Sparrow is less than paternal about the young Continental *chanteuse,* Hélène. He proves his worth (and Hélène's as a

nurse) in an improvised appendectomy on the veteran Quartermaster, and signs on for another trip . . . and so, indirectly, does Hélène.

NOTES

BB: 'It was fun living in England and learning to improve my English which I speak . . . how would you say in your calm English way?—not too bad . . . perhaps, eh? It was especially exciting because for a long time I had admired Dirk Bogarde. In films I had seen his face—so interesting—so full of emotion

and feeling. He did not disappoint me when we met.'

Nor vice versa. Bogarde told *Picturegoer*: 'She was like a breath of Oklahoma on the set every day. The kind of sex she suggests is warm, uninhibited, completely natural. With her superb figure, long legs and flowing hair, she has a gazelle-like grace. The effect? Pure enchantment.' He also noted well her future. 'Even without a French accent, Brigitte would be too much for British studios to handle. You see, Brigitte takes the trouble to put across sex as an art. With many of our girls, it's a farce!'

Vadim could not have arranged things better if he had tried; and he played no part in engineering his wife's timely export. It was Betty Box who spotted Bardot herself, catching the BB début in a Riviera cinema. 'It was her enormous vitality that attracted me. She was very young, very good-looking, and yes, very sexy, too, but in a most wholesome way.' A firm follower of Continental trends, in faces more than style, producer Box subscribed to magazines like *Cinémonde* and noted the impact of what were, in the main, Vadim's publicity manoeuvres of the time. (In like manner, Miss Box was later to import Claudia Cardinale, Mylène Demongeot, Sylva Koscina, Yoko Tani, Elisabeth Ercy, and others to Pinewood, adding international impetus to their young careers.)

Director Ralph Thomas never faulted his partner's judgement; he just got on with the imports in hand. In Bardot's case, however, neither guessed how well she would work out in the rôle refused by the late Kay Kendall. Bardot was co-operative in every department—from her eye-popping strip-off answer to the problem of undies showing through the shower curtain, to her non-stop pursuit of all publicity matters, resulting in some of the finest gallery stills of her mid-50s period. Nor did they dream her impact would be so marked on the British Press and public. If Vadim pushed Bardot, it was Box and Thomas who made her a star.

And Vadim agrees. 'The British first really saw her talent—even if it was only as a piece of French spiciness. When she went over to London . . . she was hardly known outside of France. In London, a crowd of photographers came along to take pictures and almost every paper in England carried a pin-up type picture of her the following day.'

Pinewood's tame publicity machine had her photographed tasting the prerequisite pint of beer and amateurishly labelled her 'the kind of *mademoiselle* who makes the temperature rise even in the tropics'.

Leonard Mosley, *Daily Express*, who had first really introduced her to Britain in 1953 after literally falling for her at the Cannes festival, gave his discovery a huge spread. 'She walks into camera-

Giggles. As British director Ralph Thomas and Dirk Bogarde make Bardot a star.

range as the central figure in one of the corniest clichés of the cinema. The scene is a night-club . . . On comes Brigitte, singing. It has killed many films in the past. It is the moment when most critics groan and most husbands tell their wives that they wish they had never left the cricket on TV. Brigitte Bardot turns it into achievement for herself—and establishes that elfish face, that firefly figure and that humming-bird personality into a triumph of sheer charm over a bad script . . .'

Harold Conway, *Daily Sketch*: '"You like some coffee," askes Brigitte with eyes looking as big as the Pool of London—and packs more sex-appeal into her question than Betty Grable gets into an entire film.'

The *Sunday Express* thought her—'easily'—the most charming aspect of the film; the *News Chronicle* found her delicious; the *Evening News*, 'perfectly bewitching'; and *Picturegoer* said she was 'the prettiest and sauciest girl the French have sent a British studio since Odile Versois' (star of *Act of Love*).

Raymond Durgnat, *Films and Filming*, noted that it was in this mild comedy that Bardot 'sumptuously gowned and groomed, first emerged from the rank-and-file of starletry, and her two subsequent films firmly established the BB "range"'.

She worked her charms on America, as well. A. H. Weiler, *New York Times*: 'The pert Mlle. Bardot's

features and distinctly feminine figure are guaranteed to distract any ship's doctor . . . visual proof that the beauties of France are not all geographic.'

It was, however, the geography of Bardot that Vadim was more interested in and preparing to display to the world.

Shock. Dr. Bogarde finds Bébé in his shower—scorning all the genteel 'nude scene' paraphernalia of nipple-covers etc.

Les grandes manoeuvres

1955

Franco-Italian. Filmsonor (Paris)/Rizzoli Film (Rome) co-production; 106 minutes. UK: Films de France, *Summer Manœuvres*, 1956. US: United Motion Picture Organisation, 1956. Eastman Color.
Director: René Clair. *Script:* Clair, Jérome Géronimi, Jean Marsan, *from the novel by* Courteline. *Dialogue:* Clair. *Photography:* Robert Le Fèbvre, Robert Juillard. *Editor:* Louise Hautecoeur. *Music:* Georges Van Parys. *Sound:* Antoine Petitjean. *Art Director:* Léon Barsacq. *Costumes:* Rosine Delamare. *Production Manager:* Jacques Plante. *Second Unit Director:* Michel Boisrond. *Assistant Director:* Serge Vallin. *Shooting:* April 28–July 8, 1955, Studios Boulogne.

CAST

Michèle Morgan . . . . . . *Marie-Louise Rivière*
Gérard Philipe . . . . *Lt. Armand de la Verne*
Brigitte Bardot . . . . . . *Lucie*
Yves Robert . . . . *Félix*
Simone Valère . . . . *Gisèle*
Jean Desailly . . . . *Victor*
Jacques François . . . . . *Rodolphe*
Pierre Dux . . . . *Colonel*
Lise Delamare . . . . *Jeanne*
Jacqueline Maillan . . . . *Juliette*
Magali Noël . . . . *Singer*
Catherine Anouilh . . . . *Bride*
Raymond Cordy . . . . . *Armand's Batman*
Olivier Hussenot . . . . . . *Prefect*

STORY

A French provincial garrison town, 1914. Armand de la Verne, officer and questionably a gentleman, is the Don Juan of his crack cavalry regiment. To prove his reputation, he accepts a wager that he will be the lover of any woman chosen by his fellows, in the month before their regiment leaves for summer manœuvres. Marie-Louise, milliner and divorcée, is selected as his target: no easy citadel to fall before his charms, flowers, and letters of unrequited love. By the time she warms towards him, Armand is genuinely in love, thinking of marriage not officers' mess bets. Tragically for him, Marie-Louise learns of the wager and refuses to forgive or see him again . . .

Affair. Brigitte and Yves Robert copy the romance of René Clair's star leads—though far more cheerfully.

NOTES

Where was Bardot among all this? Learning from the master René Clair, the finest director she has worked with before or since—and from the elegant playing of the illustrious leads, Philipe and Morgan. While they enacted their by turn witty and sad love story, Bardot mirrored their love and intrigue on a more joyful plane, with one of Philipe's brother officers, Yves Robert.

The film was Clair's 26th, and his first in colour. 'A film I like very much . . . because it is in the location of my youth. As a boy, I lived near Versailles where there were a lot of officers and cavalry. I've always been fascinated by that world and wanted to make a film about it.' He called it, simply, a film about love. 'But it's also a comedy that stiffens into drama,' wrote Margaret Hinxman in *Picturegoer*, 'and a deeply observed portrait of a lost age and a nostalgic way of life . . . a rare enchantment.'

The Times: '. . . a sign for lost youth, for a lost generation, and for, perhaps, *l'amour* as against love, and its only fault is that in enchanting the senses it fails to touch the heart.'

Roy Armes, *French Cinema*: 'The setting allows Clair to draw yet another portrait of bourgeois society and show its underlying hypocrisies and deceits, while the romance of Armand's friend, Félix (Yves Robert), with a pretty little photographer's daughter (BB) provides balance and light relief to the main theme.'

And across the Atlantic, A. H. Weiler, *New York Times*, also singled out Bardot, as 'the pretty object' among the stellar leads.

La lumière d'en face

1955

The Light Opposite. French. Entreprise Générale Cinématographique/Fernand Rives production; 100 minutes. UK: *The Light Across the Street*, Miracle Films, 1956; 97 minutes. US: United Motion Picture Corporation; 98 minutes. Monochrome.

Director: Georges Lacombe. *Producer:* Jacques Gauthier. *Script:* Louis Chavance, René Masson, *from a story by* Jean-Claude Aurel. *Dialogue:* René Lefèbvre. *Photography:* Louis Page. *Editor:* Raymond Leboursier. *Music:* Norbert Glanzberg. *Sound:* Antoine Archimbaud. *Art Director:* Alexandre Trauner. *Production Manager:* Fred Surin. *English sub-titles:* Mai Harris. *Shooting:* from July 11, 1955, Studios Victorine, Nice.

CAST

Brigitte Bardot	*Olivia Marceau*
Raymond Pellegrin	*Georges Marceau*
Roger Pigaut	*Pietri*
Claude Romain	*Barbette.*
Guy Pierraud	*Antoine*
Lucien Herbert	*Gaspard*
Berval	*Albert*
Jacques Gauthier	*Doctor*

and Christine Gouze-Renal.

Temptress. The siren awakes. *Via* Vadim's (in)tuition.

STORY

Forbidden *any* excitement by doctors following a traumatic lorry smash, Georges still marries Olivia as planned. They open a roadside café on his beloved Highway 7, smile a lot at each other, but sleep in separate rooms. Consummation is to be postponed until he has medical clearance. Georges's sexual abstinence mounts to frenzy as he sees how his young wife's looks and body arouse the customers at his pull-up for carmen—and bring closer interest from the virile boss of the garage opposite. Olivia meets Pietri often, though remaining faithful to Georges. Frustration drives him insane. He nearly strangles his wife, she runs to Pietri. Georges tries to shoot them only to fall under a lorry and die on Highway 7.

NOTES

Or, as Miracle Film's Tony Tenser, the man who dreamt up the sex-kitten tag, put it in his publicity release: 'A young bride, innocent yet radiating passion from every inch . . . the husband she loves who must not share her bed . . . how each glance, each gesture incites in him that which must not be . . . and when she walks, the travelling eye is transfixed and the husband's feelings become your feelings.' Tenser wasn't entirely wrong. With this treatment, and a poster of Bardot sitting on a sink, washing her feet, under the legend 'A girl has to cool down the best way she can', Miracle Films had a winner and Bardot was truly launched, and created in Britain. Goodbye to the innocence in *Doctor at Sea* and *Summer Manœuvres* and hello Bébé-doll.

In those early days of the Continental film imports into Britain (screened mainly in London and university city art-houses), Dick Michaels and Phil Kutner of Miracle Films flew to Paris at least once a month to check productions which their agent had earmarked for possible purchase. They confirmed a price for *Lumière* before their screening was over, although once back in London they had no idea what to call it. *The Light Opposite* was as weak as milk-toast; they needed something rather spicier. They mentioned the headache to a Wardour Street chum, Fred Hutchinson, of Paramount. *The Light Across the Street*, he suggested, first time. 'Perfect,' said Michaels: it had all the essential naughty connotations Continental films were then renowned for (Britain and America did not make films about streets, lights, i.e. tarts).

Publicity man Tenser got to work and Fleet Street was easily enticed into noting the considerable change in the young star, then being hailed as a gorgeous pekinese. A few critics complained about her change of image from *Doctor at Sea*; the rest had a field day, running a fistful of adjectives up and

Triangle. Roger Pigaut defends the virgin bride (and himself) from the fury of Raymond Pellegrin as the impotent husband.

down every curve of the star and the story—which remains one of the most searingly erotic in her lists.

Alan Brien, *Evening Standard,* was the most enamoured of London critics about her phosphorescent charms—'she glows in the dark like an open stove'. He called her a creature from another world, and an uncanny space-girl combination of Shirley Temple and Eartha Kitt, who might easily have been elected Miss Mars of 1956 . . . 'Though she is now 21, she still looks like a schoolgirl who has been in too many night-clubs. She had oomph before she knew how to spell it and she graduated from the sixth form with an X certificate. With her in the class, a dormitory would seem like a harem and a biology lesson would turn into a True Confessions serial . . . With a lens which must surely be shaped like a keyhole, the camera follows her remorselessly around. She is forever standing against a strong light in a nylon nightie, sitting on the kitchen table, washing her legs under the tap, bending over the ice-bucket in a loose blouse, and bathing naked in the river. These activities cause the temperature to rise all around—not least in the audience. By the time the husband and the handsome garage proprietor across the road are stoked up to fever heat with jealousy and frustration and start reaching for the guns, it is difficult to see the screen for steam. As a film . . . it is merely competent. As an illustrated catalogue of the charms of Miss Brigitte Bardot, it is

Couple. And the garage-owner, Pigaut, wins the girl . . .

hard to imagine how it got through the Customs.' Campbell Dixon, *Daily Telegraph*: 'Another French film about suffering through sex. All the characters struggled against deprivation . . . Played by Raymond Pellegrin and Roger Pigaut with an intelligence, by Brigitte Bardot with bosom.'

Fred Majdalany, *Time and Tide*: 'A not very good French film that banks on everyone being bemused by the undeniable, but in this case, misdirected, physical witchcraft of young Brigitte Bardot . . .' For the *Daily Mail*, he called it the kind of French film that people who did not go to French films would probably expect a French film to be like. 'As the Americans would say, it is warm sex-wise, cold interest-wise, boring story-wise. [BB] is formidable body-wise and pout-wise, but is not called upon to exercise any great effort acting-wise.'

C. A. Lejeune, *Observer*: 'Apart from the required display of physical charms, Mlle. Bardot is mainly occupied in opening and shutting windows, a task which she performs admirably.' (Funny, I do not remember her opening windows; mouth and dress, yes . . .)

The *Daily Mirror* found Bardot so seductive it awaited her next film with impatience and called her a dimpled poem of provocation; the *Daily Sketch*: 'she not only makes one long to eat her up but manages to suggest that nothing would delight her more than to be eaten'.

Bromley Town Council, in Kent, did not agree with anyone, including most of the population of Bromley. Their Highway and Buildings Committee ordered the film withdrawn from a local cinema because they had not found time to see it first. Said Town Clerk Lionel Keyes: 'The licensing authority does not feel that X films are in popular demand here.'

The climes, they were a-changing. Bosley Crowther, *New York Times*, noting how heavily the cards were stacked against the hero ('so is Brigitte Bardot'), called it a cheerless little picture, directed without charm or style—but with 'rather candid sub-titles by the way'. More than language was becoming candid in the cinema. And Bardot was to be in the forefront of the revolution.

Playing a bit rôle in the film was a former star of the immediate post-war French Government ministry and diplomatic circles: Christine Gouze-Renal— who later produced several BB vehicles, notably *Vie privée*, 1961. Jacques Gauthier, producer of *La lumière* . . . also played a small rôle: Pellegrin's doctor. Upon Gauthier's early death, his contract with Brigitte for two more films was taken over by Ray Ventura (uncle, incidentally, of her future lover, singer Sacha Distel). Ventura went into partnership with Raoul Levy, producer of the ultimate BBreakthrough, *Et Dieu créa la femme.*

Cette sacrée gamine

1955

That Crazy Kid. French. Lutetia/SLPF/Sonodis/SELB production; 86 minutes. UK: *Mam'zelle Pigalle*, Films de France release, 1957; 86 minutes. US: Films-Around-the-World distribution; 77 minutes. CinemaScope. Eastman Color.

Director: Michel Boisrond. *Script/dialogue:* Roger Vadim, Michel Boisrond, *from an idea by* Jean Périne. *Photography:* Joseph Brun. *Editor:* Jacques Mavel. *Music:* Henri Colla, Hubert Rostaing. *Sound:* Norbert Gernolle. *Art Director:* Jacques Chalvet. *Choreography:* Georges Reich. *Production Manager:* Georges Senamaud. *Assistant Director:* J. Poitrenaud. *Shooting:* from September 6, 1955, Studios Saint-Maurice.

CAST

Brigitte Bardot . . . . *Brigitte Latour*
Jean Bretonnière . . . . *Jean Cléry*
Françoise Fabian . . . . *Lili Rocher-Villedieu*
Bernard Lancret . . . . *Paul Latour*
Raymond Bussières . . . . . . *Jérôme*
Mischa Auer . . . . *Ballet Master*
Darry Cowl . . . . *Man with suitcase*

STORY

Wrongly suspected of forgery by the gendarmes, night-club owner Latour flees Montmartre, making sure his singing star, Jean Cléry, protects his precocious daughter—'*c'est un grand bébé!*' Jean abducts the girl from ballet class to keep one step ahead of the police, and installs her in his flat, still clad in brief ballet tutu. She is not such a baby as Papa maintains—as Jean's fiancée, Lili, quickly points out. Despite a wild series of catastrophes (she floods the bathroom, burns his evening suit, plays poker with the valet, and winds up in jail one night), Jean and Brigitte fall in love. They also trail the real forgers. In a monster punch-up at the club, the gang is netted, Latour's name is cleared and Jean left choosing between Lili and Brigitte. No contest!

NOTES

BB: 'I like this film of Boisrond. It is very optimistic —so am I!'

Floored. The 'baby' and the butler, Raymond Bussières.

Once more Vadim's talent-touting paid off as young Boisrond, René Clair's assistant on *Belles de nuit*, which helped introduce La Lollo, and *Les grandes manœuvres*, which helped introduce BB, took the plunge into direction. Boisrond knew Bardot from 1953 and *Act of Love*, in fact, and their new teaming generated their lively flair for comedy, to be underlined more superbly in *Une Parisienne* and *Voulez-vous danser avec moi?*

Vadim's section of the script obviously included naming the rollicking heroine, and providing more dancing exposure of his bride: physical exposure too, of course, in and out of Greek tunics, ballet tutus, frilly nighties and the arrival of her 50s trademark, the bath towel. Plus the one line of dialogue no one would argue with: *Latour:* She's such a baby! *Gardener:* A baby like that has always been my dream. (Vadim's dream anyway.)

This time, the longest *critique* in Britain came in, of all journals, *The Times:* '... one of those light, frothy bits of French more or less nothingness with which it is so difficult to come to grips. The director is a pupil of M. René Clair, and so satire is to be looked for. Every now and again it pops up, while it enjoys a field day during the last sequence which shows the wrecking of the night-club ... by gangsters, police, performers and anyone else who cares to join

Crazy. Vadim co-wrote the script, filled with bath-towels, jails, dances, and he called the 'crazy kid' Brigitte. What else?

in. This is a scene to end all club-wrecking scenes and while it is funny enough, it is funny at one remove, so to speak, from the audience's appreciation . . . leaves us with the uneasy impression that we have seen it before. Brigitte is a schoolgirl, who proves before the end that she is hardly the kind of girl to captain the hockey team . . . and Mlle. Bardot lends a vivid, mischievous personality to the part . . .'

Jympson Harman, *Evening News*: 'A good deal of what we should call Goonery is injected into the treatment of the obvious farcical situations. Miss Bardot appears in a variety of kinds of strip-tease as well as figure fitting dancing tights and short tunics. For many people saucy Miss Bardot will be enough. But I found the humour forced and untidy.'

Gordon Reid, *Continental Film Review*: 'It is a vehicle that allows Brigitte . . . to pass from provocative pout to expose poses to border-line ballet—very attractive she is too . . . a light entertainment trifle that by taste and shrewdness transforms a modest production into a neat spectacular one . . . a vehicle . . .'

Ivon Addams, *Star*: 'A champagne comedy . . . Miss Bardot is youth. She is beauty. She is every man's idea of the girl he'd like to meet in Paris.' Peter Burnup, *New of the World*: 'As gay and sparkling as you could wish . . . light as a soufflé, refreshing as champagne.'

Reg Whitley, *Daily Mirror*: '. . . She spends most of her time in various stages of undress—as a tomboy schoolgirl who develops a crush on her father's best friend . . . She describes herself as 'thirteen years old—but forward for my age'. You're telling me. She swims and dances in the near nude and figures in several naughty situations . . .'

And a warning from *Monthly Film Bulletin*: 'The lavish upholstery . . . fails to obscure the deficiencies of the script, which undermines even [BB's] likeable, scatter-brained performance.'

Richard W. Nason, *New York Times*, saw it in 1960, after *Et Dieu créa la femme*: 'Those in charge of the film assets of Brigitte Bardot, which are known to be considerable, have done a rather strange thing . . . They have cast their valuable little bombshell against type as a romantic and prankish schoolgirl. This is, of course, a rôle that does not allow for the sort of wanton animalism upon which her popularity has been built . . . It presents nothing that can take the place of a serious study of Miss Bardot's form. There are some tongue-in-cheek jokes in the script . . . At other times the tongue is struck right out. When all is said and done, Miss Bardot is seen as a mother, wedded to the crooner, complete with a baby and bassinet. Who's kidding whom?'

Mio figlio Nerone

1956

My Son Nero. Italo-French. Titanus-Vides (Rome)/ Les Films Marceau (Paris) co-production; 105 minutes. Released in France as *Les Week-ends de Néron.* UK: *Nero's Weekend.* Gala Films, 1957; 90 minutes. CinemaScope. Eastman Color.
Director: Steno (Stefano Vanzina). *Script:* Rodolfo Sonego, Alessandro Continenza, Diego Fabbri, Ugo Guerra, *from a story by* Steno. *Photography:* Mario Bava. *Music:* A. F. Lavagnino. *Art Director:* Puetro Filippone. *Shooting:* Rome.

CAST

Alberto Sordi	*Nero*
Brigitte Bardot	*Poppea*
Vittorio De Sica	*Seneca*
Gloria Swanson	*Agrippina*
Giogia Moll	*Lidia*
Ciccio Barbi	*Anicetus*
Mario Carotenuto	*Creperius*
Mino Doro	*Corbulo*
Farnalette	*Segimanius*
Maria Pellegrini	*Acceronis*

STORY

Nero's lackaday (orgy-every-night) existence with his luscious mistress, Poppea, is ruined by the arrival of his domineering mother, Agrippina. She will keep on so about the great empire! Nero aims to conquer the world with his music, not war. Seneca remains busy keeping Nero's alliance with Poppea from Agrippina and assisting the emperor's attempts to be rid of Mamma. She remains impervious, however, to vipers in the bed, deadly poisons, collapsible beds and sinking ships. And why did Nero fire Rome? The city did not appreciate his singing!

NOTES

Steno called it 'a new look into the strictly private life of Rome's enthroned madman', and in the wake of all the other big, serious (if often risibly funny) epics, it was a refreshing piece of farce. *Carry On Nero*, with all the pitfalls such a title would imply. Bardot's inevitable bathing scene as Poppea made all the papers, with stories, many engineered by Vadim, being different in every country. Steno, with his budget in mind, ordered a pool filled with chalk

all' Italiana. Third time around. But the style was more frenzied actually as Brigitte lived it up, campily. In good company. Vittorio De Sica as Seneca and Alberto Sordi as a mother-in-law-infested Nero. Bardot was his plaything, Poppea. And playtime in the bath meant asses' milk—or else! Of such publicity, headlines are made and films sold...

and/or whitewash to look like milk. Vadim, so one version goes, ordered Bardot to insist on real milk. Cow's milk quickly turned rancid under the klieg lights. Steno suggested lime and water—that didn't work either. Rome reports insisted that Bardot stamped her pretty foot and demanded historical reality: asses' milk. But where do you find asses enough for 400 quarts of milk? Apparently they did, plus fridges aplenty to store the stuff. Whatever the truth of the milky wastes, the publicity did nothing but good for the movie. In Italy, at least.

Anthony Carthew, *Daily Herald*: 'The unlikely combination of [BB] and Gloria Swanson makes a highly un-likeable film. Roman orgies were surely never as tame as this.'

Sarah Stoddart, *Picturegoer*: 'As Nero's favourite, [BB], despite a bath in asses' milk, is no match for sizzling Swanson.'

Monthly Film Bulletin: 'A tasteless, vulgar charade, which provokes a certain number of easy laughs during the first few minutes . . . but soon becomes a pitiable affair.'

The Times: 'Mlle. Brigitte Bardot, as Poppea, seems a little out of her depth and class.'

Campbell Dixon, *Daily Telegraph*: 'The acting is deliberately farcical . . . [BB's] Poppea, running the gamut from pretty smile to pretty pout, is the madcap of the Lower Fifth.'

En effeuillant la marguerite

1956

Plucking the Daisy. French. Films EGE/Hoch Productions; 101 minutes. UK: *Mam'selle Striptease*, Miracle Films, 1956; 100 minutes: re-issued, 1962; 94 minutes. US: *Please Mr. Balzac*, Distributors' Corporation of America; 1957. Monochrome.
Director: Marc Allégret. *Producer:* Pierre Schwab, Claude Ganz. *Script:* Roger Vadim, Marc Allégret, *from an idea by* William Benjamin. *Dialogue:* Roger Vadim. *Photography:* Louis Page. *Editor:* Suzanne de Troeye. *Music:* Paul Misraki. *Sound:* Jacques Carrère. *Art Directors:* Alexandre Trauner, August Capelier. *Production Manager:* Claude Ganz. *Shooting:* from February 13, 1956, Studios Éclair.

CAST

Brigitte Bardot . . . . *Agnès Dumont*
Daniel Gélin . . . . *Daniel*
Robert Hirsch . . . . *Roger*
Darry Cowl . . . . *Hubert*
Nadine Tallier . . . . *Magali*
Luciana Paoluzzi . . . . *Sophie*
Mischa Auer . . . . *Taxi-driver*
Jacques Dumensil . . . . *Général Dumont*
Georges Chamarat, Anne Colette, Jacques Fervil, Jacques Jouanneau, Madeleine Barbulée, Yves-Marie Maurin. Guest star: Françoise Arnoul.

STORY

Merry, madcap big-city adventures of bourgeois beauty Agnès Dumont, fleeing her small-town home once her general father discovered she wrote the best-selling scandal book of the hour. In Paris, she breaks into her brother's big house and pawns one of his big books to tide her over. Big mistake. The house is the Balzac Museum; Hubert is merely caretaker. Agnès sees more of journalist Daniel; and although he does not realise it, he sees much more of her—winning an amateur striptease contest (in a mask) to raise money to buy back the Balzac first edition. Daniel flirts with the mystery stripper, which infuriates Agnès behind her mask. At the contest finals, Général Dumont is among the judges and the mask must come off . . .

NOTES

Vadim's last stand—as far as traditional French cinema went. Once again, Allégret submitted to his assistant's creation, on paper, flesh and screen; and a vast improvement was seen from the BB of their first venture the previous year. More confident than ever, Vadim knew what star-quality he had in his wife; this, therefore, was to be the end of the coy comedienne as far as Vadim was concerned.
His script, which derived in part from Irene Dunne's *Theodora Goes Wild* (1936), included a Hitchcock walk-on, audio-style, for Vadim—his name was heard as scriptwriter of a play on the radio. He also insisted on a big-name co-star: Daniel Gélin accepted with relish, repaying the couple's walk-on in his 1952 début as director. In Britain, Darry Cowl won the best reviews, as BB's stammering, hesitant, absent-minded and continually smoking brother: a marvellous cameo, repeated too often in later films. Françoise Arnoul, another big name of the time, agreed to a guest walk-on in a night-club scene with Gélin. The remarkably sensual Françoise was sadly overtaken, demolished, in the rapid rise of the BB legend—although Vadim replaced Bardot with her in his second feature, *Sait-on jamais*, the following year.
In Italy, the poster for what they called *Miss Spog-*

Poster. The Italians tore their ads. down—from disgust or admiration was never made clear—and so the new poster became that of a poster being torn down...

liarello was torn off Rome walls for being 'audacious, shameless, offensive and immoral'. In France, *Cinémonde* headlined their coverage '*Brigitte . . . vedette d'une comédie française de style Americain!*' In America, Howard Thompson, in the *New York Times,* moaned that the lady who suggested a caged panther was behaving like a caged country dove. And *Time* found her too sisterly—'Still she's a fetching little hussy and the language she speaks can be understood without sub-titles.'

In Britain by now she was billed as 'the one and only' and found a new home when the film was selected to open the revitalised Cameo-Royal, in London's Charing Cross Road (September 26, 1956); a surprising A-certificate feature for the home since then of strictly X-film fare. A leader in the development of news-theatres since 1932, the cinema inaugurated the West End's first all-cartoon programme in 1937, as well as packing 'em in with another programme honestly headlined: 'Fourteen really bad pictures.' In the halcyon 50s days it was the major West End home of BB films—with a life-size pin-up statue of her in the foyer to prove it. While the *Daily Mirror* had to agree the movie

Mentor. Marc Allégret's influence on Bébé—and Vadim—was immense.

123

Outrage. Her parents disapprove ... (Sound familiar?)

Esteem. The Press approved ... (Well, Vadim wrote it.)

was not as saucy as it sounded, 'the title is the best thing about this film', the *Monthly Film Bulletin* pulled nary a punch: 'The recent noticeable decline in the quality of French screen comedy reaches a new low in this lengthy, stultifying unfunny rig-marole.'

The Times, in another verbose treatise, felt that students of international terminology would be intrigued to see the French borrow an Americanism to describe the age-old tradition of undressing in public. 'Here, then, is an essay in Le Striptease ... The exact sequence of events leading to her physical dénouement need not be described here in detail, for this is no more than a routine French farce, translated by transatlantic influences from the bedroom to the stage dressing-room. Suffice to say that there are some comic French newspapermen, playing artless pranks upon each other, and a comic general who is Agnès's father, all engaged in what can reasonably be described as good, clean fun, while Agnès herself remains a simple innocent whose activities in the striptease field never suggest that she is in danger of losing her amateur status.'

Or in short, as the *Daily Sketch* reported: 'The striptease competition is supposed to be a big climax. Don't be fooled. At essential moments the camera—like Brigitte herself—goes all coy on you, and cheats.'

Not any more. Vadim was already deep in negotiations—indeed calculations—with Raoul Levy. And God and the Devil were being brought into the act ...

Et Dieu créa la femme

1956

French. Iéna/UCIL/Cocinor production; 95 minutes. UK: *And Woman . . . Was Created*, Miracle Films, 1957; 91 minutes: re-issued as *And God Created Woman*, 1967; 93 minutes. US: *And God Created Woman*, Kingsley International, 1957; 92 minutes. CinemaScope. Eastman Color.
Director: Roger Vadim. *Producer:* Raoul J. Levy. *Script:* Vadim, Levy; *adaptation dialogue:* Vadim. *Photography:* Armand Thirard. *Editor:* Victoria Mercanton. *Music:* Paul Misraki. *Sound:* Pierre Louis Calvet. *Art Director:* Jean André. *Production Manager:* Claude Ganz. *Assistant Director:* Paul Fayder, Pierre Boursans. *Stills:* Léo Mirkine. *English sub-titles:* Mai Harris. *Shooting:* from November 28, 1956, Saint-Tropez, Studios La Victorine, Nice.

CAST

Brigitte Bardot . . . . *Juliette Hardy*
Curt Jurgens . . . . *Eric Carradine*
Jean-Louis Trintignant . . . . . *Michel Tardieu*
Christian Marquand . . . . . . *Antoine Tardieu*
Georges Poujouly . . . . *Christian Tardieu*
Jeanne Marken . . . . *Madame Morin*
Isabelle Corey . . . . *Lucienne*
Jean Lefèbvre . . . . *René*
Philippe Grenier . . . . *Perri*
Jacqueline Ventura . . . . *Mme. Vigier-Lefranc*
Jean Tissier . . . . *M. Vigier-Lefranc*
Jany Mourey . . . . *Bonne Femme*
Marie Glory . . . . *Mme. Tardieu*
Jacques Giron . . . . *Roger*
Paul Faivre . . . . *M. Morin*
Leopoldo Frances . . . . *Dancer*
Toscano . . . . *René*

STORY

Vadim: 'I wanted, through Brigitte, to witness an epoch; the psychosis of our post-war generation. Juliette is a young girl of today, to whom the taste of pleasure is neither limited by morals or social taboos; entirely free in her sexual behaviour. In pre-war literature and cinema one would have painted her simply as a whore. Here she is a very young woman without, of course, any excuses save for those of the heart, of a generous, *desaxée*, inconsistent person.'

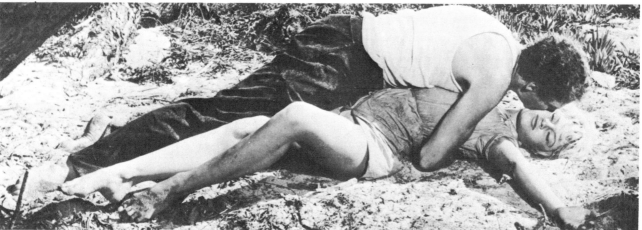

Stardom. Vadimised Brigitte staggers the world—taking Jean-Louis Trintignant for a husband and his brother (played by Christian Marquand) for her lover.

Juliette, 18, orphaned, lives in a coastal township with a childless couple, the Morins, and works in their bookstore. Permeating an effortless sex-appeal, she is desired by all the local men, from old Morin, spying on her nude sunbathing, to the Tardieu sons and wealthy shipping magnate, Carradine. She is drawn to the eldest Tardieu, but she is just a plaything to Antoine. 'I never said I wanted to be first.' She weds his gentle brother, Michel, growing to love him and trying to quell her restive, blue genes to make the marriage work. 'I need you to love me a lot.' Antoine's virility proves too strong; after his stormy beach seduction, she flees to Carradine. Michel fights his brother, shoots Carradine, slaps his drunken wife, dancing in a club, and drags her home. Carradine: 'That girl can drive men wild. But Michel's young—and he's shown her he's master. He'll make out all right I think.'

Star. Curt Jurgens was the name securing the backing. He knew whose film it was, though. 'Brigitte possesses innate femininity ... an indescribable phenomenon.'

NOTES

Brigitte enters the BBig-time. The film that created the myth, the actress who wasn't an actress but herself, as amoral, Vadim said, Bardot said, as Juliette on the screen. The film that hardly bothered the French and shook up the rest of the globe and changed the face of the cinema. Due to BB, the *fesses* that launched a thousand strips.

'My best film!' Brigitte declared frequently at the time and well into 1957/8. And so it was. So it is. Inasmuch as a remarkable original can never be repeated, nor improved upon. So it goes . . .

Twenty years later, Vadim still maintains it is her finest, her truest, her most definitive work. His own as well (followed, incidentally, by his second feature, *Sait-on jamais*; *Barbarella* and *La curée*). As for Bébé's later career, Vadim has seen nearly every film she has made, or at least the important output for him and everyone else of note, and he cannot locate a better total performance from her than in this, their astonishing début canvas.

'I have seen again *La vérité*, for example, which was a good melodrama, but very old-fashioned. But, yes, a good film: interesting. When it came out in 1960, people said, "Here, for the first time, Bardot is really an actress"—because it was a very psychological rôle. But it was still kind of old-fashioned. Yet the people, the critics, say, "Ah! Now she really acts!" But she was not, I think, ever really as interesting as she was in *God Created Woman*. All the good points in *La vérité* were just picked up from *God Created Woman*.'

The début worked so exceeding well because of the young married couple's intertwined relationship —experienced master and eager pupil in love, sex and in work. Physically and mentally, Vadim knew Bardot from stem to stern; his film was dedicated to sharing such knowledge with the world, revealing as much of her interior and her glowing exterior— and never over-extending any of her by now relative inexperience. 'Never had I been so much at ease,' Brigitte told *Cahiers du Cinéma*, in May, 1957. 'Vadim knows me so well. All the dialogue was so natural to me and the setting marvellous.'

And the censorship? 'I have not timed it but there are many cuts—*c'est dommage!* It spoils the rhythm. There was, for example, a long scene on the beach where Christian Marquand slipped off my dress and caressed me. There is hardly anything left of it and I regret it. It was not *sale* (dirty) because it was beautiful.'

She was shooting this steamy sequence when Donald Zec, *Daily Mirror*, turned up and turned in the first clue about the cinematic eruption to come. 'Brigitte, in a sea-soaked dress, stood over a handsome dark-haired actor . . . He had just rescued her

Coiffure. The looks, the lips, the hair. Vadim's message got through . . .

(for the film) from a raging sea. He was exhausted. He was wet. He was winded. He looked at her. She looked at him. Suddenly, she put a dainty foot on his face and trod his head into the sand—like an unwanted jam sandwich at Bognor. This, he didn't like. So he grabbed her ankle and with a powerful flick of the wrist sent her tumbling on to her back. "Bravo—cut," said the director.'

As befits Britain's most wry, incisive show-business reporter, Zec was also first to report on the finished film, after a private Venice screening with 20 people including Gary Cooper and a Great Dane dog. 'It's the most flagrant, suggestive, near the knuckle picture I have ever seen anywhere . . . opens with Brigitte lying prone (profile on) naked under a bamboo awning. After this, she appears in and out of clothes, in and out of bed, with the rapidity of a mannequin modelling nightdresses . . . The most extraordinary scene is her wedding night, where the camera intrudes for much longer than is strictly necessary. Her facial expressions, suggestive movements and semi-strip-teasing had the audience gasping with amazement.' Gary Cooper was quoted as saying: 'Ah guess ah ought to put a sack over my face.' The Great Dane, apparently, said nothing. To everyone's surprise in London, the retiring Censor, A. T. L. Wakins, did not say much either. It was the last film he awarded an X-certificate by trimming just a few minutes from the already censored French version. His successor, the short-lived John Nicholls, could not touch the film—but forced the Cameo-Royal cinema to remove all nude stills from display. American censors—every state a different story—went snip-happy, particularly after a wrathful indictment from the Roman Catholic Legion of Decency. Two Philadelphia managers were arrested for showing the film—'dirt for dirt's sake' said the local District Attorney.

Copine. Bébé and Isabelle Corey, her latest *confidente.*

Couple. The marriage night—a Vadim/BB classic sequence.

Bardot remained peeved only by the French cuts: 'I asked why they had cut a back view of me walking with a bicycle. They replied: "It's the way she walks. It says too much." The only thing I didn't like about the film was having to be knocked off the bike!'

John K. Newham, *Tit-Bits*, introducing his paper's long serialisation of the script: 'The most sensational film ever produced in France . . . the film that shocked the French censor so much that he banned it completely until drastic cuts had been made . . . puts [BB] into a class of her own. No other star has appeared in so many X certificate pictures. [Not exactly true in 1957.] No other actress has dared to appear in so many torrid rôles. She is all the screen vamps rolled into one. But it offers more than sensationalism. It has a message of warning for all girls who might be tempted to allow their appeal for men to dominate their lives. Only tragedy can lie ahead for those who throw caution to the winds [very true in BB's legend].

Matt White, *Daily Sketch*: 'I'm prepared to bet an overcoat to a bikini that this film will make its star Miss Sex of the Universe. In a lifetime of seeing movies, I have never seen an actress convey sex so simply and so devastatingly . . . She had me blushing in the nervous darkness of the cinema.'

Philip Oakes, *Evening Standard*: 'Running a gauntlet of wet-mouthed males, Miss Bardot shows remarkable stamina and a great deal of thigh. Her other talents have gone the way of all flesh . . . The fatal clinch takes place on a deserted beach where [her] ten button dress reaches a one button minimum.'

Cecil Wilson, *Daily Mail*: 'Censored or uncensored, this actress has a way of making her meaning clear . . . But if her performance consists largely of a smouldering pout, it must be remembered that Mlle. Bardot can smoulder to better purposes than most other screen sirens can blaze.'

Reg Whitley, *Daily Mirror*: 'I can remember few performances to equal brilliant Brigitte's vivid portrayal of an over-sexed, slinkly slut . . . Two kissing scenes, one with a fallen tree trunk setting, the other over the bonnet of a motor-car, are almost embarrassing in their realism.'

Anthony Carthew, *Daily Herald*: 'A quicker eye than mine is needed to catch the glimpses of sumptuous bosom which were promised . . . Only someone with a violently sniggering imagination would call this film sexy.'

Peter John Dyer, *Films and Filming*: 'There are three men in her life, and soon we are getting our erotic money's worth; or would be, if only the Censor would stop snipping little bits out. Actually the sex is very well done . . . The abandon of the final scene, after Juliette has forced herself successfully on the other brother who obsesses her, achieves considerable power, and there seems nothing faked about the frenzied beating she takes from her husband . . . She gives her best performance, but we see her so often nowadays; the pout-and-writhe technique is already too familiar, too calculated for any real impact. She lacks . . . oh, I don't know . . . mystery, I think.'

Gordon Reid, *Continental Film Review*: 'The *raison d'être* of this film is Bardot: the provocative wriggle of her hips, her pert mouth, her figure—revealed to the limits of an X certificate. This, let it be said, is sufficient enough to make a box-office success but not a good film . . . Although everything about Miss Bardot, from her ballet dancer, flat-foot walk, to the pout of her mouth, disturbs my male equilibrium as much as the next man's; I am still not persuaded that she is an actress of genuine depth.'

Paul Dehn, *News Chronicle*: 'For those with some eyes, Mlle. Bardot is quite a sight. She has Vivien Leigh's neck, Simone Signoret's mouth, Veronica

Lake's hair, Marilyn Monroe's walk and my best wishes for a less tediously vulgar picture next time.'

Robert Kennedy, *Daily Worker*: 'This is a crude piece of calculated pornography obviously devised to sell the sexual attraction of Miss Bardot.'

A new word joined the clichéd 'pout' in BB reviews: calculated. It was warranted. Vadim had gone to producer Lévy with a film idea about wild girls of Paris; like Topsy, it grew, way, way out of proportion. Matching the pronunciamentos issued by the two young reputation-seekers, and the varied critics and intellectuals of established reputation fast becoming sullied in over-praising, and thus creating, the BB myth. The film has been compared to strict pornography (laughable in this day and age of *The Devil in Miss Jones*); to the best of Louise Brooks, Pabst's 1928 study of debauchery, *Abwege/Crisis*. (A fair comparison, particularly when studying one *Times* review of Pabst subduing Brigitte Helm's personality to his own ends with a ruthlessness which compelled admiration—'she seems always to be registering expressions which are not hers but his'.)

It was also hailed in the tendentious manner of American hyperbole as a meaningful treatise upon the malaise of innate sexuality; vilified by the Massachusetts clergy; banned in Dallas as 'too exciting for coloured people'; and praised as the film which opened the door of much required sexual realism and permissivity in the cinema.

And yet what was it? François Truffaut said it best: '*sincère, amoral, intelligent et puritain*'. I would question only its sincerity, or that of anyone concerned with the venture, save for BB herself. From shoe-string start to gold-plated finish, here was a simple venture in which a young writer, would-be-director (with a great cameraman), decided to share (or if you prefer to flaunt) the superlative body of his gorgeous wife with the world. To prove, as he had said for years, that if in still photos she looked good, she was greater still in movement. All Vadim offered to Lévy was an outline, his own sketchy thoughts on 'sincere amorality', his wife and his *copain*, husky Christian Marquand. The perfect porno package in today's terms: turn-on chick, virile brute, and a thin skein of meaningfulness. Lévy cottoned on immediately: a fast-buck affair to make some money and in so doing cock a snoot at the Establishment by arousing their audience, male, female or neuter, to admit to their most hidden dormant desires. That's all. The first tell-it-like-it-is movie, made, by, about and supposedly for youth, in a manner calculated to make a fortune from the middle-aged and older; made not for those who had never known freedom until now, but for the generations who had seen all liberties removed and regained,

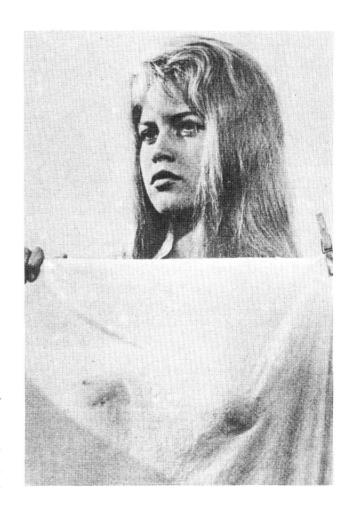

those who could never make up for lost times and dreams.

Vadim had learned his craft from de Sade; it was, for instance, no accident that Bardot's rôle was called Juliette. 'The Marquis,' said Vadim, 'was a very devoted family man and so am I.' Devoted to recording posteriors for posterity, recording his wife in candid close-up, filming her every curve, sigh, emotion and fantasy as he, and only he, knew how because he had encouraged them all. 'Nude scenes? She loves them. She finds them very funny . . . because she hates hypocrisy. She knows people will be shocked at seeing her prancing around naked: she reckons if they are shocked, they are being hypocritical. It's the child in her which does not shy away from nudity. But in the film she was undressed for no more than five minutes. Yet people insisted she was naked throughout.'

The eroticism came easily; the prurient philosophy followed later. By which time, Vadim had lost his wife to co-star Trintignant and an endless string of others. Bardot, however, would never lose BB. The philosophy-myth nearly strangled her . . .

More reviews, fascinating in hindsight of the quite revolutionary changes accomplished in world cinema because of this film; although Vadim was to match it again only the once, it eventually led other and more mature directors to unleash a tumultuous torrent of every form of sexuality, from Bergman's *The Silence* to Damiano's *Memories Within Miss Aggie*.

John Gillet, *Monthly Film Bulletin*: 'Vadim's first film as a director . . . reveals an intermittent, yet tangible talent which is here dedicated almost exclusively to the considerable physical charms of [BB], probably her best performance to date, her play still lacks force and the director's infatuation with erotic *tableaux* (the bizarre seduction on the beach and the heroine's semi-nude posturings) finally defeats its own objects.'

J.-P. Coursodon, *Cinéma 60*: '. . . full of *boule-vardière* vulgarity, badly played, and disagreeably pretentious . . . praised by the critics on the pretext that the comportment of its heroine was a little less conventional to the rule that was then in our cinema. Now that the times have changed, the film is bearable only due to its photographic qualities.'

Gene Moskowitz, *Variety*, made the great mistake of marking it 'just average' for a successful export to America. 'Film unfolds, slowly, centering on the questionable attributes of the new star here, Miss Bardot. Though a young looker, she lacks any thespian strength to get any depth into her sensual rôle . . .'

Americans, though, fell very heavily for Brigitte, although the Roman Catholic Legion of Decency found it 'an open violation of Christian and traditional morality' and condemned the film out of hand: like *The Moon Is Blue*, *Baby Doll* and *Bitter Rice* before it.

Time: '[it] opens with a shot that promises a good deal more than the picture delivers. There lies Brigitte, stretched out from end to end of the CinemaScope screen, bottoms up and bare as a censor's eyeball. In the hard sun of the Riviera, her round little rear glows like a peach, and the camera lingers on the subject as if waiting for it to ripen . . .'

Wanda Hale, *New York Daily News*: 'It takes the French to beat the Italians, Americans, Swedes *et al.*, at peddling sex on the screen . . . may I say you've never seen anything like it. If Loren, Monroe, Mansfield, Diors [sic], etc., see Brigitte in this film, they will more than likely feel so inadequate they will leave the screen . . . it leaves little to the imagination. The only word for it is brazen . . . acceptable trash benefited by good direction, bold acting and stunning photography.'

Bosley Crowther, *New York Times*: 'This round and voluptuous little French miss is put on spectacular display and is rather brazenly ogled from every allowable point of view . . . in slacks and

sweater, in shorts and Bikini bathing suits. She wears a bedsheet on two or three occasions and once, she shows behind a thin screen, in the nude. What's more, she moves herself in a fashion that fully accentuates her charms. She is undeniably a creation of superlative craftmanship . . . a thing of mobile contours—a phenomenon you have to believe.'

And didn't they just queue to do so. *Variety* soon swept the legend into headlines: SEXPOT BARDOT FROM FRANCE IS NY BO WOW! which has nothing to do with looking like a Pekinese, but Varietyese for her New York box-office triumph. The film had opened in October, 1957, in the Paris Theatre, which has 568 seats—in one week, it had $24,717 in the till. *Time* magazine soon had the 'story of a woman indiscriminately seeking a bed-mate' earning $1,500,000 from 175 bookings in America; it went on to score a full $8,000,000, which as the French Press computers worked out was the equivalent to a year's export sale of Renault Dauphines. *Life* magazine, ever ready for a simile, caught the inference and compared her to a European sports car, racier and more realistic than any domestic product. They were right; apart from the occasional, very occasional film, the kitten was to become mechanical.

La mariée est trop belle

1956

French. Production Générale de Films/SN Pathé-Cinéma; 95 minutes. UK: *The Bride is Too Beautiful*, Renown Pictures, 1957; 93 minutes. US: *The Bride is Much Too Beautiful*, Ellis-Lax Films, 1958; 90 minutes. Monochrome.
Director: Pierre Gaspard-Huit. *Producer:* Christine Gouze-Renal. *Script:* Philippe Agostini, Juliette Saint-Giniez, *from the novel by* Odette Joyeux. *Photography:* Louis Page. *Editor:* Louisette Haute-cœur. *Music:* Norbert Glansburg. *Sound:* Antoine Archimbaud. *Art Directors:* Jean d'Eaubonne, Pierre Duquesne. *Production Manager:* Fred Surin. *Assistant Directors:* P. Lary, Serge Vallin. *Shooting:* from July 15, 1956, Studios Paris and Boulogne.

CAST

Brigitte Bardot . . . . *Chouchou*
Micheline Presle . . . . *Judith*
Louis Jourdan . . . . *Michel*
Jean-François Calvé. . . . . *Patrice*
Marcel Amont . . . . *Toni*
Roger Dumas. . . . . *Marc*
Madeleine Lambert . . . . *Aunt Agnès*
Colette Régis . . . . *Aunt Yvonne*
Marcelle Arnold . . . . *Mme. Victoire*
Roger Tréville . . . . *Designy*
Nicole Guden . . . . *Juliette*

Marriage. To Hollywood's No. 1 Frenchman, Louis Jourdan.

STORY

Magazine editors Judith and Michel turn village beauty Catherine into top Paris teenage cover-girl—Chouchou. All French girls ape her style, a myth is built up, a legend required—a marriage will do. A mock wedding and for the next edition. 'Bridegroom' Patrice falls in love, however; Chouchou prefers Michel. He's impressed but thinks her a child. Chouchou proves otherwise, offering herself to Patrice and two cameramen. When the model set-up is ready at her village church—Michel is becoming her real husband.

NOTES

BB: 'I find it *cucu la praline* . . . a bit silly.'
So did her fans; such lightweight comedy nonsense after the fire of the St.-Tropez and Trintignant scandal. Vadim had not only left home and hearth, but Paris too—for Venice and his second film. Bardot could have starred, would have, save for two contracted comedies. This was the first; the second was infinitely better.
A fey beginning, then, for Bardot's long business relationship and close friendship with her new producer, Christine Gouze-Renal, who had played a tiny rôle in *La lumière d'en face*. Mme. Gouze-Renal, *chef du cabinet* to the Socialist leader François Mitterrand (her brother-in-law today) and cabinet minister in the immediate post-'45 government of De Gaulle, entered films administratively on leaving the cultural relations department of the French Embassy in Buenos Aires. She was concerned with both *La rage au corps*, 1953, and *Les amants du Tage*, 1954, both of which starred Brigitte's immediate predecessor in the Parisienne sex-symbol game, Françoise Arnoul, who replaced Brigitte in Vadim's Venetian film.
Brigitte has always succeeded with women producers (Betty Box, Mag Bodard). She feels, perhaps rightly, that they understand her better; Gouze-Renal more than any other, she thought. They made two more films together, *La femme et le pantin,* and the highly personal, *Vie privée*. Bardot also was guest star in a comedy with the producer's husband, Roger Hanin, and the actress has always retained the producer

among her intimates. 'I love Brigitte,' Christine Gouze-Renal has declared, 'and nobody understands her as I do. People everywhere in the world have an ambivalent attitude towards her. They hate her and love her at the same time. Behind all that fan worship, there is desire and envy, a kind of loathing. Brigitte, you must believe me, hates her life more than anyone can imagine. And when she is troubled, she turns to me. I have become her mother.'

This was the first Continental production bought by the British Renown distributors; they didn't lose on it. Based on a book by the one-time French star Odette Joyeux, it was pedantically directed by Pierre Gaspard-Huit, who later provided James Bond with his first French playmate in the shape of his wife, Claudine Auger.

The script, for all its fashion-world satire, was not so far from some truths about the Bardot persona— all French girls *were* copying her style. It also contained another clue about the girl papers and magazines could not print enough 'secrets' about. This exchange took place during one of her modelling scenes. *Editor:* What are you thinking of? *BB:* Nothing. *Editor:* Perhaps that's why you photograph so well.

Cast as Patrice, the enamoured juvenile lead, was Bardot's lover from her second film four years before: Jean-François Calvé. More than most he noticed the remarkable change in the stripling he once knew as *Manina*.

Critics were similarly flummoxed by the new, cool Bardot. After so hot-bloodedly serialising the Vadim film in *Tit-Bits*, John K. Newnham was fulsome in outlining his paper's dream-girl's switch from vamp to vapid. 'There's nothing sordid in either her characterisation or the story. She remains virtuous throughout. But the reformed Brigitte isn't dull. It's a happy compromise. She's still provocative, but in a nice way. She still has numerous bedroom scenes, but there is nothing audacious about them and her nightwear is most discreet. She baths in almost the altogether, but it is done without any suggestiveness. She has a quota of love-scenes, but they are far removed from the life-in-the-raw orgies of passion so often associated with her films. They are natural and wholesome. . . . I like this fresh Brigitte . . . It points the way to a more lasting film future for her. She has been too bad for too long. She is too delightful and piquant a personality to be allowed to drift into oblivion because of too persistent lack of taste.'

Ivon Addams, *Star*: 'First shot . . . shows her in a white bridal gown. The last shot shows her in the same attire. For most of the time in between, she wanders around in her nightgown looking for a bridegroom.'

Wet. Rain (and shower) drops kept falling on her head.

Dry. It never seemed to harm her hair much...

Idea! Editors Louis Jourdan, Micheline Presle create the Chouchou myth—what better follow-up than a wedding.

Jympson Harman, *Evening News*: '. . . quite a shock to see her as a comparatively nice girl . . . much more attractive than Miss Bardot's so-called sex-sensations.'

Gene Moskowitz, *Variety*: 'Perhaps for lack of anybody else, [BB] seems to be the No 1 star here these days . . . Possessed of a pouting pigeon personality, she does not seem to be dishing out either the beauteous firebrands or the wavering virgins. She appears to have been pushed too fast for her real thespic talents.'

The Times compared the film, favourably, with Donen's *Funny Face*, and felt the French improved the American theme; the *Daily Sketch*'s Harold Conway agreed, though calling Audrey Hepburn the better actress. However, Bosley Crowther, *New York Times*, felt it all surprisingly circumspect: 'admirers of Mlle. Bardot . . . have borne with her through all sorts of far-fetched and senseless banalities, so one more lapse into the childish is not likely to disappoint them. And this one is trite and inconclusive.'

André Maurois, *Playboy*: 'her first failure . . . She realised that to recapture the freshness of her early success she must work with the new generation of directors; hence her decision to join the New Wave.'

Groom. Jean-François Calvé returns from BB's second film, to be the model falling for his partner. 'An exquisite little animal,' he called her. 'All the charm of the woman, the kid and the feline.'

Une Parisienne

1957

Franco-Italian. Les Films Ariane-Cinetel-Filmsonor (Paris)/Rizzoli Film (Rome); 86 minutes. UK: *Parisienne*, Intercontinental Films release via Rank Film Distributors, 1959; 87 minutes. US: Lopert Films, 1958; 85 minutes. Technicolor.
Director: Michel Boisrond. *Producer:* Francis Cosne. *Script:* Annette Wademant, Jean Aurel; *adaptation,* Jean Aurel, Jacques Emmanuel, Michel Boisrond; *dialogue,* Annette Wademant. *Photography:* Marcel Grignon. *Editor:* Claudine Bouché. *Music:* Henri Crolla, Hubert Rostaing, André Hodeir. *Sound:* Antoine Petitjean. *Art Director:* Jean André. *Assistant Director:* Jacques Poitrenaud. *Shooting:* from March 8, 1957, Studios Billancourt.

CAST

Brigitte Bardot . . . . *Brigitte Laurier*
Charles Boyer . . . . *Prince Charles*
Henri Vidal . . . . *Michel*
André Luguet. . . . . *Premier Laurier*
Nadia Gray . . . . *Queen Greta*
Madeleine Lebeau . . . . *Monique*
Noël Roquevert . . . . *Herblay*
Robert Pizani . . . . *Ambassador*
Guy Tréjean . . . . *Colonel*
Claire Maurier . . . . *Caroline*
Marcel Pérès . . . . *Général*

STORY

Marriage is rapidly arranged for the French Premier's daughter, Brigitte, and Michel, his principal secretary, on being found (quite innocently) in bed together. Michel has a roving eye and Brigitte hits back by flirting with Prince Charles, the visiting Queen Greta's consort. They jet to the Riviera for a bathe, drink, embrace and punch-up in just enough time to catch colds. Michel does not believe one word of the escapade, until the official farewells to the royalty. Both Brigitte and the prince are sneezing. Michel's concern is obliterated by the prospect of an extended honeymoon.

NOTES

BB: 'It amused me to do *Parisienne*—it changes me from the *petit animal* I was always interpreting.

Here I have evening dresses and I'm a married woman—*c'est drôlement chouette.*'
Super indeed! Certainly it rates as my own favourite Bardot comedy vehicle, along with portions of *Voulez-vous danser avec moi?* from the same director, Vadim's brave attempt at rescuing *La bride sur le cou*, and Deville's stylish *L'Ours et la poupée.* (Perhaps, at this juncture, I should show all my colours: *En cas de malheur* and *La vérité* are my choice of her best dramas; *La lumière d'en face* and *Et Dieu créa la femme,* the finest *érotiques*; and *Viva Maria*, of course, her greatest adventure romp.)
Boisrond learned his trade at Clair's knee, and started directing with *Cette sacrée gamine.* He has an infectious feel for fluffy comedy, never better than with Bébé as his leading clown. The nervousness of his début is missing from this item; he handles his stars, including veterans Boyer, Nadia Gray, Henri

Vidal and, from BB's début, Noël Roquevert, with a control as light as a feather.

Bardot rated Boisrond highly (she made another $1\frac{1}{3}$ films with him) and in a myth-encompassing manner she was quoted by *Unifrance*: 'He's wonderful. Michel is young, like us, and he knows how to express exactly how the boys and girls of our generation behave and feel . . .'

For once, the critics, the British at least, were in perfect concert. They loved it. And her.

Peter Burnup, *News of the World*: 'I can confess now, with all due reluctance, that I've been bored now and again with Bardot and the well-known Body Beautiful; particularly in certain of her seamier sex extravaganzas. But here, in one of the frothiest French farces you're likely to see in a month of Sundays, the young lady emerges as a comedienne of the truly premier choice. . . . She is a complete, scintillating delight.'

Raymond Durgnat, *Films and Filming*: 'Her screen personality, even in the idyllic comic rôle of *Une parisienne*, gives an effect of inner conflict, turbulence, unpredictability. One can't take one's eyes off her because one never knows what she is going to do next; whether her reaction to a given situation will be tears, anger, a disarming pretty smile, an apology, a seduction, or a brusque, almost brutal reassertion of her freedom. Sweetly outrageous, yet slightly lost; petulant, yet humble; both sullen and generous; subject to whims and caprices implying not only a gaiety but also a negation of consistency akin to despair; endowed with a sensuality so vehement as to render the romantic dream superfluous; as wilful as a baby, as direct as a man—the personality of this adorable though redoubtable bundle of contradictions is as complex as Garbo's.'

Time: 'Far and away the most delightful of the seven Bardot reports that have popped into the U.S. in the past two years . . . Brigitte is still no comedienne. But she does make the most voluptuous straight man in the world, especially when playing with such pros as Boyer and Vidal.'

William Whitebait, *New Statesman*: 'Bardot rides again . . . The speed cops go after her: she shows them her licence and her knees, and goes on to show *us* what makes any Bardot film, the tease of all kinds, wedding night, bathroom, sea-bathe, nudity under the bedsheet, the big eyes and divided bosom . . .'

A woman's view from Dee Wells, *Sunday Express*: '[BB's] producers over-reach themselves. She takes baths. She swims in a bikini. She takes off her dress. She climbs into bed at least three times. She parades around wearing only a nonchalantly unbuttoned shirt. Even when she is fully—so to speak—dressed, enough Bardot is on view to remind chest specialists and bra manufacturers of what you might

Comedienne. The script dubbed her Brigitte (again).

call "shop" . . . it is a very funny movie . . .'

Charles Maclaron, *Time and Tide*: 'Why they bother to write a script in order to get [BB], as often as maybe, down to the minimum of clothing, is something I have never fully understood . . . costumes ranged from a bath towel to a brief sheath by Balmain, and her emotions from Bardot with her hair down to Bardot with her hair up . . . Mr. Boyer moved through all his scenes with a kind of wry compassion, as if he wondered what had come over films since the days when he was young.'

Far from it. At 58, Charles Boyer, the legendary great lover of every screen siren from Colbert and Darrieux to Dietrich and Garbo, was bowled over by the latest gamine. 'She is, say, lively, and impulsive: a quick study. She does not run around nude. She undresses with great amiability when the script calls for it. She is called, actually, Bri-Bri . . . and is very mature. She told me that she knew her success could not last, and when it was over she would not cry. A very *sympathique* young woman. Most easy to act with. Her secret is to act always like a girl of 18, but to do so naturally without the least archness. In my opinion she will become a very good actress. To see *Une Parisienne* is to believe this.'

Roger Watkins, *Picturegoer*: 'Scenes have obviously been cut—ones with her in the nude in bed; one where she slips out of her dress watched by film husband Henri Vidal. Even so she appears so saucy she dominates the entire screen. What chance has Vidal of being noticed? Is this, then, Bardot's lot?

...at the elegant royal receptions and the ripe royal bar-room brawls. That's why the lady is a champ!

Has she to have lesser leading men because no one else dare tangle with her? It seems so.'
So it goes. The names of any substantial male co-stars in her next 24 films can be counted on a single hand: Gabin, Delon, Mastroianni, Perkins and Connery. In fact, since *Viva Maria*, her most important co-stars have been women ... which is taking the liberation thing too far.

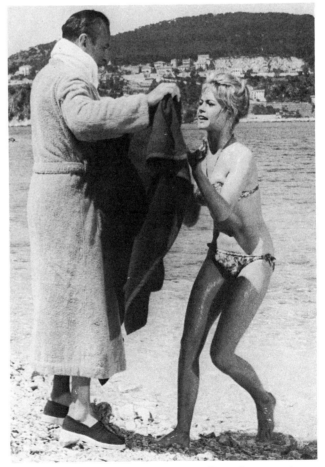

Support. In two comedies, Henri Vidal was her perfect match; at 58, Charles Boyer still lit up well as the great lover.

Les bijoutiers du clair de lune

1957

The Moonlight Jewellers. Franco-Italian. Iena Productions-UCIL (Paris)/CEIAD (Rome); 95 minutes. UK: Heaven Fell That Night, Columbia Pictures, 1958; 90 minutes. US: The Night Heaven Fell, Kingsley International, 1958; 90 minutes. CinemaScope. Eastman Color.
Director: Roger Vadim. Producer: Raoul J. Levy. Script: Roger Vadim, Peter Viertel, from the novel by Albert Vidalie. Photography: Armand Thirard. Editor: Victoria Mercanton. Music: Georges Auric. Sound: Robert Biart. Art Director: Jean André. Production Manager: Roger Debelmas. Shooting: from June 28, 1957, on location in Spain.

CAST

Brigitte Bardot . . . . *Ursula*
Alida Valli . . . . *Aunt Florentine*
Stephen Boyd. . . . . *Lambert*
Pépé Nieto. . . . . *Count Ribera*
Maruchi Fresno . . . . *Conchita*
Adriana Dominguez. . . . . *Fernando*
José Marco Davo. . . . . *Police Chief*
Antonio Vico . . . . *Chauffeur*

STORY

Spain: and the last holiday of convent girl, Ursula. She runs off with Lambert—her Uncle Ribero's murderer, her Aunt Florentine's seducer. With the girl's loving aid, Lambert evades capture. They are pursued by police, during passionate days of sado-masochistic sex in the mountains, until Ursula is killed in the crossfire.

NOTES

Bardot-Vadim-Levy, Mk. II. No time, no need for pontifical outbursts, a routine sex-thriller, nothing more, nothing less, and not as good as either of Vadim's first two projects. There were reasons aplenty: mainly the collision-course of star and director living out their own myths in reality, she with her latest lover(s), he with his new wife-to-be. Plus the worst weather in Spanish location history.
Vadim: 'We started shooting in Spain. Brigitte was perfect for nine weeks in the studio. She had just

Confidente. Older this time, though Alida Valli soon turned into a giggling *copine*, pillow-fighting with her niece, BB.

finished a picture and was genuinely tired. Also she was worried about other things. Then, the set was flooded by storm. Filming was stopped 14 times because of the weather. Brigitte became ill. She went to Paris to see doctors, came back, and worked a few more days. We went on location in Spain, the South of France and in Paris studios. It was far too heavy going. She could not take it. Few people could. It has nothing to do with Annette . . .'

Annette Stroyberg, that is, waiting to become Mme. Vadim Mk. II—and waiting on the *Bijoutiers* set. 'I expected to be very jealous of Brigitte. After all, she was not only a world-famous star but Vadim's first love, and at that time, still his legal wife. My first impression of her was that she seemed a hundred times more beautiful and desirable than I.' One reason why Annette never made the grade as BB Mk. II in Vadim's third and finest film, *Les liaisons dangereuses*, 1959.

Stephen Boyd, BB's first British co-star since 'Dr.' Bogarde, voiced—then denied—the thoughts of all male stars refusing offers of films with the world's most important female star. Boyd told Roderick Mann, *Sunday Express*: 'All I can say is that when I'm trying to play serious love scenes with her, she's busy positioning her bottom for the best angled shot . . . It's the worst thing that's ever happened to me. I've been here two months and still haven't seen a script. None of the phones work. Half the town's been washed away by floods. We're filming in three languages—two of which I don't speak. I've been terribly ill . . . This picture is a nightmare.

Duo. Back in harness, despite divorce: Vadim and Bébé.

Shocker. Stephen Boyd was a heavy hero. An Irishman as a Spaniard in a French film. And sadistic with it. Enough so for one critic to call the film pornographic!...

Bardot is having her breakdown this week. Vadim is next. Then they've promised me mine.'

Boyd later claimed poetic licence interfered with his comments. 'The real story,' he told Henry Toby, 'is I'm crazy about Bardot . . . I wish I could start work with her again tomorrow . . . I prefer her to actresses who take themselves more seriously.' The following year, he insisted in *Cosmopolitan* that Bardot was a wonderfully complicated girl, impulsive, extraordinarily beautiful 'and a little off her rocker. Since she discovered sex, she's been overboard. She used to chase me all over the set.'

Phillip Oakes, *Sunday Dispatch*, did not think much of the result: 'A dull little essay in film pornography.'

Wayland Young, *Evening Standard*: 'This one makes no pretence of being anything but contour photography of one sort or another . . . Spain is a very beautiful country and Bardot is a very beautiful girl, and no opportunity is lost for the latter to take off a record proportion of clothes in the middle of the former. She gets nakeder and nakeder as the crags and gorges and torrents get fiercer and fiercer . . . But even the pleasure of seeing a naked Bardot is spoiled by the belief her former husband . . . seems to have that a girl's back looks better with a couple of bloody welts running down it. It doesn't. And they weren't even necessary for the plot.'

Jympson Harman, *Evening News*: 'You never before saw so much of [BB] or indeed of any other girl as you can see in this box-office compendium of sex and sadism. She goes about the house most of the time clad only in the briefest of bra and bikini, cooling her slender legs with an electric fan and taking a shower after shower. In one scene she only just slips on a black lace shawl in time.'

Label. By now she was stuck with the sex-kitten tag. And played it. 'I purr. I scratch. And sometimes I bite.' On this arduous location, the biter was bit by bad weather and health.

William Whitebait, *New Statesman*: 'From the beginning when she descends from a train and leans against a car, posing, the hunt is on. Of course, it's very hot, somewhere in Spain, and soon most of her clothes are off: on, off, slipping, hitched, diaphanous, clinging—with a shower now and then to help, and the sun . . . It is called *Heaven Fell that Night* and there's no reason why it shouldn't be.'

Richard Roud, *Monthly Film Bulletin*: 'On every level this film is disappointing. The story is gratuitous and the script uninteresting. Stephen Boyd's part is unexciting and even [BB] is not very good. There remains only a few amusing scenes: Bardot in the armoury and her pillow fight with Alida Valli.'

Bosley Crowther, *New York Times*: 'The by-now-familiar landscape of brazen [BB] gets some noticeable competition from the rugged landscape of south-eastern Spain . . . For the curious fact is the famous "kitten" is miserably used in this film . . . she hasn't much else to do than occasionally peel down to the bare essentials (under pretext of the oppressive heat) and chase foolishly after Stephen Boyd . . . Under these circumstances, there isn't much zing in La Bardot. She takes her cue from the proceedings and not only acts but also looks immature.'

Finally, what of her big London fan, the critic who tripped over her at Cannes in '53? Leonard Mosley, *Daily Express*: '[BB] plays a convent girl who comes to Spain with, it seemed to me, only two ambitions —to wear as little as possible, and to get herself a man. Within five minutes of opening she achieves her first ambition and is rolling around her bedroom in her underwear, while her caddish uncle looks lecherously on . . . After a time, all the disrobing began to bore me and halfway through *Heaven Fell That Night*, I fell too—asleep.'

En cas de malheur

1957

In Case of Adversity. Franco-Italian. Iena-UCIL (Paris)/Incom (Rome); 105 minutes. UK: *Love Is My Profession*, Miracle Films, 1958; 105 minutes. US: UK-title, Kingsley International, 1959; 111 minutes. Monochrome.

Director: Claude Autant-Lara. *Producer:* Raoul J. Levy. *Script:* Jean Aurenche, Pierre Boast, *from the novel by* Georges Simenon. *Photography:* Jacques Natteau. *Editor:* Madeleine Gug. *Music:* René Cloërec. *Sound:* René Forget. *Art Director:* Max Douy. *Production Managers:* Yves Laplanche, Roger Debelemas. *Assistant Directors:* Ghislaine Aubin, Michel Pazin. *English sub-titles:* Mai Harris. *Shooting:* from November 4, 1957, Studios Joinville.

Non! Jean Gabin refused the rôle—became a fan.

CAST

Jean Gabin	*André Gobillot*
Brigitte Bardot	*Yvette Maudet*
Edwige Feuillère	*Viviane Gobillot*
Nicole Berger	*Jeannine*
Franco Interlenghi	*Mazetti*
Madeleine Barbulée	*Bordenave*
Jacques Clancy	*Durey*
Claude Magnier	*Gaston*

STORY

Summer and winter love affair springing into tragedy . . . Top Paris lawyer Gobillot compromises marital and legal life by defending street-girl, Yvette, on a robbery charge. He wins the case; she pays the only way she knows—with an eager body. Gobillot revels in his fee and finds release from his elevated society snob status in his infatuation for Yvette. A clumsy liaison at best: a married man with a girl with casual infidelities, both seeking shelter amid conflicting youthful passion and aged tenderness—until a stray lover, Mazetti, stabs her to death.

NOTES

The turning point . . . The *Daily Herald* called it 'the end of the Bardot legend'. Jean Gabin, on hearing producer Levy's (obvious) choice of star for the *putain*, exploded: 'What? That thing that goes around naked?' And the screen-lawyer had to be taken to court to force him to turn up for work.

The *Herald* and Gabin were wrong; and would later admit it, too.

Here was the film, the performance, which proved the talent, thin perhaps, widely spread agreed, but tangible and effective opposite class players; here, too, was proof of her screen persona—the topless, bottomless flagellant of hypocrisy, the innocent in a corrupt world, recognised and exploited by Vadim.

Autant-Lara and Simenon were veterans at the game, and knew better the cause and effect of the youthful free spirit upon the pre-war generation; more than Vadim ever could. In just two films, Vadim had formulated the raw identikit and then blown it; he had, though, shown the veterans how; and how far

Snip! Gabin won't defend BB in court. 'You have no money.' Nonchalantly, she lifts skirt to show her fee ... transfixing Gabin to the spot. Too much for world censors. They all cut the naked *derrière*, though allowing the finale, proving Bébé and not Quant invented the mini...

to go. They knew enough to mould it into reality.
Yet the *Daily Herald*'s Anthony Carthew, covering the 1958 Venice festival, predicted Bardot would be 'just another Continental bosom-and-wiggle girl' in two years, and that people would have completely forgotten her in five. In two years she added more veteran fuel to her youth and shook everyone up (the *Herald* included) with *La vérité*; in five years the public were queuing around the block for *Viva Maria*.

Critics were simply aghast at the brash newcomer daring to work in the company of Gabin and Feuillère: '*Révolution à Joinville*' headlined *Ciné-monde*. Such august horror clouded their vision. In most European polls, Bardot and Gabin were voted top stars by the end of 1957. She moved up four places to top the Belgian *Ciné-Revue référendum de popularité*, keeping Michèle Morgan in second place (Mme. Feuillère was nowhere in sight). Sophia Loren also moved four places to fifth place; Marilyn Monroe was obliterated to second from last, 14th. In Britain even the *Picturegoer* fan-magazine came out, claws bared. 'Things have come to a pretty pass in the French cinema if the box-office prestige of being in a [BB] movie is so great that even artists of Gabin-Feuillère calibre are prepared to play second and third fiddles . . . [to] the most irritating mannered little actress on the screen.'

Derek Monsey, *Sunday Express*: 'Petulant and wilful, insolently sensual, she flicks through . . . like a Sex Symbol in need of a good polishing.'

Reg Whitley, *Daily Mirror*: '. . . another of her off-the assembly line performances . . . often heavy going.'

Evening Standard: '. . . there is no reason for assembling the talents of Gabin and Feuillère to support what is essentially a 105-minute look through one of those seaside-viewers with titles such as "*Up In Mabel's Room*".'

Paul Dehn, *News Chronicle*: '[BB] in cinematically unusual circumstances—viz., stark naked from behind, stark naked from in front, except for a mackintosh, and being sick into a wash-basin. The greatly gifted actor, Jean Gabin, may also be glimpsed, pulling a lavatory chain.'

Bosley Crowther, *New York Times*: 'This is supposedly the picture in which [BB] acts . . . a matter of opinion. If flirting in a few crucial scenes, pouting when she is supposed to be unhappy and throwing her chest out when she is supposed to be aroused may be calculated as acting, that is the word for what she does. But if getting across a complex creature, charged by many hungers and moods, is the measure of an acting performance, this one falls far short . . . Face it folks, this is a disappointing film.'

Campbell Dixon, *Daily Telegraph*: 'Let's not blame M. Simenon . . . I'll lay odds that his story . . . isn't vulgar and unconvincing, like the film based on it . . . Why the others concerned should have put their great gifts to tawdry use is another matter . . . I'm not thinking of Miss Bardot, who frankly wants to get rich quickly and whose charms, like Phryne's, are their own defence. What puzzles me is why . . . two of the greatest artists that ever graced the screen, should be mixed up in it . . . The director doesn't help. The lawyer's *affaire* with the little *putain*, hotted up with symbols of sex and perversion familiar to anyone who has glanced at Kraft-Ebing—high heels, complete nudity, nudity sheathed in shining black silk mackintosh, and so on—proceeds from the sensual to the silly.'

Peter John Dyer, *Film Monthly Bulletin*: '[BB], however, remains only too clearly the price that the director has had to pay in order to make the film. It is something of a tribute to his detached, photographic realism that so much of this glacial record should have remained effective in spite of the tedious and mechanical familiarity of Bardot's mannerisms.'

The Times: 'Mlle. Bardot does not have Miss Monroe's gifts. She is, rather, in the Diana Dors class—and with her hair and pout, she has a distinctive look of her—and the obvious efforts M. Autant-Lara has taken to make her act affect the spontaneity.'

She had some friends, all the same. Not least, Gabin himself—'she's a real pro.; a girl who needs affection' —and the director, Autant-Lara. 'I have to go softly

Foil. Said Franco Interlenghi, 'I love my wife, but a man is a man...'

Fuel. The master French actor—and his screen mistress.

with her because she seems so afraid. She has no confidence in herself. Playing a long scene with Jean Gabin frightens her. She asks me: "What if I look ugly? What if I forget my lines?" And yet she will be a good actress. They told me such terrible things about her that I was afraid to make this picture. I find she is not terrible at all. She is nice. A nice child.'

Time magazine: '. . . easily the peep-showiest, cheap-thrillingest of [BB] pictures—and probably the best.'

Ernest Betts, *People*: 'Brigitte avoids the crudity that marred her earlier pictures. It is intended for adults. It will satisfy adult minds. And in it Brigitte is fully adult at last.'

Hollis Alpert, *Saturday Review*: 'There has been a good deal of junk written and talked about [BB] representing some sort of spirit of modern young womanhood and I suspect a lot of it to be simply a justification of the voyeuristic use made of her redoubtable body by people who pretend that their motives are more artistic and philosophical than commercial. [BB] has never seemed to me a beauty but her face is intriguingly animalistic, and she gets through the message less broadly and vulgarly than, say, Jayne Mansfield . . . She has a rôle with more scope for portrayal than any yet given her. The

Veteran. *Cinémonde* in Paris asked Jean Gabin what it was like to hold Bardot in his arms. 'What? That kid? Let's rather talk about my sheep, my chickens, and my wife!'

characterisation, in other words, outweighs the exposure. Not that the latter is missing by any means.'

Observer: 'The contrast between [BB] and the sophisticated woman of the world, played by Edwige Feuillère, is revealing. The clash is between the fundamental honesty of the child from the gutter and the hypocritical discretion of the grown-up bourgeois world. The Bardot child-woman is never sentimental or mysterious. She has no time for the tantalising wiles of a Cleopatra. She is a rank man-hunter and her methods of seduction are forthright—she lifts her skirt and bites her partner's shoulder to indicate what she has in mind.'

French critics found closer affinity between Bardot's Ursula characterisation and Hélène in *Douce*, Autant-Lara's best film during the Occupation (1943); another intriguing simile as the remarkably perverse ingénue played by Odette Joyeux, later the author of *La mariée est trop belle*. Hélène's screen lover was Roger Pigaut—performing similar duties opposite Bardot in *La lumière d'en face*.

Raymond Durgnat, *Films and Filming*, appreciated what everyone else had missed: a hymn of joy to liberty and love, if shot through by its climactic jealousy and suffering. 'It is disconcertingly frank (the hero at one point beset with *ejaculatio praecox*, and another scene implies BB having Lesbian tendencies, drawing Gabin into an orgy *à trois* with their maid). In effect, it is the story of Gabin emancipating himself from a hypocritical, corrupt and unjust "respectability" (this famous lawyer, presented to the Queen on her Paris visit, knowingly perverts justice and disgraces the innocent victim of a smash-and-grab raid as a frequenter of prostitutes!) into an eccentric but egalitarian and happy little society of misfits and outcasts (a household consisting of an elderly lawyer, a 20-year-old ex-prostitute and the fresh, docile, innocent maid, straight from the convent orphanage, who is quite happy to be corrupted).'

As Durgnat added, the script was packed with disconcerting insights into psychological relationships—and Bardot more than held her own with both cast and scenario; if anyone was swamped it was Feuillère only. Yesterday's *élégance* would be a long time coming back, and when it did—Bardot would be exemplifying it. Fully dressed, according to producer Levy. His comment after the *Malheur* première: 'I have made my last sex film. You will never see Bardot nude or nearly nude or jumping in and out of bed in any film of mine again.'

La femme et le pantin

1958

The Girl and the Puppet. Franco-Italian. Société nouvelle-SN Pathé-Cinéma-Gray Film (Paris)/ DEAR Films (Rome); 101 minutes. UK: *A Woman Like Satan*, United Artists, 1960; 90 minutes. US: *The Female*, Lopert Films (UA subsidiary), 1960; 86 minutes. CinemaScope. Technicolor.

Director: Julien Duvivier. *Producer:* Christine Gouze-Renal. *Script:* Jean Aurenche, Julien Duvivier, Marcel Achard, Albert Valentin, *from the novel by* Pierre Louÿs; *dialogue*, Marcel Achard. *Photography:* Roger Hubert. *Editor:* Jacqueline Sadoul *Music:* Jean Wiener, José Rocca. *Art Director:* Georges Wakhevitch. *Sound:* William Sivel. *Production Manager:* Fred Surin. *Shooting:* from April 8, 1958, Studios Boulogne; locations in Camargue and Spain.

CAST

Brigitte Bardot . . . . *Eva*
Antonio Vilar . . . . *Don Matteo*
Españita Cortez . . . . *Maria-Térèsa*
Michel Roux . . . . *Albert*
Lila Kedrova . . . . *Manuela*
Jacques Mauclair . . . . *Stanislas Marchand*
Dario Moréno . . . . *Arbadajian*
Jess Hahn . . . . *Sidney*
Claude Goddard . . . . *Mercédès*
Germaine Michel . . . . *Woman in car*
Rivers-Cadet . . . . *Man in car*

STORY

Seville, Spain. During the Feria festival, rich bull-breeder Don Matteo seeks flamenco student Eva as his mistress. She refuses to be bought. She supports her exiled French novelist father; is refused a job at Arbadajian's seedy night-club for being a virgin. With lies and wiles, she convinces him otherwise and tours the provinces with his second-rate company. Don Matteo gives up position, wealth and invalid wife Maria-Térèsa to follow her. His humiliation becomes complete when he finds Eva dancing private nude shows. He wrecks the club and is hauled off by the police. Eva is satisfied. Now that he is humbled, she loves him and agrees to become his mistress, and apparently, mother-substitute.

Cover-up. Brigitte's strip-tease as shot in the multi-mirrored tavern (tribute to Orson Welles?) and as issued by a staid United Artists in America, complete with painted panties.

NOTES

Bardot meets the Thirties, part two. However, what 54-year-old Autant-Lara wrought so well, Duvivier, 62, plainly failed at. The posters crowed about 'The girl with the magnificent body and no heart . . . fiery, dramatic . . . more jungle cat than kitten'; this was all BB, not Eva. Duvivier just wasn't up to it.

The Pierre Louys story which von Sternberg made into a minor masterpiece (*The Devil Is a Woman*, 1935, his last film with Dietrich; later re-made in Mexico, 1950, with Maria Felix) ended up here as something of a dirty old man's nightmare, lacking verve, style, credibility (despite four writers, including the venerated Marcel Achard), or a leading man with believability. First Fernando Lamas was set for Don Matteo; then Tyrone Power. Both were too wary of the Bardot screen and man-eating image, and the task of falling victim to her casually displayed charms fell to Spanish star Antonio Vilar. He dislocated Bardot's jaw when slapping her around in one scene, and she got her own back by helping him slip a disc in a hectic bed encounter. Throughout it all, Vilar looked forlorn enough to be attending a funeral. His own.

Making full use of her new-found reputation of super-legend, Bardot refused to see the gathering Press either on location or back in Paris. 'Who,' she said at the studio, 'is Hedda Hopper?' She did, however, allow London columnist Ken Passingham on her bedroom set; it made an amusing *Sunday Dispatch* report: 'At this moment 25 people are grouped around a four-poster bed containing [BB] and Spanish actor Antonio Vilar. And five of them are telling her how to make love. All of them, of course, are French . . . Underneath the bed a prop-man lies prone and outstretched waiting to catch a bedside lamp as Miss Bardot knocks it down in an excess of passion. This is too much for Miss Bardot. . . . "Let me," she says, "make love in my own way. I know how to love." "Do not be silly, Brigitte," says the director. "This is for CinemaScope. It has to be big. I will show you." He shows her. I feel quite exhausted.'

Although winning a typical BB nickname, Dudu, Duvivier should have left well, and Bébé, alone. Bardot knew the game and her fame better than most. A pity she was not allowed to go her own way; and odd that she wasn't, considering the producer was, perhaps, her greatest ally in France. Opening in Britain after the joyously received *Babette*, the film was roasted alive in the critics' pit as a Technicolor burlesque of puerile eroticism. Said Campbell Dixon, in London's *Daily Telegraph*: 'One of the worst films I ever saw.'

'One of the most vulgar films to be encountered outside the pornographic black market', underlined David Robinson, *Financial Times*. At least he attributed full blame to the right quarter: Duvivier and Marcel Achard—'both old enough to be Bardot's grandfather. The least one might expect from men of their age is subtlety.'

Robin Bean, *Films and Filming*: 'Duvivier seems to have taken [it] too seriously, with the result that it is less crudely and sensationally made than most of Bardot's films with an all too familiar plot of rich man ruined by his attraction to exiled French girl . . . all designed either to send your blood pressure up or send you to sleep.'

Nina Hibbin, *Daily Worker*: 'Static, heavy-handed and unconvincing, it has [BB] no longer a kitten, but a cat—practising a particularly feline form of perversion. She dangles herself temptingly, in varying forms of undress, before the man she loves.'

The Times: '[BB] is fast becoming the victim of that legend of the irresistible voluptuary which has been built up around her. Her stories now follow an inevitable pattern. Provocation is followed by procrastination, seduction is encouraged, seduction is resisted, seduction is even enforced.'

Paul Dehn, *News Chronicle*: 'Bardot reverts to type . . . sporting a neckline which plunges deeper than a bathyscape, silhouetting herself nakedly against a frosted bathroom and dancing a number of cautious flamencos with her feet well out of range but her torso well in.'

Picturegoer: 'Oddly enough, while throwing her body around like a football at a cup final, she's really pure all through. But there isn't much she doesn't know about driving a man out of his mind. Thus Brigitte enslaves her wealthy charmer, promising much and delivering nothing at all through the picture . . . she pouts, preens and prances, provocatively in a tawdry flamenco show, while darting upstairs every so often to perform a nifty striptease for the pop-eyed tourists. At its best, she's a cut-price *Blue Angel*. But for the most part, you won't have seen anything like it since Pola Negri gave up luring men to their silent doom.'

Derek Monsey, *Sunday Express*: 'Not exciting. It is dull. It is also vulgar and unpleasant in much the least interesting sense of those words. It is dubbed so badly into a curious American-English that the discrepancy between lip-movements and words is the most disturbing thing (Bardot's fundamental

shape and funny walk excluded) in the film.'

America did not think much of it, either—the dubbing or the playing—when the film opened at pricey neighbourhood theatres.

Eugene Archer, *New York Times*: 'In one of her innumerable love scenes in this turgid Spanish romance, Mlle. Bardot writhes away from her lover and sighs, with all the passion she can muster, "Oh how I wish I would make you suffer!" She succeeds entirely too well, in a manner guaranteed to dismay her American admirers. M. Duvivier's main directorial contribution to this consists in keeping the star's anatomy scrupulously in focus. He tries for technique only when he attempts to imitate her walk, by allowing his camera to sway rhythmically from side to side. The effect, like the film and the actress's performance, is briefly hypnotic and ultimately indigestible.'

Meanwhile, Raoul Levy was preparing a more palatable confection to sweeten the soured . . .

Babette s'en va~t~en guerre

1959

French. Iéna/Films Ariane; 103 minutes. UK: *Babette Goes to War*, Columbia, 1960; 98 minutes. US: Columbia; 103 minutes. CinemaScope. Eastman Color.
Director: Christian-Jaque. *Producer:* Raoul Levy. *Script:* Raoul Levy, Gérard Oury; *adaptation,* Jean Ferry, Jacques Emmanuel; *dialogue,* Michel Audiard. *Photography:* Armand Thirard. *Editor:* Jacques Desagneaux. *Music:* Gilbert Bécaud. *Sound:* William Sivel. *Art Director:* Jean André. *Production Manager:* Louis Wipf. *Shooting:* from January 14, 1959, Studios Joinville, London locations.

CAST

Brigitte Bardot	*Babette*
Jacques Charrier	*Gérard*
Hannes Messemer	*Von Arenberg*
Yves Vincent	*Captain d'Arcy*
Ronald Howard	*Fitzpatrick*
Francis Blanche	*Schulz*
René Havard	*Louis*
Jacques Hilling	*Captain*
Alain Bouvette	*Emile*
Max Ellroy	*Firmin*
Mona Goya	*Mme. Fernande*
Pierre Bertin	*Duke*
Viviane Gosset	*Duchess*
Françoise Belin	*Mado*
Noël Roquevert	*Gustave*
Jean Carmet	*Antoine*
Michael Cramer	*Heinrich*
Charles Bouillaud	*Pierrot*
Robert Berri	*Sergeant Bill*
Roland Bartrop	*Dispatch Rider*

STORY

1940. Bordello maid Babette is among Dunkirk *evacuées* working at the Free French HQ in London. Major Fitzpatrick maintains she is a double for German General Von Arenberg's ex-lover and she agrees to act as kidnap bait with her new boyfriend, Lieut. Gérard, as her partner. Parachuting into France, she gives her owl's hoot signal—the only answer is a cow's moo. She has lost Gérard and nearly her freedom when

Love. 'My first sexless film,' Bébé decreed. She still married her leading man, Jacques Charrier, and gave birth to the most celebrated baby of post-war France.

brought before Paris Gestapo Chief, 'Papa' Schultz. He also recognises her as a *doppelgänger* for the general's mistress and insists she spy on Von Arenberg, suspected of plotting against Hitler. Babette, in a brunette wig, acts as a double-agent—capturing the general and Gérard's heart. Which, apparently, is the 125th movie reason why Hitler called off his British invasion plans . . .

NOTES

BB: 'I am sick of sex. And of what they have made me out to be. [A not altogether surprising statement after the last film.] I do not like it any more—and I think maybe other people are sick of it, too. This is my first sexless film. I want everyone under 16 to be able to see me.'
Such was the Levy premise: second time around. Originally, producer Levy's occupational therapy had Babette as Bette, a prostitute. Stripping . . . ? Perhaps. 'Just a little. Brigitte will be trained at a Commando

Spies. BBabette lures Nazi General Hannes Messemer into a trap peculiarly designed by a French officer, Jacques Charrier, and a Gestapo chief—comically etched by the late Francis Blanche.

school, where she will, of course, wear battledress. It will be explained to her that in an emergency a battledress can be taken off and used as a rope for climbing a wall. In one scene we will show her doing this.' Unfortunately for the 209 airmen who gave up their week-end passes from RAF Station Abingdon when BB arrived for her parachute training locations, the script had been changed—via the witty Gérard Oury, currently the director of France's biggest grossing comedies. The battledress and all other clothes stayed firmly on; not enough inducement, though, for the then-boyfriend, Sacha Distel, to agree to co-star. 'I may be the only man in France who would turn down such an offer, but I will not play opposite, or appear in a film and act with Bardot.' She went to the theatre and liked the leading man in *The Diary of Anne Frank*: Jacques Charrier. He took Distel's disclaimed part—and his girl. They were married within six months, in less time than it took for the film to be ready for its Paris première.

For the first non-nude BB vehicle, Levy ironically selected veteran 'sexy' director Christian-Jaque; *Babette* was his 56th film since 1933. He had made his name, and Martine Carol's, by directing his then-wife in six movies; she was nude in every one, making her France's first post-war sex-siren. Martine soon tired of the obligatory nude (usually bath) scenes and, anyway, had been pushed well out of frame by the onsurge of Bardot.

A dab hand at comedy light comedy, Christian-Jaque (real name: Christian Maudet; BB's surname in *En cas de malheur*) is perhaps the most cosmopolitan of Paris directors, working in Italy, Germany, Spain, Sweden and Britain. He went on to make another BB vehicle in 1970, *Les pétroleuses*. 'She's absolutely charming and adorable. What you need to do is to make her feel easy and create a happy atmosphere, and to tell her exactly what she is expected to do. Other directors have shown you Bardot the stripper. I'm going to show you Bardot the comedienne ... not once does she remove her clothes in this film. Originally it was to have been like all the others—but now we have changed our minds.'

Levy kept all options open. One scene had Brigitte changing clothes before going out to trap her Nazi quarry. She opens a wardrobe door and selects a new dress—and the fade-out is sharp. Presumably she changed on-camera, disporting in undies or less, just in case it was required. It was not. The only time she was seen under the sheets—she was using her radio transmitter. And her rarely exploited talents as a light comedienne dressed up the rest of the finished film—stolen from under her covered bosom by Ronald Howard's British army officer and the late Francis Blanche's hilarious Gestapo chief.

According to the media—one headline ran: Brigitte

keeps her clothes on and throws off the X-label. Bardot was about to become Bernhardt. Some journalists, angered by her continuing disdain of interviews, began calling her Brigitte Garbo. 'To get by,' warned *Picturegoer,* 'she'll have to act well.' She did. The film was shown at the Moscow festival, from where *Sight and Sound,* that most esoteric of British film organs, was moved to report: 'A gem of satire, wit and imagination—all this and Bardot too.'

In Britain, Columbia was annoyed with the Censor for giving the mild comedy an A (adults) certificate rating instead of a U (family trade) certificate. 'It's a harmless little comedy,' said the company, 'with no naughty dialogue and NO undressing.' With the reviews, Columbia had nothing to complain about. 'The deftest farce I have seen for a long time,' praised John Waterman, *Evening Standard.* 'I have not myself been a Bardot fan,' admitted Ivon Adams, *Star,* 'this film has made me one . . . exquisite.'

There were, though, those rash enough to moan about the absence of the very aspect of Bardot films about which they more usually complained. A. H. Weiller, *New York Times*: 'But Mlle. Bardot is clothed almost as abundantly as an eskimo . . . A switch such as this could lead to disaster . . . the director appears to have allowed Mlle. Bardot some freedom in her characterisation. As such, she is again, the pouting innocent with a slight, if not entirely memorable, flair for comedy. Her natural endowments are noticeable when she is seen occasionally in a form-fitting frock, but Mlle. Bardot fully-clothed is a definite distraction. A word to the wise producers should be sufficient. Watch it, gentlemen.'

Derek Hill, *Tribune*: 'Even the cover-up act by Bardot seems a mistake; a little of her usual striptease would have at least livened things up. It might even have disguised the fact that, robbed of her gimmick, she can't hope to carry a film.'

The Times: . . . '[it] sets out to prove that [BB] is quite capable of sustaining a film on her powers as a light comedienne and without resorting to any scenes of unrestrained passion or uninhibited dishabille. The aim is certainly laudable, but the proof is not altogether forthcoming. Miss Bardot makes a charming scatterbrain, a pouting and disarming incompetent who is yet a long way from being in the same class as either Miss Marilyn Monroe or Miss Judy Holliday. The script, it is true, does not give her much assistance and having presented her with several potentially funny situations, does not develop them.'

Some older fans thought otherwise. Nina Hibbin, *Daily Worker*: '. . . looking even more provocative in khaki than she used to in her scanties—she proves once again, that, in addition to her more obvious attributes, she has a sparkling sense of comedy.'

Paul Dehn, *News Chronicle*: 'Here, all of a sudden, is Bardot the polished comedienne; and the week's nicest surprise is to see her squaring her incomparable shoulders in readiness to receive the mantle which Danielle Darrieux must one day, alas, pass on. . . . A whole armoury of variously calibred moves, pouts, frowns, scowls, beams, smiles, hand-flaps, wrist-flicks and tones ranging from the dulcet to the deafening has been moved up the Bardot line to serve a brilliant story's strategy . . . I laughed fit to bust. Best comedy of the year.'

Even the subscriber of her supposed impending doom, Anthony Carthew, *Daily Herald,* changed his tune. 'The perfect film for her. It is wildly funny, skilfully made and has a script far above the strip-cartoon level of her previous pictures.' Agreed; but as I commented at the time: 'Deft comedy lines, brunette wig and other wrap around clothes were not enough to change her essential spark, although the script was aimed, of course, at the men and she was not well served . . . her part could have been a fella's.'

Voulez~vous danser avec moi?

1959

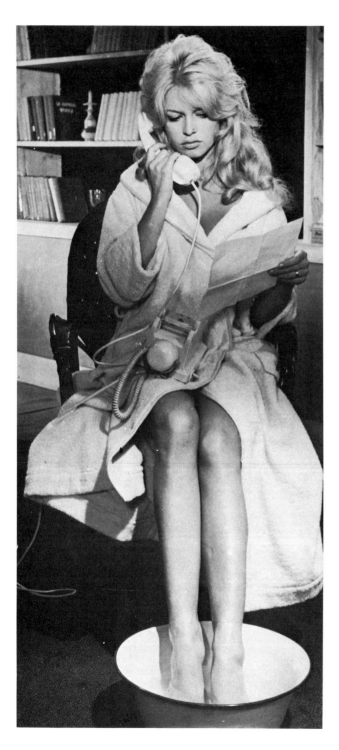

Do You Want To Dance With Me? Francos Film (Paris)/Vides Films (Rome); 91 minutes. UK/US: *Come Dance With Me,* Columbia, 1960; 91 minutes. Technicolor.
Director: Michel Boisrond. *Producer:* Francis Cosne. *Script:* Annette Wademant, L. C. Thomas, Jean-Charles Tacchella, Gérard Oury, *from the novel, 'The Blonde Died Dancing'* by Kelley Roos; *dialogue:* Annette Wademant. *Photography:* Robert Lefebvre. *Editor:* Claudine Bouché. *Music:* Henri Crolla, André Hodeir. *Sound:* William Sivel. *Art Director:* Jean André. *Assistant Directors:* Jacques Poittrenaud. *Shooting:* from July 15, 1959, Studios La Victorine, Nice.

CAST

Brigitte Bardot . . . .*Virginie Dandieu*
Henri Vidal . . . .*Hervé Dandieu*
Dawn Addams . . . .*Anita Flores*
Noël Roquevert. . . . .*Albert*
Dario Moréno. . . . .*Flores*
Philippe Nicaud . . . .*Daniel*
Serge Gainsbourg . . . .*Léon*
Paul Frankeur. . . . .*Police Inspector*
François Chaumette. . . . .*Assistant*
Pascal Mazotti . . . .*Barman*
Maria Pacaume and Georges Descriéres.

STORY

Virginie knows her dentist-husband, Hervé, is innocent of the murder of exotic dance-instructress Anita Flores. Even if she was blackmailing him after some extra-marital canoodling. Even if Virginie did find Hervé next to the body, gun in hand. But how to unmask the killer before the police arrest Hervé? She joins the Flores dance school as an instructress and soon has suspects aplenty: Anita's husband, a widower all too readily consoled; sinister photographer Léon; dancer Daniel; shady barman Pierre; and others among Anita's blackmail victims. Together with an extremely patient police inspector, Virginie finds her man: Daniel, drag queen at a gay club. He killed Anita to help his boyfriend gain an inheritance.

Drag. Philippe Nicaud's make-up technique amuses Bébé—not so Papa Noël Roquevert watching her make-out with dentist Henri Vidal (below).

NOTES

Her first film as Mme. Charrier and her last before the birth of Nicolas; her third with Boisrond, every one a champagne-fizz comedy winner; and her 24th film in all, one fraught with tragedy . . . with worse to come after her next.

Rising Italian starlet Sylvia Lopez, best-looking muscles in the *Hercules Unchained* thud and blunder epic, had been playing the silky blackmailer, Anita Flores. She fell ill after a few days' work and died from leukaemia. Soon after shooting was completed, Brigitte's co-star, Henri Vidal, husband of Michèle Morgan and one of the best among BB's screen partners, also died. By the time the film reached Britain—September, 1960—Bardot had finished 25 films in eight years, lost two husbands, a reputed seven other lovers, also in eight years, and had tried to kill herself.

Yet it began so frothily. With Bébé selecting her ginghams, Vidal and Noël Roquevert (as her father this time) back on the BB strength, Dario Moréno re-treading his oily club-owner from *La femme et le pantin*, and Boisrond running the most madcap screen-tests yet of Bardot's leading men. The twist was that the killer was a transvestite: Philippe Nicaud came over better than Claude Brasseur or Claude Véga in the

drag-tests. (The film was made in the same year as Curtis and Lemmon starred in drag opposite Monroe in Billy Wilder's classical *Some Like It Hot*.)

Director Boisrond said: 'Our first two films were pure comedy. This time I wanted a change—a suspense film with some comedy touches. Because for me, Brigitte is one of the rare actresses who can combine humour and drama.'

For once in America, it was not Bébé's exposure causing the routine censor group condemnations, but a flash close-up of Vidal handling Dawn Addams' unfettered breasts. Dawn Addams, Britain's leading Europhile export of that time, had taken over the Lopez rôle, and shook several British critics with this sequence—'a fire that has rarely been evidenced in her other films', said one. For the record, the exposed bosom was not Dawn's nor indeed Sylvia Lopez's, but that of a stand-out stand-in. More British critics took exception to the homosexual dénouement, although Hollywood had already begun riding its homo-cycle, with the euphemistic *Tea and Sympathy, The Strange One* and *Cat on a Hot Tin Roof.*

Time magazine saw all this, Bardot in Le Fétiche Bleu Club's dressing-rooms with a bunch of under-dressed and rather muscle-bound drag queens, as connected with what eventually became known as Women's Liberation—and this before Germaine Greer had left the colonies or Gloria Steinam found her hip sunshades. In a review (the rest of which was riddled with puns even more execrable than my own), the still then anonymous *Time* critic commented: 'B.B. cannot be seen naked in this film, but there is a brief restaging of the memorable scene from *And God Created Woman,* in which Brigitte's nakedness, though coyly hidden from the audience, is reflected in the bulging eyes of her lover. In a praiseworthy attempt to reach a wider audience—some unrest has been reported among wives and girl friends dragged to previous BB films—the producers have included several shots of handsome naked men.'

Monthly Film Bulletin: 'With a pert sprinkling of comedy, this is a colourful *policier* boasting a few neat twists and surprises, conventional enough in every sense until the dubious intrusion of a homosexual element in the closing night-club sequence. [BB] is very much at ease as the high spirited heroine and the acting is very good . . .'

Derek Monsey, *Sunday Express*: 'Bardot dances, pouts, kisses and displays all that engaging urchin attractiveness which even big men find irresistible, but she does not undress. Or rather, she discards her clothes at one moment, but all you see is the clothes mounting in a very small pile and her husband watching where they fall . . . Not a very good film, but modestly amusing in, at times, a rather immodest way.'

Roy Nash, *Star*: '[BB] as a brave little Goody-two-shoes playing hunt-the-murderer in a shady Paris dancing school and, with her waterfall of yellow hair tumbling down her back, reminding me of nobody so much as Mary Pickford.'

Apart from *Time,* the Americans seemed to have had sufficient of BB. Bosley Crowther, *New York Times,* found it 'a shoddy piece of mystery writing that calls for its shapely star to be more seductive than deductive and believe us that isn't much'. And in *Esquire,* Dwight MacDonald attacked Bardot for becoming 'a grotesque, a production of biological over-specialisation, like a borzoi; her face has been reduced to the sexual essentials and is, objectively considered, by now rather terrifying.' Incredible!

Memoriam. A very tragic comedy. One star died during shooting; Henri Vidal (above) soon after; the ebullient Dario Moréno (below) a few years later.

L'Affaire d'une nuit

1960

French. Progefi. UK: *It Happened at Night,* Bargate distribution, 1962; 95 minutes. Monochrome.
Director: Henri Verneuil. *Producer:* Christine Gouze-Renal. *Script:* Jean Aurenche, Henri Jeanson, *from a book by* Alain Moury. *Photography:* Robert Lefebvre. *Editor:* Léonide Azar. *Music:* Martial Solal. *Art Director:* Robert Clavel. *Assistant Directors:* Michel Wyn, Armand Velin.

CAST

Pascale Petit. *Christine*
Roger Hanin . . . . *Michel*
Pierre Mondy . . . . *Antoine*
Uncredited guest appearances: Brigitte Bardot, Jacques Charrier, Christine Gouze-Renal.

STORY/NOTES

Bébé turns up in an un-credited walk-on during this lightly saucy comedy caper, produced by her good friend, Christine Gouze-Renal—and starring her husband, Roger Hanin. The leading lady, Pascale Petit—who like Belmondo, Charrier and others got her first break in *Les tricheurs*—was one of the few newcomers on the French scene who did not purposefully ape Bardot, apart from her initial celebrity.

P.P. was the young wife caught between middle-aged husband (Pierre Mondy) and his good pal (Hanin). The friend looks after the wife one night while hubby is out of town; passion proves too strong and, rather than fight it out, the husband leaves for foreign parts.

Brigitte was a close friend of many in the Progefi unit, particularly of producer Gouze-Renal, whom she had known since *La lumière d'en face* (1955), and her choice of director, Henri Verneuil. Hence Bardot being asked to help supply a touch of Paris-by-night celebrity in the background of a restaurant sequence featuring Pascale Petit and Roger Hanin. 'Okay,' she told the producer, 'I'll do it—but you must come along, too.' And so Christine Gouze-Renal joined the star's (mute) table; so did Bébé's husband, Jacques Charrier.

The scenes were shot at La Grille in Les Halles region of Paris—and proved very similar, in fact, to BB's later and similarly uncredited walk-on (or sit-down) in Godard's *Masculin-Féminin,* in 1965.

Guests. Bébé agrees to a sit-in rôle. If producer Christine Gouze-Renal joins her—hubby Charrier, too.

Stars. The producer's husband, Roger Hanin, and the newest initials in Paris: P.P.

155

La vérité

1960

Franco-Italian. Iéna (Paris)/CEIAP (Rome); 130 minutes. UK: *The Truth,* Columbia Pictures; 125 minutes. US: Kingsley International; 127 minutes. Monochrome.
Director: Henri-Georges Clouzot. *Producer:* Raoul J. Levy. *Script:* Clouzot, Jérôme Géronimi, Simone Drieu, Michèle Perrein, Christiane Rochefort. *Photography:* Armand Thirard. *Editor:* Albert Jurgenson. *Music:* Stravinsky, Beethoven. *Sound:* William Robert Sivel. *Art Director:* Jean André. *Production Manager:* Louis Wipf. *Assistant Director:* Serge Vallin. *Shooting:* from May 2, 1960, Studios Joinville.

CAST

Brigitte Bardot . . . . *Dominique Marceau*
Charles Vanel . . . . *Maitre Guérin, Defence*
Paul Meurisse . . . . *Prosecutor*
Louis Seigner . . . . *President of the Court*
Marie-José Nat . . . . . . *Annie Marceau*
Sami Frey . . . . *Gilbert Tellier*
Jacqueline Porel . . . . . . *Defence Lawyer*
René Blancard . . . . *Attorney*
Jean-Louis Reynolds . . . . *Michel*
André Oumansky . . . . . . *Ludovic*
Fernand Ledoux . . . . *Court Doctor*
L. Arbessier . . . . *Professor*
Jacques Perrin, Claude Berri, Barbara Sohmers, Suzy Wills, Christian Lude, Jacques Hilling, Colette Castel, M. Cavalier.

STORY

Dominique Marceau is accused of killing her lover, her sister's fiancé, Gilbert. Murder or *crime passionnel*? Witnesses relate her life-style in a distorted mirror of flash-backs. A rebel against her bourgeois family existence, Dominique shared a Paris room with her virtuous sister. While Annie studied the violin, Dominique led a foot-loose, amoral, morose Latin Quartier life. Embarrassed by her frankness and beauty, Gilbert falls into a searing affair with her, doomed from the start. He studies Bach, she digs Brando, and comes home late, in other men's shirts. He leaves her. Soon he is engaged to Annie and making his name as a conductor. Dominique, realising he supplied her greatest happiness, returns for an ecstatic night together. Then he throws her out. She threatens to kill herself in front of him. He laughs, she shoots. He falls, dead. Now, who among the elderly gentlemen arrayed to weigh the evidence can understand the confused mind before them and realise the love behind the violence? Not the judge, impartial, formal; not the prosecutor, coldly seeking death for premeditated murder; not her defence, making her seem innocent by demolishing the object of her love. Unable to articulate the truth, Dominique slashes her wrists in jail.

NOTES

BB: 'This is my favourite film. Very important to me. It is the first really dramatic picture I have made.

Bardot on trial for *her* life. *Prosecutor:* You spent weeks seducing him, didn't you? Weeks! *Defence:* Objection! What length of time should she have spent? Is there any legal limit on how long a seduction ought to take?

I can act in it. There are two parts for me in it. One is like BB—dancing the cha-cha and all that. And there is another part in court where she is accused of murdering her lover. In the first part of the film, I'm very gay—like BB—but in the second part, I'm very serious. I end up killing myself in jail. I have had to work harder than I have ever worked before in my life.'

Cinémonde called it: *'Et Clouzot créa la tragédienne.'* The *Daily Herald* screamed: 'This is Bardot PLUS!' The ad. copy ran 'Bardot reveals the SHATTERING TRUTH about today's young lovers! "Suppose I'm a tramp . . . why can't I be in love?" ' The film won the Grand Prix du Cinéma Français. Clouzot won the best director award at the 1961 Mar Del Plat festival in Argentina. Bardot won the best foreign actress David di Donatello award in Italy. The *Evening Standard*'s rave review headline told it all: 'When they ask "What was Bardot like?" this is the one to show.' Yet how it was ever made, finished, put together and finally screened is worth a book in itself. The off-set squabbles and headlines put even the Brando *Mutiny on the Bounty* and the Taylor–Burton *Cleopatra* scandals to shame. Such nefarious side-issues are rarely aired in critical reviews; critics write about what they see (or think they see), not what they hear from the studio battlefront, although one heavily impinges upon and affects the other. A short recap of events

Winner. Sami Frey won the steeplechase of tests—and the girl. Not that he talked much about either. 'I never like discussing my love affairs. It is above all public confession. Our love scenes in *La vérité* began the biggest emotions of my life. How could they be else? It was a bewitching film and it engaged all my future.'

157

during production should be considered when examining in any way the phoenix triumph emerging from the ashes of this final Levy—Bardot combination.

She started work within a fortnight of becoming a mother and almost immediately walked off the production, when the actor she wanted was rejected by Clouzot, who wanted a completely new, raw partnership. Sami Frey won the part, and inevitably the girl. Not content with that juicy enough item, the French papers insisted Clouzot was also having an affair with Bardot—a fact not helped by the absence of both spouses involved. Actress Vera Clouzot and Jacques Charrier were both in hospital; Vera later died from her illness. On his release, Charrier was in a (perhaps, rather too well) photographed street affray with Frey; and Bardot, emotions taut and worked to a frazzle by Clouzot to excellent effect on-screen, fled to the country chased by the cannibalistic French Press, and repeated the end of the script and slashed her wrists. She was acting in two, if not three, lifelike scenarios at once: two much for any girl.

That her performance (or any in the film) is so persuasively impressive, grippingly true, and painful in its realism, is then something of a miracle. On Clouzot's part; and even more so on Bardot's. She had, let it be clear, rarely been given credit for being able to act at all up to this point. She proved her talent—it was, as Vadim said, natural, emotional spontaneity, not acting *per se*—in a screen season later dominated by powerhouse performances by women: Loren's *Two Women*, Monroe's *The Misfits*.

Clouzot had covered amoral youth in *Manon* (1949, with Cécile Aubrey at 16) and he had reported a murder trial for a Paris newspaper in 1959. His script was a melodramatic plea for a change in the antiquated French legal system, where judges, usually elderly, bourgeois, far removed from the modern life they see paraded before them, judge the criminal, *never* the crime. As Autant-Lara before him, having been given the Vadim package of sensual delights, Clouzot used them to social as well as erotic ends. The script's murder was not what was on trial, but the morals of the newly liberated French youth. Of Bardot herself. Could BB's rôle have felt genuine love? Was, in fact, love at all possible in a permissive society rejecting the old ground-rules? (Even Bardot was having trouble with that question.) If amorality was incongruous with love, then *crime passionnel* became an impossibility to prove. The truth of the scenario was, of course, that the couple were genuinely in love, but never at the same time—a failing Bardot had often remarked upon within her own love-life.

Bearing *Babette* in mind, Raoul Levy's brief was simple: drama, tragedy, yes, but sex, too. 'Actually it would be a pity for her *not* to strip,' commented Clouzot. 'She has the most beautiful back and bottom

I have ever seen. But even undressed, Brigitte is an actress. Also, she is very easy to direct. Very obedient. I was far more worried about the leading boy than I was worried about Brigitte.'

So was Bardot. Choosing the musical student who had to be equipped with all the traits of a future conductor (jealousy, ego, possessiveness and a plodder to boot) was a long haul. Bardot wanted the man she had left Vadim for, Jean-Louis Trintignant; an inspired choice, he certainly had the steely talents to add the credibility missing from only this rôle in the film. Her husband, Charrier, was reportedly incensed at her suggestion, noting the explicit love scenes and realising—who didn't?—what had happened last time.

Clouzot did not agree; instead he tested her in a (dressed) bed clinch with all the young hopefuls of the new wave: Marc Michel, Charles Belmont, Gérard Blain, singer Hughes Aufray; Jean-Marc Bory, Moreau's lover in *Les amants,* and BB's fiancé in her next Vadim project; inexplicably Jean-Pierre Cassel, a light comedian and her co-star later in, aptly enough, a light comedy; and even Jean-Paul Belmondo. Clouzot settled instead upon Sami Frey.

Chosen as opposing duellists in the highly theatrical and antiquated atmosphere of the French courts, were two of the French acting circle's most respected veterans—stars, both, of previous Clouzot triumphs. Paul Meurisse (from the director's definitive horror study, *Les diaboliques/The Fiends,* 1954) was the icily wry counsel for what is most simply labelled

Life-style. Bardot's favourite role. Her most successful at the French box-office. Clearly, her finest (and most awarded) screen acting. Even if, as many chiding critics and other foes believed, the actress was merely playing herself. Partly true, perhaps. Certain aspects of Dominique Marceau were allied, or became so, to the essential Brigitte media-image. In particular, her tragic vulnerability or inability to cope with the heavy demands of fame, and life in a goldfish bowl. And so, like Dominique, Bébé attempted to achieve solace in suicide....

as the prosecution; his lawyer was, in fact, appearing on behalf of the slain victim's family, and attacking anyone, the accused Bébé in particular, in order to defend the dead man's good name. And Charles Vanel, from that very first Continental film to win a general-release ticket in Britain—Clouzot's suspenseful *Le salaire de la peur/The Wages of Fear*, 1953—took on the Bardot defence, twisting the simple truth of the affair to suit his own (and the judges') generation-gap comprehension of the case.

Interesting names, too, among the supporting cast of Brigitte's café *copains,* two of whom have since excelled themselves on both sides of the camera: Jacques Perrin, best remembered as the crusading journalist in Costa-Gavras's *Z,* which he also produced; and Claude Berri, who acts these days in his own productions, which he writes and directs with humorous insight about the Jewish background he was raised in: *Mazel Tov ou le mariage, Le Cinéma de Papa, Sex-Shop, et al.*

Shooting began in an atmosphere charged with rumours of unabated affairs. On the set, however, Clouzot's major passion was to make the film—and make it right. His way. Even if the new-wave critics thought him old-fashioned: 'I'm very friendly with Truffaut and Godard but the whole *Cahiers* [*du cinéma* critics] is against me and I don't know why ... They are only interested in making films for 20,000 people.' Clouzot aimed higher and pushed Bardot like she had never been pushed before. One story had him dissatisfied with her breathing when arriving at the

top of some stars. 'You are not panting as if you had *really* been running. To the microphone which is, in fact, the ear of the audience—you sound artificial.' He grabbed her hand and charged her around the Joinville studios courtyard to the amazement of the people on the lot. Back into the set, shouting for the camera to start running before they reached the base of the fake staircase, and only then shot the scene to his complete satisfaction.

Everything was worth it.

Alexander Walker, *Evening Standard*: 'Brigitte comes wobbling carnally out of the provinces and hip-flips her way through the pads of Paris *beatnicks*. No job can hold her. No man either . . . she gives a stunning performance as herself. Posterity will turn to this film to see why we marvelled at the sight of B.B. stretching out her toes to be kissed by morning callers, or letting the soap slip out of the shower to lure on the timid visitor, or simply jigging to jazz music as she gets out of bed. What she would make of the normal person's daily dozen I dare not think.'

James Breen, *Observer*: 'The girl that Bardot plays—an aimless provincial who drifts to Paris, goes to bed with practically everybody and ends up by murdering her true love—has no human reality. She is put together from bits of old celluloid and newsprint . . . The question is how does Bardot rate as a sex-symbol? To me she never for a moment conveys the innate-sex-in-the-bone radiance of Marilyn Monroe. The scene . . . where she lies in bed listening to a record and rotating her bottom under the sheets in time to the music, while M. Frey smoulders nearby, isn't a patch—for sheer sex waves—on the scene in *The Misfits* where a tightly jeaned Monroe plays ecstatically with bat-and-ball. Bardot energetically does what she's asked, but her movements are contrived and emotionally cold. She lacks aura and so directors have to calculate it for her.'

Bosley Crowther, *New York Times*, found the story banal. 'The truth about a so-called "crime of passion" is what [Clouzot] is supposed to be trying to fathom . . . But a viewer might easily get the notion that what he is really out to do is crowd the screen with the scorching sensuality of his star performer . . . For never had this famous Gallic siren been so frankly and ferociously employed as a symbol of sexual intemperance and rebellion . . . what a story! And what a field day for Mlle. Bardot. By comparison, *And God Created Woman* is a fable for children in school . . . Familiar as are her mannerisms and attitudes in those scenes that display erotic implications, their shameless candour is meaningful here, suggesting the anarchism of a stratagem of contemporary youth.'

Pauline Kael, *Sight and Sound*: '. . . a tired and trite mechanical piece of slick movie making. Conceptually, it's rather like *Of Human Bondage*—seen from Mildred's point of view. Although the title and the film's structure suggest that we are going to see the relativity of the truth, the movie seems designed to show us the truth about [BB], just as *The Misfits* was written around Marilyn Monroe. (These ladies are then congratulated for their histrionic achievements in playing themselves; certainly they are perfect in the rôles—no one else could play them so well—but then, could they play anything else?) This confusion of art and life which takes the form of sensationalism is becoming very popular in this Freudianised period . . . The new heroine of our films is becoming the wretched star herself . . . The "mass" audience looks up at the "stars", the educated audience looks down sympathetically, as if reading a case history. They all share in their own narcissism.'

And from my own review of the time, *Bournemouth Times*: 'When she's in the courtroom this is a BB you've never seen before—powerfully compelling. In the flashbacks, there is much of the more familiar Bardot that we all love—reminiscent at times of her previous films and more than once of her own jumbled life.'

Life, as the off-set brouhaha had shown, was a film in itself. And shortly it would be so.

Director. Henri-Georges Clouzot (top) found his name besmirched by incessant rumour-headlines. All he had set out to do was film modern youth, matching Bardot with newcomers Marie José-Nat, her sister, and Sami Frey—their boyfriend.

La bride sur le cou

1961

Loose Reins. Franco-Italian. Production Jacques Roitfeld, Producteur Associé Francis Cosne (Paris)/ Vides (Rome); 85 minutes. UK: *Please Not Now!* 20th Century Fox, 1963; 72 minutes. US: *Only for Love.* CinemaScope. Monochrome.

'Direction Artistique': Roger Vadim. *Producer:* Jacques Roitfeld. *Associate Producer:* Francis Cosne. *Script:* conceived by Jean Aurel; *adaptation,* Claude Brule, Roger Vadim; *dialogue,* Claude Brule. *Photography:* Robert Lefebvre. *Editor:* Albert Jurgenson. *Music:* James Campbell. *Sound:* Robert William Sivel. *Choreography:* Michel Renaud. *Art Director:* Robert Clavel. *Production Manager:* Louis Wipf. *Shooting:* from January, 1961.

CAST

Brigitte Bardot	*Sophie*
Michel Subor	*Alain*
Jacques Riberolles	*Philippe*
Joséphine James	*Barbara*
Claude Brasseur	*Claude*
Mireille Darc	*Marie-Jeanne*
Edith Zetline	*Josette*
Serge Marquand	*Prince*
Jean Tissier	*Concierge*
Bernard Fresson	*Serge*
Claude Berri	*Bernard*

STORY

Further madcap adventures of the wild 'n' whacky Bri-Bri persona: Agnès/Chouchou/Brigitte/Babette/ Virginie, here called Sophie (what else from a Vadim reunion—*The Wise Sophie,* etc.). A cover-girl once more. 'I'm not,' she says, 'made for the life I'm living.' When her photographer lover, Philippe, leaves her and Paris for a winter sports holiday with an American heiress Barbara, Sophie sets out to make him jealous. She selects Alain as her partner for an affair. Philippe does not give a hoot—he's really in love with his Barbara. Sophie, meantime, falls heavily for Alain, and following a knockout succession of improbable happenings, featuring a gun, grandmother, Ferrari, custard-pie, one bobsleigh, three go-karts and an Indian swami, everybody ends up with the partner they deserve.

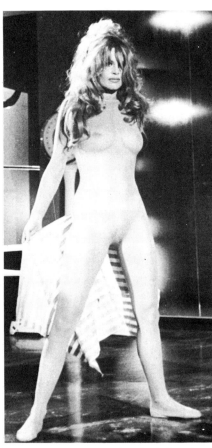

Exposure Deleted. Bébé dances as Vadim pulls the strings anew. In soft focus, she may have appeared naked, but there were stills aplenty to prove otherwise. The British censors were not amused, nor appeased, and ordered the entire segment cut from the film. Vadim was not surprised, he was used by now to the unkindest cuts of all; Bardot, though, had hoped censorship was becoming more liberal. 'It's not a good thing to ban. Banning just encourages curiosity and increases temptation. You don't stop children from smoking by putting a ban on children smoking—they'd respond by smoking in secret. Far better to discourage them. Offer them a cigar or pipe—they won't want to try again after the first puff. Same with cinema. For instance, I've never taken drugs, but if I had the desire to do so, just seeing the film *More* would have cured me of it.'

NOTES

The comeback started quietly, with Bardot co-producing with Jacques Roitfeld and Francis Cosne—the producer who protected her from the world's Press on leaving hospital after the suicide attempt. After a long rest, with Sami Frey ever in attendance, she wanted some—light and airy—fun. She chose a comedy of the Boisrond class, and written by one of the *Parisienne* scripters, Jean Aurel. She talked of wanting to encourage new creators, a second stage of the new wave, and showed enough confidence in Aurel by signing him as her director.

But the kind of *Babette Goes to Peace* went to pieces. After a few days working, she summarily dismissed Aurel and pleaded for Vadim to save her skin. Boisrond would have been better, but he was preparing something bigger, with her in mind. Hence, for contractual reasons Vadim is listed as supplying 'direction artistique'. Vadim and Claude Bruel changed Aurel's script, on the move, into genteel slapstick and ridiculous dialogue—*Man:* Undress please. *BB:* What for?

Vadim explained his ideas in a long dissertation to *Variety,* long that is by *Variety* standards: 'There wasn't a chance to polish lines or anything. Our comedy situations are made up right on the set because they seemed funnier than in the script. It gives us a great deal of spontaneity. I don't think we've ever made such a comedy in France before. French audiences love Hollywood slapstick, it's done with a great deal of skill, but French directors usually get their laughs from dialogue. With us, the lines must be funny. That's the theatrical tradition and it requires a kind of rigid logic that is very inhibiting . . . I am trying something that I have never done before and that is quite alien to the French cinema. This is situation comedy. Actually there isn't very much dialogue in the picture. I am quite convinced that we French can be every bit as funny as the Americans if we permit ourselves to let loose. I don't think Americans

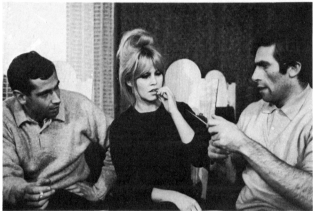

Direction. Together again: Bébé, recovered trom her near-fatal brush with her overbearing image, and Vadim—replacing her original choice of director (Jean Aurel) and scoring the rare screen credit of *'direction artistique'*. He wanted to make 'something quite alien to French cinema'—a situation comedy. He had the perfect star. 'Brigitte is a natural when it comes to comedy. She has that undefinable knack of being funny and pathetic at the same time. Very few actresses have it.'

today particularly like to laugh at themselves. The same is true of the French. The only people who can really see themselves in the mirror and occasionally be amused by the image are the British!'

Shooting went on amid a welter of new-wave anger directed at Bardot for the sacking of Aurel, and at Vadim for appeasing her action by taking over the film. On-set all was calm; for once. 'It was obvious she was happy he was around,' remarked actor Claude Brasseur, finally working with Bébé after losing his drag-queen test on *Voulez-vous danser avec moi?* 'He shows so much enthusiasm. I don't think Vadim could ever be bored when he's making a picture. It means too much to him.'

Exactly what the wise, fast-maturing Bardot had banked on. Apart from the slapdash slapstick, Vadim also engineered a continuance of his peep-show displays to expose all possible facets of the BB body beautiful—a dreamy dance routine, choreographed by Michel Renaud, principal dancer at the Paris Opéra.

Co-star Michel Subor (from Godard's long-banned *Le petit soldat*) dreamed and Bardot seemed naked behind the intentionally blurred soft-focus.

Buying the movie for the United States, 20th Century Fox made a few publicity noises alleging these dancing reels were resting longer than necessary in Customs' hands. Actually the film cleared Customs with nary a hitch: it was obvious that BB was garbed from the neck down in an all-over body-stocking—but devilishly diaphanous. The sequence showed how much she had grown, both physically and as a *danseuse*, since the celebrated mambo in *Et Dieu créa la femme*; it also showed how little Vadim had moved on in style . . . or the British Censor in common sense. British fans saw little of the 'offensive' dance number in a release print 15 minutes shorter than available in France and elsewhere; an astonishingly infantile slice of censorship, considering the era. Brigitte, however, won long, if not necessarily good notices, it being the only film unveiled to the London critics that

Partner. The new co-star was the Jean-Luc Godard discovery, Michel Subor. 'Even today,' he told *Cinémonde* three years later, 'when looking at the old stills of our loves scenes—some very daring—I feel my heart jump. She is a splendid creature. As soon as she appears on a set everyone from the cleaner to the director catches their breath.'

particular week in 1963. If it was not welcomed for the comeback it was, this was due to the fact that it opened two years late, following both *Vie privée* and *Le repos du guerrier*.

Ian Wright, *Guardian*: '. . . what the paperback trade would call a "breast-seller". The only possible reason for making this trite little tale is to display the near-naked charms of Bardot but the present production has been so cut as to obliterate its main point. The distributors are left with a film not worth distributing to the public with a collection of publicity poses which are as lurid as they are misleading.'

Alexander Walker, *Evening Standard*: '. . . plainly meant to be one of Bardot's lighter efforts. It could have been an enjoyable piece of self-burlesquing inconsequence. Instead the soufflé has gone flat because the film has been dubbed into vile American and then cut to 72 minutes. The X-certificate must cover what was taken out.'

Felix Barker, *Evening News*: 'In which [BB] undresses in a photographic studio, her flat, a railway sleeper, the linen cupboard of an hotel, and in a public restaurant. But each time the censor was too quick for her. Terrible rubbish. Unworthy of our favourite sex-kitten.'

The Times: '. . . one welcomes the return of these old gags, but the plot, which is no more than a standard bedroom farce of the 1920s, unfortunately wears unbearably thin . . . Throughout this exercise, she is required to retain an air of virginal innocence, while constantly getting in and out of her clothes or someone else's bed and it says much for her abilities as a comédienne that she almost succeeds in giving the character credibility and life; but the story, unlike its leading lady, is quite shapeless . . . Whereas Mlle. Bardot may be given any old clothes and still look enchanting, she cannot be given any old situation and still remain interesting.'

Margaret Hinxman, *Today's Cinema*: 'The film presents [BB] in the kind of rôle that should please the fans who've never quite cottoned on to the idea of B.B. as a serious dramatic actress . . . naturally she has to peel off fairly often—and she still sports the prettiest shape on the screen. Although she's flighty, she's really a home girl at heart: but not so homely that she doesn't dazzle the men. Also, she's a bit of a nut who drives a car like Stirling Moss with hiccups and isn't above landing a custard pie on her lover's kisser. She goes box-car racing, winter sporting and looks a dish in manly sweaters, usually

Model. For the umpteenth time, Brigitte was a whacky model-girl—a relaxant rôle, the utter antithesis of *La vérité*. Fun and games, very casual, rarely working, from skiing to night-clubbing with (above) Josephine James, Jacques Riberolles, Michel Subor. And Vadim's re-tailored script called her, as he used to, Sophie.

without benefit of pants . . . adds up to a crushingly cute performance which is the be-all and end-all of the film.'

Philip Oakes, *Sunday Telegraph*: '. . . the word which springs instantly to mind—and remains there—is contemptible. Clumsy, prurient, appallingly acted and execrably dubbed, it is interesting only as the end to a myth, which for ten years or so has infatuated world film-makers and audiences alike . . . Despite its X-certificate, it seems to have been heavily censored and its erotic content—which, let's face it is the whole reason for both making and going to see a Bardot film—is nil.'

Brigid Brophy, *New Statesman*: 'Processed, odourless and seemingly untouched by human hand (no director is named . . .), the new Bardot film . . . might have come from an international supermarket—a shoddy one where the plastic bags won't hold water . . . Inside this soiled and sweating synthetic container there is a genuine, unchemicalised, organic article—the long legs, bursting torso and *boucher* pout of [BB], who has the earthy, sensual and quite sexless charms of a fine turnip.'

Slapdash. Vadim turned to slapstick situations 'made up right on the set because they seemed funnier than the script'. *Sunday Express* critic Richard Barkley thought otherwise: 'A piece of slapstick was never more unfunny. It is performed with the indifference of someone who has had to rehearse it a dozen times and still cannot time it right.'

Les amours célèbres

('Agnès Bernauer' sketch)

1961

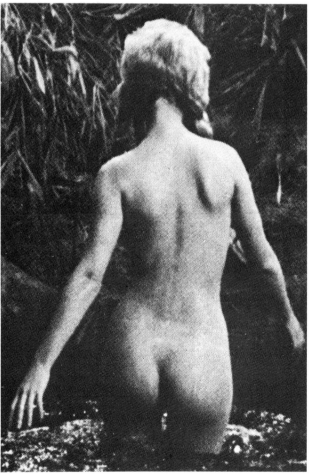

Famous Loves. Franco-Italian. Générale Européenne de Films-Unidix Productions (Paris)/Cosmos Films (Rome); 130 minutes. UK/US release: none on record. Dyaliscope. Eastman Color.
Director: Michel Boisrond. *Producer:* Gilbert Bokanovski. *Script:* France Roche; *dialogue,* Jacques Prévert. *Photography:* Robert Lefebvre. *Editor:* Raymond Lamy. *Music:* Maurice Jarre. *Sound:* William Sivel. *Art Directors:* Georges Wakhevitch, Lila de Nobili. *Production Manager:* Armand Bécué. (Other sketches: *Lauzun*—dialogue, Marcel Achard; starring Jean-Paul Belmondo, Dany Robin. *Jenny de Lacour*—dialogue, Françoise Giroud; starring Simone Signoret, Pierre Vaneck. *Les Comédiennes*—dialogue, Michel Audiard; starring Edwige Feuillère, Annie Girardot, Marie Laforêt.)

SKETCH CAST

Brigitte Bardot . . . . *Agnès Bernauer*
Alain Delon . . . . *Prince Albert*
Pierre Brasseur . . . . *Duke Ernest*
Jean-Claude Brialy . . . . *Torring*
Suzanne Flon, Michel Etcheverry, Jacques Dumesnil.

STORY

Agnès Bernauer, a simple village girl, is the secret wife of the Duke Albert de Wittelsbach, Prince of Bavaria. News of his marriage has him immediately disinherited; his cousin, Adolph, is placed first in succession to the throne. Civil war breaks out with Albert fighting with the radicals. Adolph dies and his father swears that Agnès's expected child will never sit upon the Bavarian throne. The ladies of the court, wildly jealous of the girl's extraordinary beauty, have Agnès arrested and cast into the river as a witch. Albert arrives too late to save her and rides straight into the torrential waters to die with the woman he loves more than life: the woman whose beauty all had envied to the point of murder.

NOTES

History was big in France that year. With the overloaded *La Fayette* starring Michel LeRoyer, Pascale Audret, Jack Hawkins and Orson Welles repeating

Chemistry. Despite the demands, the chemicals were all wrong and BB+Delon refused to blaze. Delon joined the ranks of the Bébé-smitten, however. 'Who is the boy of my age who dare admit he does not feel anything for Brigitte? In her, it is the beautiful woman who first attracted me. Her beauty, the charm of her silhouette, and her attitudes, the frankness of her behaviour and her true sensuality. The actress side only conquered me progressively. After *En cas de malheur* and *La femme et le pantin*, I'm sure it is the actress people now think of. She is a person who makes the whole world dream.'

his *Versailles* portrait of old Ben Franklin; and Bernard Verley as Napoléon II, *L'Aiglon*. This one had 20 stars, boasted *Cinémonde*. Actually 16 recognisable stars only, including another of the ever-growing force of BB lookalikes, Agnès Laurent. Much was expected of the venture—and probably still is. Much of a muchness it remained.

'BB + Alain Delon = ?' ran one *Cinémonde* headline. They equalled absolute *zéro*. But nothing! On paper, the chemistry seemed unparagoned, and looked it, too, in early publicity photo-sessions. On the screen, however, ignition never took place. Both stars, the No. 1 female and male heart-throbs of their nation, were basically far too pretty (and similarly guarded) to set each other off. Bardot won the contest—in acting and looks. Easily. The rôles called for a duet, though, not a battle of solo symbols.

Based on a highly popular newspaper strip running for ten years (one year longer than Bébé herself), the film could have told a dozen love stories and lasted for hours. Instead, director Michel Boisrond settled for the better scripting (and co-starring) possibilities,

Stars. On-camera they included Jean-Claude Brialy (top left) and Alain Delon. Off-set, visitors included Gene Kelly directing Jackie Gleason in *Gigot* on the *plateau* next door.

avoiding the more obvious sagas to enable the film to maintain a certain freshness for its local audience. His quartet covered varying moods of *l'amour*: the gallant, dramatic, romantic and a touch of fantasy with an adoitly applied Stars' Day Out atmosphere in his casting.

Bardot's rôle—in the fourth sketch—was the most touching tale of them all, the surprise not only of her sequence, but of the film itself. She felt safe in Boisrond's care as always—even if he had lately launched the Israeli BB, Daliah Lavi, in *Un soir sur la plage*. This was, though, the fourth and, thus far, last film Brigitte made with the doctor's son and disciple of René Clair—a man Boisrond matches in calmness and courtesy.

Paris-Jour: 'Boisrond proves you can make a commercial film of quality. *Les amours célèbres* is a treat for the eyes, a joy for the spleen and satisfactory for the spirit.' In other words, so good that no English-speaking market would buy it.

Not that *Variety*'s Gene Moskowitz felt that any outsiders would be that interested. 'BB appears in the guise of a medieval barber's comely daughter . . . But Miss Bardot's pouting, kittenish sensuality is sadly amiss in old Bavaria. And her trial for witchcraft is unintentionally risible. The whole thing needed a tongue-in-cheek approach. It is only intermittently so. Colour is well used throughout with subtle difference in each episode . . . Boisrond tends to leave all this talky, and flat in direction, depending mainly on his actors to put it across. This keeps things on a theatrical, almost comic-strip level, because of the lack of character build-up. Then, too, there is the papier-mâché feeling of the period sets.'

Vie privée

1961

Private Life. Franco-Italian. Progefi-Cipra (Paris)/CCM (Rome); 103 minutes. UK/US: *A Very Private Affair,* MGM, 1962; 95 minutes. Eastman Color.
Director: Louis Malle. *Producer:* Christine Gouze-Renal. *Script:* Louis Malle, Jean-Paul Rappeneau, Jean Ferry; *dialogue:* Jean-Paul Rappeneau. *Photography:* Henri Decaë. *Editor:* Kenout Peltier. *Music:* Fiorenzo Carpi. *Sound:* William R. Sivel. *Art Director:* Bernard Evein. *BBcostumes:* Les Maisons Marie-Martine and Real; *hats,* Jean Barthet; *make-up,* Maud Begon; *hair-styles,* Jean-Pierre and Odette Berroyer. *Production Manager:* Fred Surin. *Assistant Directors:* Philippe Gollin, Alain Gouze, Volker Schloendorff. *Stills:* Paul Apoteker. *Shooting:* June 1–August 30, 1961, Franstudio, St. Maurice, Paris; locations at Geneva and Spoleto.

CAST

Brigitte Bardot . . . . *Jill*
Marcello Mastroianni . . . . *Fabio*
Grégoire von Rezzori . . . . *Gricha*
Eléanore Hirt . . . . *Cécile*
Ursula Kubler . . . . *Carla*
Jacqueline Doyen . . . . *Juliette*
Jeanne Allard . . . . *Charwoman*
Dirk Sanders . . . . *Dick*
Nicolas Bataille . . . . *Edmond*
Paul Sorèze . . . . *Maxime*
Antoine Roblot . . . . *Alain*
Mario Naldi . . . . *Grocer*
François Marié . . . . *François*
Christian de Tillier . . . . *Albert*
Gilles Queant . . . . *Tovar*
Elie Presman . . . . *Olivier*
Fred Surin . . . . *Director*
Paul Apoteker . . . . *Cameraman*
Claude Day . . . . *Publicist*
Louis Malle . . . . *Journalist*

STORY

Carefree Jill forsakes her Geneva bourgeois background because she's in love with publisher Fabio, married to family friend Carla. Jill goes to Paris with Dick, a dancer friend. Her own individualism and

Demystification. Bardot shows the world what it was like to be BB. And leaves Marcello Mastroianni in the shadows—for Loren and Ponti to rescue.

uneven temperament mark her a failure in the dancing world—and triumphant as photo-model and sudden, instantaneous sex-star movie sensation. In three years, she is Europe's highest-paid actress ('she brings in as much foreign currency as Renault') and the world's sex-symbol ('looks tarty . . . that hairdo!'). She has everything—and nothing. Desperately lonely and unhappy, she casts off her friendless world to find Fabio again in Geneva. Now separated, he is free to begin an affair. They go to Italy where he is designing and directing Kleist's *Katchen von Heilbronn* at the Spoleto festival: a blissful idyll until the Press uncovers them and moves on to their doorstep. Pressures on their privacy mount to hysteria—until Jill finds relief in a death caused, ironically, by the kind of photographic flash which began her career.

NOTES

BB: 'I am in an impossible situation. I don't know what I'm supposed to do when I meet men. If I even put an arm around them, gossip says I'm trying to break up another home. If I defend myself . . . I'm immediately accused of being a snob. Believe me, it is not easy being Brigitte Bardot. *Alors, c'est final!* This is my last film. Maybe one more with Vadim, that's all. After this, I retire. It's the best thing for me.' It was supposed to have been Noël Coward's *Private Lives,* about which plan there was surprising little to be heard from The Master himself. There was, however, no *vie privée* more public, mixed up, misun-

derstood, misconstrued, misjudged, mashed about and mass-produced than Bardot's; and she, more than Malle or Rappeneau, developed the story into a monstrous mosaic of a Bardography. The new heroine *was* the wretched star herself.

As with Vadim, Brigitte dictated much of the scenario herself, in particular the one sequence which left critics and public with a bitter taste in their mouths: where Jill is berated in a lift by a charwoman. This was a direct incident from BB's often *Huis Clos* of a life. She had, she said, no idea she was, or could be hated so much. . . .

Charwoman (Jeanne Allard): 'Oh, now I recognise you. So it's you. Well, it's no honour to be with you, you have no shame. What have you got in your body? Oh there's no need to look like that . . . when I think my son was killed in Algeria for the likes of you. Yes, I recognise you all right, and not from your films. I wouldn't lower myself to go and see them. But from the papers, although there's no need to read or buy them, it's enough to see your ugly face on every front page . . . I can't understand how creatures of your type exist. What have these poor boys done to you, you want all of them. Can't you leave them in peace? I know what ought to be done to you and you could scream and cry your fill and I wouldn't stir a finger to help you. You should be locked up, you whore— whore, do you hear? Yes, whore! I don't know why I'm controlling myself . . . this creature thinks she's beautiful. You slut . . .!'

BB, this is your life. *Jill:* I don't care! I don't care about people! Don't you understand? I don't want to stay in here any more. I want to get out! Out! I'm fed up of being locked in all the time, always, all my life! I've had enough of shut doors, shut shutters, shut curtains. . . . I can't go on any more. I'm going mad, do you understand? Mad, mad, mad! *Fabio:* Tomorrow we shall be gone. *Jill:* Tomorrow it will be another room and it will be the same.

Sole mistake on the project: the director. This is one film Vadim should have been almost forced to make. Too close to home, of course; but he knew the pain and the not infrequent joy of this saga best of all. Louis Malle was still more technician than humanist at this time; a craftsman with a painter's eye, honing Hitchcock's narrative experiments of short-takes ('photo-grams' as the French critics call them), fading one into the other, 'as if told from memory with stops and leaps and a light mist in the photography'. Malle prefers awkward themes (his best work remains *Zazie dans le métro,* 1960, and 1974's *Lacombe, Lucien*), impossible subjects, usually larger than life in his interpretation. After shooting fish for Cousteau for three years, everything on dry land obviously seemed immense to Malle.

He admits his friends tried to prevent him making the film: 'and I should've listened to them. I like the ending but most of it is lousy.' It flopped in France because, he surmised, BB was such a contemporary myth that everyone was expecting to see their own elaborate scenario of her private life—and it won major impetus abroad only when released in the wake of Monroe's death. (And then not helped by some strange dubbing; Bardot's 'voice' was totally inappropriate, while in France, Mastroianni had been dubbed

so expertly in French, it was well nigh impossible to tell he was speaking his own Italian lines himself.) Louis Malle: 'A film with BB is difficult; how can anyone resist the invasion? It might have been more interesting to make a film strictly on Bardot herself— but that would have required someone other than her in the part. Anyhow, all the public and critics were expecting to see a film (*their* film) about the private life of BB. Hence the 'deception' . . . I'm not interested in mediocre characters. I've sublimated the character of Jill because I prefer heroes. It is the film in which I improvised most and I don't much like that—too nerve-wracking.'

He defended the climax against all comers: Jill falls to a beautifully Decaë-photographed death. Many critics found it absurd; audiences too. Malle called it a lyrical conclusion, 'an end of a mythological heroine —I couldn't have shot a scene where she was seen really falling, smashing on to the ground.' And his stars? 'Brigitte and Mastroianni were supposed to be lovers in the film, but they wouldn't speak to each other . . . which made the whole thing impossible.'

They talked, a little, though. Mastroianni, during Spoleto locations: 'There are two Brigittes—the sex-symbol which the world thinks it knows—the girl who eats up men for breakfast every day—and there is

Real Life. Bardot's Jill is swamped at a première. Brigitte has always been terrified of crowds, steeling herself to face Press conferences and location shooting in front of hordes of spectators. 'They fill me with fear and that's difficult because, by all the laws of our profession, a star is expected to live in the glare of publicity surrounded by a vast public. For me, this is a special strain. I was not brought up to it. I did not seek it. I do not want it.'

Brigitte, the simple, ordinary girl. The only trouble is, Bardot herself doesn't know the difference between the two sometimes. She has these two opposite personalities—and one lives in fear of the other. Once she told me she never really wanted to be a movie actress. But, as with the girl in the film, one thing led to another and it just happened. Perhaps it was all Vadim's fault. When he created her, he set out to make an impossible dream for all men. Unhappily for Brigitte, he almost succeeded. And now she can't be a real person unless she gives up acting for good. She can only be something for people to giggle at and gossip about. She has become the object of scandal and of prying eyes, and of finger-pointing. She hates to be lonely—but now that is what she has to be most of the time.'

Mastroianni again, after the première: 'I'm sorry I ever made the film. The script sent to me was not the one they finally used. I didn't go to the première in France and I don't wish to be associated with the publicity. It was the first time I had made a film outside Italy and I don't intend to make another one. BB? She is pleasant. That's all I can say. I can add no more.'

James R. Silke, *Cinema*: 'With it, she *invites* the audience to examine her private life . . . as a desperate woman in search of a single, secret place where she can touch her lover with the private passions of her desperate heart—where she can give her one real gift, love, without fear of its sudden death in the flash of the celluloid exposure . . . In making the film, the actress Bardot wears the same mask that has brought her own personal tragedy; rather than discarding it,

she uses it here to inform her audience that her life *is* her private affair. The extreme innocence and dazzling eroticism of her performance compels us to grant her the pedestal she seeks, out of reach of those who would desecrate the image.'

Pierre Marcabru, *Combat*: 'A great director of actors borrows from reality. This is what Roger Vadim did with Bardot; this is what Louis Malle has not done. So *Et Dieu créa la femme* remains the best Bardot film; so *Vie privée* although cinematographically interesting, only catches an actress in her movements as an actress, and not in her tyrannical truth.'

Time: '. . . a very sad affair. [BB], the once cuddly sex kitten, has grown into a sullen tabby . . .'

Margaret Hinxman, *Today's Cinema*: 'Coming so soon after the death of Marilyn Monroe, the film is grimly topical and its picture of the tormented life of a star at the mercy of the voracious fans, photographers and gossip writers who helped create her, seems only too accurate . . . But in the end you long for something substantial to hang your sympathy on. [BB] acts the part with a feeling undoubtedly based on experience, though the portrayal lacks real warmth and her tragic end seems merely inevitable.'

Penelope Gilliat, *Observer*: '. . . it probably gives a good many members of the American and British public an easy way of relieving our pain about Marilyn Monroe. But at its best, the film is a real neurotic fable, a story of damage and sleeping pills and uncomforting awakenings that communicates the anguishes of living out a difficult life in public and controlling a hysterical personality in a blaze of flash bulbs.'

Claude Mauriac, *Le Figaro littéraire*: '. . . a film which, instead of feeding the legend as her previous films, feeds upon it . . . For want of the masterpiece we could have had, we have in large measure a document . . . Malle has come a bit too late. First, because of the phenomena of simultaneous attraction and repulsion, of which [BB] is the object, and which formed the reason for this film, has already lost its virulence . . . Then, because this very young actress is not so young any more. It was her adolescent face and body, preserved beyond adolescence, which made her a success. Now the child-woman has become a young woman, to whom we would wish another hairstyle, some other *mimiques* and different mannerisms.'

Bosley Crowther, *New York Times*: 'Its star does bear some resemblance to the nature of the French star's life, in that it details the personal disillusionment and public harassment to which a popular movie actress is exposed . . . But, alas, what is supposed to pass for drama in this magnificently photographed film is not only infinitesimal but is also deplorably banal. . . . The unspoken irony of the picture is that an actress who is so poor at her job should be the representation of the bitterness of fame in such film.'

Jean-Louis Bory, *Arts*: 'That life is contrary to myth, that myth devours life, this is understood. On this theme, Louis Malle has built an interesting film. Always very agreeable to look at. First, because what we have to look at is almost always Brigitte Bardot. (Mastroianni does what he can to face the sun and death, and the little he does, he does well.) . . . Malle has come close to a real film: The Mob and Bardot. Duel of two monsters: one, the most hideous, the most inflamed, the less studied, is this mob, regularly brainless, regularly fed with newsprint, hate, envy, brutality, stupidity, enjoying itself at capital executions, ready to tear apart what is young, beautiful and free . . . Malle's eye is not savage enough.'

Gordon Reid, *Continental Film Review*: '. . . his use of soundtrack and symbolic music quotes, the mobile camera of Decaë and some brusque editing making an interesting account of the problems and nightmares of a young star which some, all too tragically, find too much to bear.'

Thomas Wiseman, *Sunday Express*: 'The story could just as easily be about Rin-Tin-Tin as about Miss Bardot for all its understanding of feminine psychology. Of the curious love-hate relationship that obviously exists between a Bardot and her audience, the film offers not a hint; of the drive that induces a girl to exhibit herself in public—to offer herself to the world—the film has nothing to say. M. Malle has been content to allow his camera to follow Miss Bardot around as if it were a love-sick schoolboy, but it shows us no more of this fascinating girl-myth than is to be found in any fan magazine.'

Alexander Walker, *Evening Standard*: '. . . the aim is to show what stardom is like—the answer is sheer hell. A life lived in the flashlight incandescence, with no moment to call one's own. The pity is that once this not too erudite point is made . . . most frighteningly in a scene where a charwoman spews a stream of abuse at Bardot . . . the film has nothing to add, except to perpetuate the Bardot myth. A clear case of a director being seduced by his subject.'

Lucky him—but what the subject got was the full weight of her message across to the people, the Press, the public: the mob. Not according to Gordon Gow, *Films and Filming*. 'The effect was to dwarf the issue in sensationalism . . . it didn't work. Not for me, anyway. Not for the audience of which I made one at a provincial cinema in France during a Sunday matinée. The general reaction was divided between cries of rapture for every moderately sexy view of Brigitte Bardot (who has never been photographed to better advantage) and loud yawns of derision for everything else.'

Exposing the cancer does not necessarily kill—nor even affect—the malignancy.

Le repos du guerrier

1962

Franco-Italian. Francos Film (Paris)/Incei Film (Rome); 102 minutes. UK: *Warrior's Rest*, Gala Films, 1963; 99 minutes. US: *Love on a Pillow*, Royal Films International, 1963; 102 minutes. Franscope. Eastman Color.

Director: Roger Vadim. *Producer:* Francis Cosne. *Script:* Vadim, Claude Choublier, *from the novel by* Christiane Rochefort; *dialogue*, Vadim. *Photography:* Armand Thirard. *Editor:* Victoria Mercanton. *Music:* Michel Magne. *Sound:* Robert Biart. *Art Director:* Jean André. *Production Manager:* Paul Joly. *Shooting: from February 5, 1962, Studios Billancourt.*

CAST

Brigitte Bardot . . . . *Geneviève Le Theil*
Robert Hossein . . . . *Renaud Sarti*
James Robertson Justice . . . . . *Katov*
Macha Meril . . . . *Raphaële*
Yves Barsacq . . . . *Hotel Manager*
Jacqueline Porel . . . . *Mme. Le Theil*
Jean-Marc Bory . . . . *Pierre*
Jean-Marc Tenberg . . . . *Coco*
Christian Melsen . . . . *Police Inspector*
Michel Serrault . . . . *Varange*
Ursula Kubler . . . . *Nurse*
Robert Dalban . . . . *Police Sergeant*
Jean Tuscano . . . . *Jazz Musician*

STORY

Geneviève, 25, precise, matronly bourgeoise, much loved by Maman and her fiancé, Pierre, rescues a would-be suicide by opening the wrong door at her Dijon hotel. In hospital, he says he belongs to her: she saved his soul, she can have it. Renaud does not have much for a soul. Given a bed, a stack of thrillers, whisky, occasional sex, and he's a tame enough animal. She lives with him, fascinated by this nihilistic thug, coarse, neurotic, maliciously ironic and, as her own innate reserves are lowered, devastatingly erotic. She's in love; he refuses love as he refuses life, the point he was trying to make when she had so rudely interrupted him. He sets out to destroy her. Their bouts of frenetic, if servile, lovemaking are punctuated by Geneviève discovering his genius for sculpture and jazz, his infidelity and drunkenness as well, in his

Mousey. Robert Hossein swamps all traces of her frigidity.

Musky. Rochefort's heroine soon becomes Bardotish.

alternately sophisticated and sordid milieu. They pile up huge demands upon one another until he sobs, 'You've won. I'm defeated. Marry me' as they face each other amid a raging wind in a ruined church—which has to be the most obtuse climax of 1962 . . .

NOTES
BB: 'This is my last film—I promised Vadim I'd do it.' She spelled it out, slowly, for *Cinémonde*: '*Ma décision est ir-ré-vo-ca-ble. Après Le repos du guerrier, le repos de Brigitte.*' Why? 'I haven't found anything good in the scripts I've been shown lately, but even if I had I wouldn't have accepted. In life it is sometimes necessary to step back; I've been filming for ten years without a pause. I need to get my bearings.'

Vadim, as ever, was more interested in her barings—often disturbingly truncated in this, their fourth film together. '*Et Vadim recréa Bardot,*' said *Cinémonde*; at times her nude scenes were more reminiscent of an autopsy than creation, sectionalised in bits and pieces fashion.

Brigitte felt she owed Vadim this film, her 30th, to repay his 7th Cavalry-like rescue of *La bride sur le cou.* She refused his first suggestion, *Le vice et la virtu,* preferring this novel by a Vadim *copine,* Christiane Rochefort, one of the *La vérité* scripting quartet. Her book hailed as so bold that Mme. De Gaulle was reported as saying she would never let the Général read it, despite it winning the new literary Prix de la Nouvelle Vague, and missing the Prix Fémina and Prix Goncourt by a handful of votes.

The old team were back in nude harness then, and

Witness. The Rabat-born Macha Meril played the all-important girlfriend, watching Bardot's Geneviève switch from drab to decorous, from droll to domineering.

that was enough to break every box-office record along the Champs-Elysées. (British advertising was built on the legend that 1,000,000 French could not be wrong—though the Censor forbade use of the American title, *Love on a Pillow*.) The fact that Bardot was far from Rochefort's mousy, tubercular heroine hardly bothered anyone. BB–Vadim was a going concern once more—and both in excellent form, although her post-suicide maturity was visibly overtaking his noticeable decline. His camera was rarely where his mouth was.

Vadim: 'What really interests me in the relationship between a man and a woman: their language. *Et Dieu créa la femme* was the language of a girl; *Sait-on jamais,* the language of a boy; *Le repos du guerrier* is the language of a couple.

'We have remained faithful to the mood of the novel, while attempting to develop certain marginal themes. This has given me the opportunity of illustrating one of my theories that man is abstract and woman concrete; to determine to what point man can reject the laws of society and still survive. Renaud wants to be free . . . He finds himself faced with a woman whose reactions are completely logical and moral, since they are the reactions of love. Conflict. He tries to destroy the woman. She is too sound, too healthy . . . women are always much more solid than men. This is the victory of bourgeois values over anarchy, not in the political sense but because, in an organised society, loners are losers. Individual freedom, even in a society that calls itself free, is impossible. To be totally free, it is necessary to make an abstraction of the rest of society. An unrealistic attitude—because in that event one destroys everyone else or oneself.'

Co-star steeplechases were concerned with the second female lead for once, and not the leading man. The sturdy, satanic Robert Hossein, though older than necessary, was the perfect Renaud Sarti; and he repeated much the same sado-masochistic playing in the last BB–Vadim reunion, *Don Juan 1973*. Hossein was also booked by Vadim as a riper still s/m type for his following film, his long-planned, much-touted and eventually somewhat weak-kneed Nazification of de Sade's *Le vice et la virtu* (1962).

Vadim had been courting Bardot for this particular de Sade venture since 1957; *Les bijoutiers du clair de lune* was something of a dry-run for it. He always saw BB as his Juliette, vice rewarded, opposite his then-wife, Annette Stroyberg, as Justine, virtue punished. By now, Catherine Deneuve had replaced Stroyberg as his BB Mk. III; and she would be the face and body of abused virtue. Vadim, therefore, intended another dry-run by casting Deneuve as the heroine's friend in *Guerrier*, a rôle replete with Lesbian overtones, slight but, in Vadim's hands, highly evidential. Brigitte vetoed the suggestion; she had had enough attacks on her public and private persona without sharing love-scenes, genteel, garish or otherwise, with her ex-husband's latest mistress.

The BB girlfriend, an essential rôle in most Bébé vehicles (from Isabelle Pia in *Futures Vedettes,* Isabelle Corey in *Et Dieu* through Nicole Berger in *En cas de malheur* and Ursula Kubler in *Vie privée*) went to Macha Méril—born Princess Macha Gagarin, a distant cousin of astronaut Yuri Gagarin. And to complete major casting, BB's co-defence counsel from *La vérité*, Jacqueline Porel, became her mother; and Jean-Marc Bory, one of the many men tested for that film, played her fiancé. And Scottish character actor James Robertson Justice renewed his *Doctor at Sea* friendship with Bardot, in a father-confessor rôle in yet another BB 'farewell' film.

Vadim: 'Brigitte thought if she retired and took up interior decoration—it was her aim—she would be left alone. But, of course, it would not have been so. Personally, I never thought she would retire for good; for six months maybe and then she would have become bored. As it is I'm delighted: she acts better now than she ever did. When I first discovered her, she had temperament but not talent. Now she has the talent. She will never, of course, be a great actress because she can never be anything other than herself. She has worked hard and while there are still things she doesn't do well, there are moments when she says things with a feeling that is all her own. In *Guerrier*, you see her for the first time as a woman—not as a girl. The critics loved her.'

Not all of them.

Thomas Wiseman, *Sunday Express*: '. . . Vadim's vulgarity of style, his preoccupation with plush and titillating effects, his obsessional inability to keep his camera off Miss Bardot and his Hollywood-French commercialism which permeates every scene—all combined to make [it] heavy and bloated when it should have been subtle and sparse. . . [BB] is obliged to act with those comparatively few portions of her anatomy that are not censorable. The most expressive part of her, judging from the frequency with which it is shown in close-up, is the small of her back.'

A. H. Weiler, *New York Times*: '. . . the steamy, photogenic BB again is grappling with a new *amour* as though love were going out of style. The results are graphic but hardly new or penetrating . . . She is, for the most part, a pouting child figure, which is caught in more than one revealing pose. Except for rare occasions, her reasoning does not indicate a high I.Q.'

Bournemouth Times: 'In close-up there are now a few crow's-feet under Brigitte's eyes. No matter. She is still divine and devilish . . . perkily peeling off her clothes. It's BB's new idea on coat-tail warming and hoovering which helps cuts out three minutes . . . Not without faults . . . largely in the atmospheric-ruining English dubbing and from Vadim's co-adaptation. Much of the wit is gone—though Vadim adds a superb shot of BB's lover fishing in a gold-fish bowl.'

Italian critic Ugo Astolfo: 'No thinking person can explain why a country like France seriously accepts Vadim who has the culture of a platypus, the taste of a Jayne Mansfield and no talent. The film contains enough boredom to last an entire generation. How could even the most innocent viewer believe that Bardot could, as did the mousy, frigid heroine of the book, reach the age of maturity ignorant of carnal pleasure. The scenes are disconnected and silly except where Bardot appears nude. If we had to understand what it was all about from the film, we would remain ignorant for the rest of our lives.'

Jack Bentley, *Sunday Mirror*: 'It's a sizzler that makes

previous Bardot films look like lantern slides of life in a bird sanctuary . . . It is flavoured with the expected sight of Brigitte's bare torso—only this time more so. It's what she does with it, however, that's going to give the British censor a headache. Among the mildest of the film's sequences are shots of her doing housework in the nude and full views of orgies in which she has affairs with members of both sexes. All this—in spite of Brigitte's statement after her last film that she had finished with bedroom pouts—seems to point to the fact that Vadim's powers of persuasion are still as strong as the day she became Mrs. V.'

He had a point there. After the première, Bardot retracted all comments about retirement.

Le mépris

1963

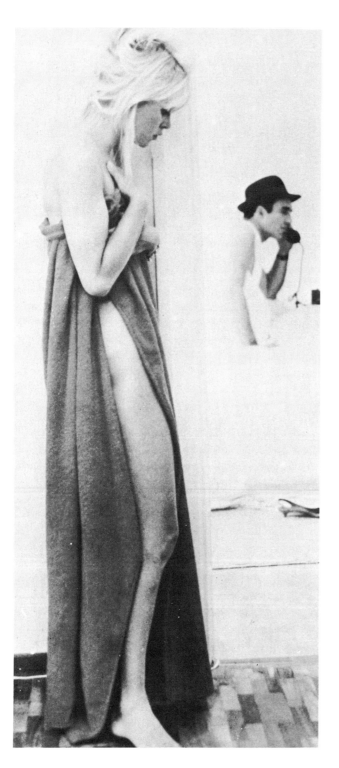

Mistrust. Franco-Italian. Les Films Concordia-Rome-Paris Film (Paris)/Compania Cinematografica Champion (Rome); 103 minutes. UK: *Contempt,* Avco Embassy Pictures, 1970; 103 minutes. US: Embassy Pictures, 1964; 103 minutes. Aka. *A Ghost At Noon.* Franscope. Technicolor.

Director: Jean-Luc Godard. *Producers:* Georges de Beauregard, Carlo Ponti. *Executive Producer:* Joseph E. Levine. *Script:* Jean-Luc Godard, *from the novel 'Il Deprezzo' by* Alberto Moravia. *Photography:* Raoul Coutard. *Editors:* Agnès Guillemot, Lila Lakshmanan. *Music:* Georges Delerue; *in Italian version,* Pierro Puccioni. *Sound:* William Sivel. *Art Director:* none credited. *Costumes:* Tanine Autre. *Production Managers:* Philippe Dussart, Carlo Lastricati. *Assistant Director:* Charles Bitsch. *Shooting:* from April 22, 1963.

CAST

Brigitte Bardot . . . . *Camille Javal*
Jack Palance . . . . *Jeremy Prokosch*
Michel Piccoli . . . . *Paul Javal*
Giorgia Moll . . . . *Francesca Vanini*
Fritz Lang . . . . *Fritz Lang*
Jean-Luc Godard . . . . *Assistant Director*
Linda Veras . . . . *Movie-clip Siren*

STORY

Alberto Moravia: 'The psychological evolution of a couple divided by misunderstanding, first hesitant, fragile, then ultimately irreparable. The wife has contempt for the husband without really understanding why. This contempt, perhaps without sound basis, brings tragic consequences.'

Jean-Luc Godard: 'A fleeting feeling of the vanity of things, all that happens and is of no importance. All this in a space well defined by the Odyssey, the sea, the Mediterranean sun, etc. It is the rapport of these concrete realities with something indeterminate.'

Paul Javal, a weak, existential figure, writer of hack 'tec fiction and one bad film script, has lost depth, belief, in himself. To provide, he maintains, security for his wife, he accepts the archetypal untenable assignment of re-writing scenes for Fritz Lang's *The Odyssey.* The Javals, though, are already too far adrift.

Surprise. 'C'est formidable,' she said. 'I've joined the new wave now!' And about time, too. Although few expected that of the available *nouvelle vague* directors, her choice would rescue a Jean-Luc Godard project. He was not all the American backers hoped. They saw the Moravia tale in their own manner. Hence the publicity-kit cartoon of the rôles.

He is losing the ability to love her. And suddenly, she, Camille, distrusts his every motive in or out of their unsatisfactory coitus. He believes she is merely jealous of producer Prokosch's secretary, Francesa, and Paul's haunted determination to trace the roots of this contempt only make him more malleable to a Prokosch thirsting after Camille. On the producer's invitation, and minus any decision by Paul, Camille visits the Capri locations where a clear parallel is drawn between Paul, Prokosch and Camille and the legend of Ulysses, Penelope and her suitors. In an impossible narrative cut, Paul sees Camille kissing Prokosch and decides to leave film, wife and island. She goes first— to her death in a car crash with the producer. Lang continues filming . . . with Godard as his assistant.

NOTES

BB: 'C'est formidable—I've joined the new wave now! Godard was really scared, you know. Me, too. He came to see me; we call each other Monsieur Godard and Mademoiselle Bardot. He watched me serve tea—he said he had to get to know me as I really am. Later, he wouldn't say anything at all.'

Godard: 'A simple film without mystery, an Aristotelian film, stripped of appearance. *Le mépris* proves in 149 shots that in the cinema, as in life, there is no secret, nothing to elucidate, merely the need to live—and to make films.'

Personally, I do not yet know which is the more exasperating—Jean-Luc Godard or the cant-coterie of

critics worshipping in non-step genuflection at his shrine, writing endless book-length reviews and indeed books, based on his notorious collection of film essays. Then, more exasperating still, he makes his first 'commercial' film—with Bardot of all actresses— and staggers the conscience and the consciousness with probably his finest work, before or since *A bout de souffle* (1959). Although, as so many of her previous directors, it is Brigitte who should share much of the triumph. Most of it, said *Le Figaro*.

His sixth feature would not have been made without BB; and the film that was made is all the more remarkable in both their careers, because of her. Any Bardot film is worth viewing more than once (well, not *any*); with *Le mépris*, this is not only advisable, it is essential. Godard has often said one must listen to the people talking in his movies. Here there is incessant conversation. (Even the credits were spoken in the style of Welles's *Magnificent Ambersons*.) There was, though, scant communication. Giorgia Moll served as interpreter for the four protagonists who, apart from the Javals, did not speak the same language; Miss Moll's pivotal rôle became absolutely nonsensical when the film was dubbed in one tongue.

The project grew out of a solo film pact between Godard and Carlo Ponti, as mystifying a pair of pactees as Godard and Bébé. The director suggested a chapter-by-chapter adaptation of the Moravia book. Ponti said yes, 'then out of fear, no'. Godard wanted Frank Sinatra and Kim Novak, 'her completely passive

side as in *Vertigo*'; Ponti preferred Loren and Mastroianni—*quelle surprise!* Impasse—until Bardot expressed interest in the script. 'Thanks to her, everything suddenly became easy and everybody was delighted,' said Godard. Particularly the main American backer, mighty Joe Levine, who was guaranteed a 'very commercial' film by Ponti.

Bardot, then, trailed into Loren country: Capri, a Moravia novel and Ponti co-producing. Shooting was completed in six weeks at Curzio Malaparte's villa, and later in Rome where Ponti added two hefty BBodyguards to his budget to combat the cyclonic *paparazzi* photographers screaming for Bardot to come out on her balcony, with or without Sami Frey. *Vie privée* had changed nothing . . .

Ponti thought the finished film more normal than Godard's other ventures; Joe Levine's New Yorkers did not. 'Very artistic but not commercial—you'll have to change it.' Godard refused, telling Ponti to take his director credit off the film and then he could do what he liked with it. The Americans would not give up and made concise demands: two new scenes, one with Bardot nude with Michel Piccoli. Godard saw some sense, apart from capitalistic, in this, and agreed. 'It was as if I had given them a Christmas present,' he said of their reaction.

'They wanted a love scene which would open the film,' he told *Le Monde,* 'and which to an extent would explain and justify the contempt. Basically, the Americans had realised they had paid more for [BB] than she was going to bring . . . The problem did not come from [BB] herself—from the very beginning, she assumed responsibility for the risks she had taken and she always backed them up. Rather, it arose from what she represented in the cinema and in the industry.' And, of course, in Paris he, she, they, were accused of selling out to the dollar and the Bébé image. *Esquire*'s review said much the same: 'Those interested in Brigitte Bardot's bottom—in Cinema-Scope and colour—will find ample reward . . . the film seizes every chance to display Miss Bardot nude and prone to suggestion.' This was overstretching the truth, even though the American print was three minutes longer than the French. (In Italy, Ponti cut his version, with re-scored music, to 87 minutes. Godard never went the 'commercial' route again.)

The director was given space to defend himself in *Le Monde:* 'The simple presence of nudity was not foreign to the film, which is not erotic. On the contrary. But it was possible, even fitting to show [BB] that way at the beginning . . . since at that moment, it is she who is undressed: she is not yet the moving, intelligent and sincere wife of the scenarist . . . who at one point in the film—through sheer coincidence— says more or less, "In life, you see women dressed, whereas on the screen you see them naked!" Under other conditions I would have refused this scene; but here, I shot it in a certain way, using certain colours . . . red lighting, then a blue . . . so that [BB] would become something else, so that she would become more unreal, more profound, more serious, than simply [BB] on a bed. I wanted to transfigure her, because the cinema can and must transfigure reality.'

Eleven years before, writing in *Cahiers du Cinéma* as Hans Lucas, Godard had commented: 'Cinema does not enquire about a woman's beauty, it only casts doubts about her heart, it records her perfidy . . . it only watches her movements.'

It would take more, much more, than a raw Brigitte Bardot on a rug and bed to get the Godardists raving, and he gave it to them—mainly when condensing all the novel's wife–husband scenes into one vast sequence lasting 30 minutes, about one-third of the film, and which, like Godard, you either love or hate.

Stanley Kauffman, in *Esquire*, called it an archetype of arrant egotism and bankrupt imagination in a director. 'Godard has nothing to say here that could not have been done in about three minutes. He has deliberately spun it out, ostensibly to recreate the languor of one kind of marital quarrel, but really (in my view) to draw approval from his clique.' Godard won that all right, from José Luis Guarner to Richard Roud, while the American distributors built up the sequence as a 35-minute love-scene, 'the longest bedroom scene ever recorded on film'.

Toby Mussman, in perhaps the finest, most objective treatise on the film, suggested it confronted us with a myriad of ambiguities, contradictions, and what

amounted ultimately to a metaphysical labyrinth of existence. 'We have ceremonies to celebrate marriages, to celebrate our found love; *Contempt* is a ceremony depicting a love lost, and therefore, a tragedy in the classical sense.'

José Luis Guarner, in *The Films of Jean-Luc Godard*: 'Conscious of [BB's] limitations, he has avoided adapting the character of Camille to the personal legend of BB and has tried the opposite course, starting from the fact that it is BB who plays Camille . . . we never forget that we are seeing BB and not Camille, but we soon grow accustomed to it; we accept her acting just as we accept that Palance "is" Prokosch and Lang "is" Lang . . . Her reactions are more physiological than rational, and she doesn't try to dominate really, like Paul, but simply to live it. It is the relative simplicity of her reactions that start the drama.'

Bosley Crowther, *New York Times,* located the major flaw in both film and book. 'Evidently, Mr. Godard has attempted to make this film communicate a sense of the alienation of individuals in this complex modern world. And he clearly directed to get a tempo that suggests irritational ennui. His characters are specific. Miss Bardot as the wife is restless errant. She moves about nervously, wears wigs, takes baths and has a penchant for sunning herself in the nude . . . But out of it all comes nothing—or very little that tells you why this wife is so contemptuous of her husband. Maybe he should be contemptuous of her.'

Godard's cameraman, the ace Raoul Coutard, was closer than most to another secret of the film. 'I'm convinced that Godard is trying to explain something to his wife [then, Anna Karina] . . . It's a sort of letter—and one that's costing . . . a million dollars.' The mail took seven years to be delivered to Britain, by which time Bardot had made another film for Godard, a walk-on—more precisely, a sit-in—during *Masculin-Féminin*, 1966.

Husband. Michel Piccoli in, sadly, his sole BB movie.

Seducer. Jack Palance in one of his few good outings.

Paparazzi

1963

French. Films du Colisé; 22 minutes. US/UK release: none on record.
Director/Script: Jacques Rozier. *Photography:* Maurice Perrimond. *Music:* Antoine Duhamel. *Commentary:* Michel Piccoli, Jean Lescot, David Ronelli.

CAST
Brigitte Bardot
Jean-Luc Godard
Michel Piccoli
—as themselves.

STORY/NOTES
As Fellini had shown the world in *La Dolce Vita* *paparazzi* are the scourge of celebrities in Rome: freelance photographers using any method permissible, and several that are not, to obtain the most exclusive, and thereby the most invaluable to sell, candid news-photos. They revel in their pejorative nickname and some have become instant-celebrities, every bit as much (and rapidly) as their unfortunate subjects. Bardot had run into them during the 1958 Venice festival, when she was with Sacha Distel and kept meeting Vadim with Stroyberg—the camera-clickers had a field day.
During May, 1961, when shooting *Le mépris* in Capri and Rome, Bardot ran into them again and had to be guarded from the dread telephoto lenses by whatever means the film unit could best supply. While Godard was making his film—and his film-within-the-film—Jacques Rozier was shooting his parallel documentary, covering the cold war hotting up between three of the most inspirational of the *paparazzi* and their quarry: Godard and Piccoli, if and where necessary, but most urgent of all, Bardot.
Neither Godard nor Bardot objected to Rozier hanging around; since his first short, *Language de l'écran,* 1947, and three more following from 1954 to 1958, he had become a favourite of the *nouvelle vague.* Godard and Truffaut both publicly supported his 1958 documentary, *Blue Jean,* and encouraged his feature début, *Adieu Philippine,* 1961. Indeed, it was widely expected that Rozier would forge ahead and join his more celebrated fans with a prolific and influential film output; instead of which he went back to television for ten years until *Du côté d'Orouet,* 1971, and *Les naufragés de l'Île de la Tortue,* 1974.
Rozier is in favour of ideological cinema. 'I want to start with the characters, not with an idea represented by the characters. They have to make reality felt . . . The cinema has the power to invent behaviour and language which can be recreated in the real world. Fashion, for instance, has been influenced by films.' By BB films, to be even more exact.
Cahiers du Cinéma called his Capri reportage a romantic story on the fringe of science-fiction; with the invisible enemies and their unsettling degree of inventiveness on the one side, and on the other, their prey: Bébé.

Tentazioni proibite

1963

Italian. Wonder Films production; Release: Indipenti Regionali, 1965. UK/US release: none on record. Totalscope. Eastman Color.
Director: F. Oswaldo Civirani.

STORY/NOTES
Two documentaries at the same time. Once Rozier had completed his study of a star besieged, Civirani moved his cameras in to delve into The Star and her *vie privée.* Such as it was with *paparazzi* and documentary crews all over her.

Une ravissante idiote

1963

Franco-Italian. Belle Rives (Paris)/Flora Film (Rome);
110 minutes. UK: *A Ravishing Idiot*, Gala Films,
1966; 99 minutes. US: No release on record.
Aka. *Adorable Idiot* and *Bewitching Scatterbrain*.
Monochrome.
Director: Edouard Molinaro. *Producer:* Michel Ardan.
Script: Edouard Molinaro, Georges and André Tabet,
from the novel by Charles Exbrayat; *dialogue,*
Georges and André Tabet. *Photography:* Andreas
Winding. *Editor:* Robert Isnardon. *Music:* Michel
Legrand. *Sound:* Robert Biart. *Art Directors:* Jean
André, Robert Clavel. *Production Manager:* Robert
Florat. *Assistant Directors:* Pierre Cosson, Antoine
Jacquet. *Stills: Paul Apoteker. Shooting:* from
October 21, 1963, Studios Billancourt.

CAST

Brigitte Bardot	*Penelope Lightfeather*
Anthony Perkins	*Harry Compton*
Grégoire Aslan	*Bagda*
Denise Provence	*Lady Barbara Dumphreys*
André Luguet	*Sir Reginald Dumphreys*
Hans Verner	*Farrington*
Charles Millot	*Balaniev*
Jean-Marc Tenberg	*Cartwright*
Hélène Dieudonne	*Mamy*
Jacques Monod	*Surgeon*
Paul Demagne	*Bank Manager*

STORY

Young Russian spy Nicholas Mukouline (alias Harry
Compton) wants simply to enjoy capitalism during
his London posting. Instead, he's thrown into
fascinating Marxist-Leninist experiences by a
grumpy, irate boss, Bagda. How, though, is Harry
going to steal the precious Avalanche File from the
home of the Admiralty's D Bureau chief, Sir Reginald
Dumphreys? Simple really. By falling head over Krem-
lin in love with that most adorable idiot, Penelope
Lightfeather, dressmaker to her ladyship. Penny will
help Harry because she is naive and pretty, oh so
pretty . . . lovely as dawn and pure as an entire nun's
convent. *And* a member of the Party . . .

NOTES

Havoc! Sophia Loren could work quite safely in London, on location and in the studios. So could Gina
Lollobrigida, Marilyn Monroe, Jayne Mansfield, even
the Burtons. BB could not. She had been in and out
often enough, peaceably enough, before. For the

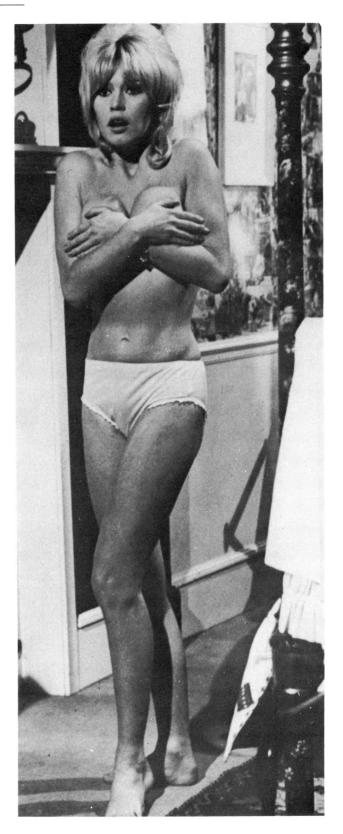

Action! Down in the forest, something stirs. It's the Franco-Italian unit scurrying around for new locations for the Perkins–Bardot embrace, after fleeing a fan-happy London town ... in a manner unheard of in film history.

Babette locations, for *Doctor at Sea,* for various publicity appearances in those early days of premières and royal film performances. By October, 1963, however, six months and one change of boyfriend after the *paparazzi* riots in Rome and Capri, she could hardly move out of Suite 506 at the Westbury Hotel. The fans outnumbered the world's Press 50–1. All hopes of London exteriors for the latest fluff comedy were aborted ... and London streets built at Billancourt, *rapidement.*

Her rarely impeccable sense of timing did not exactly help matters. Brigitte was due to start shooting at Hampstead at 2.15 pm, Friday, October 25. Naturally, a small crowd of locals and intrigued passers-by gathered as the unit made ready. News photographers arrived and waited. The words spread right across Hampstead—if not, most of London itself—that *she* was coming. When she did—it was 4 pm. The cameramen and journalists, still smarting from the chaotic Press conference the night before, wanted their slice of the action, first. Producer Michel Ardan allowed his star to pose awhile. Director Edouard Molinaro tried to commence work. The crowd, by this time, had increased to danger-point. The police stepped in and ordered the unit to disband. Molinaro yelled 'Coupez' and ran. Bardot dived into a limousine. Ardan threw up his hands in Gallic fury: 'That's that. *Fini!* We return to Paris!' And co-star Anthony Perkins looked on incredulously.

Back at the Westbury, Bébé calmly sipped Scotch and held a Press conference. 'I never thought it could happen. In Italy, yes. But not in London. I've never known anything quite like it before. It was frightening. I can never say the English are unemotional again. Perhaps, though, it's a compliment that people should crowd around me like this. But why? Why me? I don't know ... but I know I have something. Publicity? Is meaningless, *stupide!* If you have something you will get on by yourself. If not, you will always be unknown. A sex-symbol? Am I really? *Non, non,* I'd rather be known as an actress, a serious actress. No, I lie—I'd like to be known as both actress and sex-symbol. But what I want most is a *vie privée.'* And off she flew back to her Paris nest.

Some inkling of the trouble ahead—to anyone without their heads in the Thames—was seen at Bardot's circus of a Press conference on arrival in London. Once again she was late, 90 minutes late. First question, after some booing: 'Do you normally keep the Press waiting over an hour? First answer: *'Pardon?'* Apologies over, 250 reporters and cameramen (who had been denied their traditional photo-call before the writers had their chance) pushed forward as if auditioning for a re-make of *La Dolce Vita.* I know; I was caught in the thick of it and managed at one point to lead Bardot to a safe corner until producer Ardan rescued his VIP property. (Me: 'Okay luv?' BB: *'Oui, merci.'* End of exclusive interview.)

'Gee,' said Perkins, 'this could never happen in Hollywood.' Something akin to a semblance of order was later achieved and Brigitte began fending off questions being hurled thick (some, very) and fast, and mainly about the new man in her life, Bob Zaguri. 'Him, I'm not in love with him. It's just nothing.' And so it went on, silly questions, frank questions, rude questions, sensible questions; predominantly asinine questions. Yet the girl who avoided circuses as a tot because she hated crowds handled the Press with devastating ease.

Will you marry again? Never; twice is enough. *Will*

you fall in love again? I fall in love every time. *Who's your favourite man?* Tony Perkins—it would be rude to say anyone else at the moment. *Do you fall for all your leading men?* I've made 30 films. I couldn't love all of them. *Are you still going to retire?* I can't. You won't let me. *Going to Hollywood?* Too far. *From where?* From home. *Which one?* All of them. *Do you look English enough to play this English girl?* No, that's the trouble. There are many lovely English girls here. I don't look like any of them. But then the film, you see, *c'est une comédie.*

Not so much as the visit. Said her agent. Mme. Olga Horstig-Primuz: 'In ten years with Bardot, she has never had a reception like this. Something must have gone wrong.' Something did. *L'organisation*—on the part of the BB camp. Two months before, director Molinaro had warned that London could present problems. Brigitte disagreed: 'The English are much kinder to me than the Italians.' So the magical mystery BB circus arrived with only a couple of crowd-cheating ploys: vans with concealed cameras for street-shooting and a bevy of decoy-BB's to draw any sightseers in the wrong direction. Neither was used. No time!

Still, they got what they wanted. Publicity. Globally. Fan worship had never forced a film back to cover before. The film? That took three years to reach the country it had fled from, winning her first U (family-ticket) censor-rating since *Doctor at Sea,* in 1955, and being forgotten as quickly as the trouble it had caused. Even the novel's author, playwright Charles Exbrayat, was said to have been far more impressed by being elected president of the International Federation of Gastronomic Press!

Critics did not say much at all. In Paris, *Image et son* devoted six pages of varied documentation to the script and characters (the French preferring to use Perkins' Russian name, Mukouline, instead of his anglicised alias) and *Variety*'s man on the spot, Gene Moskowitz, complained that Brigitte was 'only caught in her scanties twice'. In Britain, everyone laughed in the wrong places—at the idiosyncratically French-eye view of London, where the Bobbies stopped people and asked to see their papers, among other notable gaffes. 'That apart,' said *Monthly Film Bulletin*, 'the production is no joke.' Nor it was.

Margaret Hinxman, *Daily Cinema*: 'The plot is strictly Marxian (Groucho not Karl), but the treatment is something less than sprightly and the chatter a bit over-bearing . . . but no film's ever found BB a handicap. And though she's sacrificed steamy sex for pert fun, she's still a jolly girl to have around.'

Monthly Film Bulletin tied it all up: 'Molinaro has made as little as possible of an unusually witless and improbable script and the dubbed performances do nothing to counteract irremediable boredom.'

The star needed a hit. Fast.

BBuy. All she did in London was shop with director Edouard Molinaro.

185

Marie Soleil

1964

French. Production de la Guerille; 85 minutes. UK/US release: none on record. Monochrome.
Director/Script: Antoine Bourseiller. *Photography:* Claude Beausoleil. *Editor:* Sylvie Blane. *Music:* Francis Seyrig. *Art Director:* Bernard Dayde. *Assistant Director:* Yves Boisset.

CAST
Danièle Delorme . . . . *Marie Soleil*
Jacques Charrier . . . . *Axel*
Chantal Darget . . . . *Kafka*
Michel Piccoli . . . . *Raoul*
Roger Blin. . . . . *Kark*
Daine Levrier. . . . . *Elise*
Geneviève Brunet . . . . *Polish Woman*
Christian Barbier, Michel Huilard, Brigitte Bardot.

STORY/NOTES
Another uncredited stroll-on in this French entry to the Vancouver festival of 1965. The project was the film-making début of Antoine Bourseiller, the stage actor and director with whom Bardot shared her guest sequence in Godard's *Masculin-Féminin*.

Star of the feature was Brigitte's second ex-husband, Jacques Charrier. He played an engineer from the North, visiting the Riviera and falling in love with a local girl of dubiously promiscuous habits. (Sounds familiar.) She breaks off the relationship, however, before his disillusion is total. The title-girl rôle was something of a comeback for Danièle Delorme, at whose screen marriage Bardot had played witness to in her first guest-spot in 1952.

Gene Moskowitz, *Variety,* liked it and—inevitably—did not mention the BB appearance. 'The love scenes are done with tact and maturity. Danièle Delorme is spunky, touching and vital . . . Jacques Charrier has the right rigidity and coolness for an ambitious young man caught up in a society defying patterns for the first time.' And in charge of himself once again, Charrier stayed in movies—in production.

Dear Brigitte

American. Fred Kohlmar productions/20th Century Fox; 100 minutes. UK/US release: 20th Century Fox. CinemaScope. Eastman Color.
Director/Producer: Henry Koster. *Script:* Hal Kanter, *from the novel 'Erasmus with Freckles', by* John Haase. *Photography:* Lucien Ballard. *Editor:* Marjorie Fowler. *Music:* George Dunning. *Sound:* Alfred Bruzlin, Elmer Raguse. *Art Directors:* Jack Martin Smith, Malcolm Brown. *Photographic effects:* L. B. Abbott, Emil Kosa Jr. *Assistant Director:* Fred R. Simpson.

CAST

James Stewart . . . . *Robert Leaf*
Glynis Johns . . . . *Vina Leaf*
Fabian . . . . *Kenneth*
Cindy Carol . . . . *Pandora*
Billy Mumy . . . . *Erasmus*
John Williams . . . . *Upjohn*
Jack Kruschen . . . . *Dr. Volk*
Charles Robinson . . . . *George*
Howard Freeman . . . . *Dean Sawyer*
Jane Wald . . . . *Terry*
Alice Pearce . . . . *Unemployment Clerk*
Jesse White . . . . *Argyle*
Gene O'Donnell . . . . *Lieut. Rink*
Ed Wynn . . . . *The Captain*
Orville Sherman . . . . *Von Scholgg*
Maida Severn . . . . *Schoolteacher*
Pitt Herbert . . . . *Bank Manager*
Adair Jameson . . . . *Saleslady*
Marcelle de la Brosse . . . . . *Taxi-driver*
Brigitte Bardot . . . . *Brigitte Bardot*

STORY

Erasmus Leaf is eight: a mathematical prodigy with a rare gift of a compelling obsession. He predicts horse-racing results—and he's crazy about Brigitte Bardot. When the lad's horse-sense becomes exploited by a gang, his father, Prof. Leaf, takes him off to France—where Erasmus meets Brigitte and receives

a puppy from her menagerie. Back home, the Professor smashes the con-men's game and saves the family fortune on a last throw of Erasmus's predicting gifts.

NOTES

Bond was big. The Burtons bigger. The Beatles biggest of them all. Having set America on its 45 and $33\frac{1}{3}$ rpm ear, the Liverpool mop-popheads climbed aboard Richard Lester's free-wheelin' train to Devon and took over the movies, as well. Their title was a good chapter-heading for Brigitte '64: *A Hard Day's Night*. Bardot, so the tired-out pundits ceaselessly intoned, just hadn't got it any more. She wasn't so hot. On the way out. *Passée*. Forgettable. *Forgotten!*

At 'Home'. Brigitte refused to film in Hollywood. So Tinseltown came to her, and changed the title because of her.

And yet, of all the big B's in the screenworld, it was to Bébé that Hollywood succumbed—'humbled itself,' reported an amazed *Daily Mail*.

This is Brigitte Bardot's 36th screen appearance and, cameo rôle or not, her first and only true Hollywood production. She still refused point-blank to go to Los Angeles, no two ways about that, and so the movie mountain had to come to her. And it did. Never had so many travelled so far for so little screentime. About four minutes. Charming every last one of them.

Brigitte, as always, knew exactly what she was up to. The cameo stole the film. And the title.

The movie was still named after a John Haase book, when as the London *Daily Mail* explained, 'Someone in 20th Century Fox seems to have underestimated the French sex-kitten's contempt for California. It was presumed that she would willingly fly over for two days to appear as herself. . . . Easier scripted than filmed. For nothing could persuade Bardot to go to Hollywood.'

If Film City wanted her—and it did; badly—then it would have to come to her neck of the woods. Take it or leave it. In many respects, it is strange that Fox gave in and went to shoot at Bardot's feet. Her box-office allure was plainly not all that it had once gloriously been. But without her guest appearance, their film would have remained just another mildly routine Jimmy Stewart-cum-Disneyesque crazy-family formula comedy number. Truth to tell it didn't improve that much; but the surprise BBonus was delightful.

Her message was clear enough in all the transatlantic dealings. *No* photographers on the set, apart from the necessary stills-man. *No* publicity of any kind. Her participation in the affair was to be kept secret until the film was released. (Obviously no deals had been made with the *Mail*; their man in Paris, Robin Smyth, broke the secrecy and the story.)

And so, director Henry Koster, his star James Stewart, ten-year-old freckled boy actor Billy Mumy, his chaperon, and a complete camera and technical crew, flew into Paris—with the kiddy star losing out on title-rôle status to Brigitte as a consequence. What had begun life as *Erasmus With Freckles* on the Fox lot along West Pico Boulevard in Los Angeles became—*naturellement!*—*Dear Brigitte* in a studio on the outskirts of Paris. Or rather, upon release the following year.

'Dear' Brigitte was exactly right. She didn't come

188

Gift. She received Jimmy Stewart and son Billy Mumy, said a few cute words and handed the prodigy a puppy.

cheap, no matter what it had cost Koster's unit to reach her. She won what was described as 'a Liz Taylor-size salary' of at least £1,000 an hour for a full working day. Then, there was all the work her *chauvinisme* led to: hiring a French studio; a partial crew because of the unions; a security force, as well; plus the expensive reconstruction of Brigitte's St. Tropez lounge on the set. This is where young Erasmus Leaf finally gets to meet his pen-pal idol: BB 'How nice to meet you?' says Brigitte, her first English dialogue for nine years. 'I loved your letters. . . .'

Harmless enough stuff. So much so, the *Daily Mail* felt her fans would be disappointed. 'She remains fully dressed throughout. Her neckline never plunges.' (What else, when faced with an eight-year-old fan and his professorial father?) Henry Koster found very little to object to, though. For him, and for Fox, it was a great coup. They were delighted with themselves.

The British Press hardly shared Hollywood's ebullient enthusiasm.

Leonard Mosley, *Daily Express*: 'There is a five minute sequence in which BB makes a sinuous appearance in a short silk dress that almost makes up for the banalities of the rest.'

Nina Hibben, *Daily Worker*: 'The brief appearance of [BB] may, I suppose, be considered something of a bonus . . . But even she is somehow transformed into the sweetest little lady you ever saw.'

Patrick Gibbs, *Daily Telegraph*: 'Nothing in my memory is so embarrassing as this scene—and I might say the same for the film as a whole.'

John Russell Taylor, *The Times*: '. . . plodding, arch and discursive, it muffs nearly all its chances and demonstrates conclusively just how right Mlle. Bardot has been heretofore in resisting the blandishments of Hollywood.'

No blandishments for Miss Bardot then. A fairly unique kind of tribute from Hollywood all the same— and meeting Jimmy Stewart was 'great fun'. Even so, Bébé made sure her next guest spot was in far more rarified company—Godard's. No more of a success, though.

Viva Maria

1965

Franco-Italian. Nouvelle Éditions de Films-Production Artistes Associés (Paris)/Vides (Rome); 120 minutes. UK/US: United Artists, 1966. Panavision. Eastman Color.

Director: Louis Malle. *Producers:* Oscar Dancigers, Louis Malle. *Script:* Louis Malle, Jean-Claude Carrière. *Photography:* Henri Decaë. *Colour Consultant /Costumes:* Ghislain Uhry. *Editors:* Kenout Peltier, Suzanne Barone. *Music:* Georges Delerue; *lyrics,* Louis Malle, Jean-Claude Carrière. *Sound:* José B. Carles. *Art Director:* Bernard Evein. *Special effects:* Lee Zavitz. *Production Managers:* Alain Queffeléan, Pascal Aragones. *Assistant Directors:* Volker Schloendorff, Manuel Munoz, Juan-Luis Buñuel. *Shooting:* from January 26, 1965, Cuautla, Cuernavaca, Mexico.

CAST

Brigitte Bardot . . . . *Maria II*
Jeanne Moreau . . . . *Maria I*
George Hamilton . . . . *Florès*
Grégoire von Rezzori . . . . *Diogène*
Paulette Dubost . . . . *Mme. Diogène*
Claudio Brook . . . . *Rodolfo*
Carlos Lopez Montezuma . . . . *Rodrigues*
Poldo Bendandi . . . . *Werther*
Francisco Reiguera . . . . *Father Superior*
Jonathan Eden . . . . *Juanito*
Adriana Roel . . . . *Janine*
José-Angel Espinoza . . . . *El Presidente*
Fernando Wagner . . . . *Maria II's Father*
José Luis Campa, Roberto . . . . ⎱
Campa, Eduardo Murillo, ... ⎰ *The Turcos*
José Esqueda . . . . ⎰

STORY

'San Miguel', 1903. Maria Fitzgerald O'Malley, explosive anarchist daughter of an exploded anarchist father, joins an energetic caravan of travelling French artists and partners another Maria in a singing act: Maria y Maria. Maria I turns the Irish lass into less of a tomboy, on-stage at least, and with a new-found callously sensual bloom, Maria II discovers men with a nymphomaniacal relish. Their act accidentally invents strip-tease and becomes more revolutionary still in aiding Florès's fight for the oppressed peasants. On her lover's death, Maria I continues Florès's crusade in words at least. The deeds, explosive every one, are Maria II's department. They become the heroines of the land, revered as saints in praise and prayer ('Ave Maria . . . *and* Maria'), and fall into the fortunately rusty torture chambers of the Inquisition, escape, win the final battle against the wealthy landowners—and return to Paris with their (stage) act.

NOTES

BB: '*Paf!* I'm not worried about the billing. Nor is Jeanne Moreau. The whole thing delights me. I like Jeanne very much. Perhaps you could say we are two aspects of the ideal woman. I hardly knew her until the film was proposed. Then we dined together, listened to songs together and hit it off immediately.'

Louis Malle knew they would. He had worked with both. He became Moreau's lover while rescuing her screen career from the Pigalle thriller doldrums with his first two features: *L'Ascenseur pour l'écha-faud/Lift to the Scaffold* (US: *Frantic*), 1957, and *Les amants/The Lovers,* 1958. And while directing Bardot's *Vie privée* he first noticed the marked similarities about the two women. A likeness beyond the obvious fact that most top stars are alike: both were thorough professionals, 'very, very sensitive', and both had 'terrific sex, though of a different kind'. What bound them as one for Malle, was their common horror of exposure: 'they feel always in danger, all the time they live on the edge of their nerves . . . it's frightening, really'.

Viva Maria grew out of these musings and took shape during the making of Malle's finest early film (*Le feu follet,* 1963), and thereafter into constant wooing of both celebrities into an agreement. Until he had that, he did not write a line of his premise: a big, brash, entirely frivolous, outdoor show-business film. 'I thought it would be funny to have Bardot and Moreau in the same picture. I needed the chemistry between the trained actress and the film star, the sophisticated woman and the instinctive child.'

Both stars noted the virtue of the project, particularly Bardot, her career on the wane, no peace in her so-called retirement and yet no male star capable of competing with her. They also noted all inherent dangers, particularly Moreau, the Actress in awe of the Myth; though Brigitte, also, was worried at the prospect of working with the new Anglo-French superstar, the highest paid actress in France apart from herself, and one who knew Malle better, having made three films with him to her one. In the scenario, both had fairly equal shares of the action and close-ups, but alas— Malle's big mistake—no direct conflict. On the set, well, women being women and egos being egos . . .

Almost inevitably, the start of shooting in Mexico was delayed a full week, as both stars went through nervous preamble ploys, trials of strength. Brigitte contracted laryngitis, Moreau discovered an allergy to pineapples. Indeed, she was ready to pack up and go home. Bardot, not for the first time, saved the film: she phoned Jeanne and persuaded her to stay. Brigitte was, of course, fully cognisant of how vital the production was to her career. She required a box-office triumph, and to obtain that, she needed some chemical fire to burnish her mettle upon. No man dared take her on; so it had to be a woman . . . and Moreau was the best around, having already usurped BB's position as queen of the French industry. *Time* magazine said the only thing wrong in calling Moreau the French Garbo was that 'she is so much better an actress than Garbo ever was'. Now, if Bébé could hold her own with Moreau, the darling of Malle, Brook,

Bang! Bardot plus Moreau. An explosive combination.

Bingo. Brigitte's Maria discovers men.

191

Bango. Moreau settles for George Hamilton. Bardot blooms after three men in one night: *Je suis brisée!* Moreau: *Moi, je suis plus difficile!*

Antonioni, Truffaut, Welles, Buñuel—even of Vadim—she could prove she was not yet finished.

Malle certainly understood the situation (he had, for instance, seen Bardot eat up Mastroianni). 'For Brigitte, this is the most important picture of her career. Two years ago she tried to retire—she's very rich, she need never make another film—but she just couldn't leave. Now she must make the transition from sex-symbol to . . . well, something else.'

She did so—sublimely. From sex-symbol to actress, in her element as a knockabout, tomboy comedienne. As usual, she preferred the cash to the publicity and hid, with her 'body-and-soul-guard' Bob Zaguri, from all save the French Press. Which is how Moreau won the *Time* cover-age instead. Bardot hardly cared. She had £100,000—*and* the film, wiping the floor with Moreau, stealing the movie from all Malle's *Zazie*-slapstick and politico-barbs in a script which also put the Roman Catholic Church heavily upon its own rack. Bardot v. Moreau was no set battle. Moreau's Maria I, the older, more sullen, kinkier beauty, gave as good as she got, yet proved no match for Bardot's typical hoyden, blonde child of nature, swinging from lianas with bombs betwixt her teeth and directing machine-gun battles with the poise, precision—and enthusiasm—of all her previous strip routines.

George Hamilton, Hollywood's current errant pretty-boy idol, was eclipsed by both—tied to a wooden cross, to say nothing of a wooden performance, while Moreau made love to him at one point. He had no complaints, doing very well out of the publicity and only being cast in the first place as he happened to be around on a Mexican vacation. 'I was water-ski-ing over a lake when some guy on the beach started waving at me like crazy. I was wanted on the phone. It was some girl. "How would you like to make a movie in Mexico?" she asked. No, I told her, I could do without a Mexican picture right now. "No, no, it's a French production." I don't speak French—anyway who's in it? "Bardot and Moreau——" I'll learn the language immediately . . .' He learned a lot more. (So did Malle's assistant directors: Volker Schloendorff went off to direct back home in Germany, and Buñuel's son, Juan-Luis, has since started features in France.)

In London, the film re-opened at Mayfair's Curzon cinema, redesigned since *Parisienne* and *Les bijoutiers du clair de lune* played there. In the main, critics adored Malle's bravura casting and his black comedy whirlpool of starry stunts and stints.

Alexander Walker, *Evening Standard,* expected a combination of Lady Godiva and Lady Macbeth. Instead, he relished both stars in the nimblest job of comedy-making since René Clair's fingers got stiff. 'Instead of locking them in rivalry, [Malle] has joined them arm in arm in a duet. They don't compete for the camera, but share the honours so evenly that it is impossible to prefer one to t'other . . . the only rivalry they engage in is in inciting each other to take off that little bit more of her costume. Win or lose, the spectators are the gainers . . .'

Bosley Crowther, *New York Times,* was stunned to find 'the two most formi-DA-ble female figures in French films' in the same movie: 'you must have imagined the ladies to be too serious, too dignified, too concerned about the possible damage it might have done to their valuable physiques . . . For the most part, they are amusing because of the incongruity of their being here, acting farce with almost as much insignificance as anonymous Mack Sennett bathing girls.'

Pauline Kael, *The New Yorker*: 'Frivolous, picaresque . . . lavish and visually beautiful, but the subsequent bombings and shootings weren't so funny; the central conceit involved in the pairing of Bardot and Moreau didn't work out, so the slapstick facetiousness was just left there, with nothing under it. But Bardot—not because of any *acting*—has never been more enchanting than in parts of this movie. When Malle puts her into boys' clothes, with a cap and a smudge on her cheek, she was a tomboy looking for fun: Zazie grown up but still polymorphously amoral.'

Kenneth Tynan, The *Observer,* was not amused at all. '. . . the film suffers from a central, invalidating flaw; it entirely fails to justify its basic gimmick, the casting of Dionysiac Bardot opposite Appollonian Moreau. There's hardly any plot conflict between them . . . The expected confrontation simply does not take place: the script would be much the same if the two parts were rolled into one . . . Their routines together, despite anything you may have heard to the contrary, are not anthology items but self-conscious fiascos, of the sort that you politely applaud at charity matinées. The number in which Bardot 'invents' strip-tease, is especially contrived; her costume splits quite implausibly, and the subsequent stripping is minimal and sadly unteasing . . . A big opportunity has been fumbled—the kind of opportunity, perhaps, that an artist would either not have sought or not have muffed.'

Malle and Moreau played safe, therefore; Bardot played her usual poker game—and took the pot.

Twogetherness. Ave Marie . . . *and* Maria. Said Moreau in Mexico: 'Films have never shown the kind of relationship that can exist between two women. Men like to think that women must be constantly jealous of each other, never trusting, never in rapport. That is not true, of course, certainly not today . . .'

Masculin~Féminin

1965

Franco-Swedish. Anouchka Films-Argos Films (Paris)/Svensk Filmindustri-Sandrews (Stockholm); 110 minutes. UK: *Masculine-Feminine,* Gala Films Distributors, 1967. US: Royal Films International, 1966; 103 minutes.

Director/Script: Jean-Luc Godard, *from two stories, 'La femme de Paul' and 'Le Signe' by* Guy de Maupassant. *Photography:* Willy Kurant. *Editor:* Agnès Guillemot. *Music:* Francis Lai. *Sound:* René Levert. *Production Manager:* Philippe Dussart. *Assistant Director:* Bernard Toublanc-Michel. *Shooting:* November–December, 1965, Paris.

CAST

Jean-Pierre Léaud . . . . . *Paul*
Chantal Goya . . . . *Madeleine*
Catherine-Isabelle Duport *Catherine*
Marlène Jobert . . . . . . *Elizabeth*
Michel Debord . . . . *Robert*
Birger Malmsten . . . . . }*Couple in film*
Eva Britt Strandberg . . .}
Brigitte Bardot . . . . . . }*Couple rehearsing play*
Antoine Bourseiller . . . .}
Chantal Darget . . . . . . *Woman in métro*
Elsa Leroy . . . . *Miss 19 of 'Mademoiselle Age Tendre' magazine*
Françoise Hardy . . . . . . *American's friend*

STORY

Godard: 'It's not a dissertation on youth or even an analysis . . . but it's a piece of music, a "concerto on youth" . . . I have no idea what I wanted to do. I wanted, it seems to me, to use cinema to speak of youth, or else I wanted to use youth to speak of cinema; I don't know. For me, cinema is at the same time, life. It is something that photographs life. Résumés of life, once they have been put together, are what we call a film.'

Boy meets girls: Paul and Madeleine, and her flat-mates, Elizabeth and Catherine. Boy switches jobs, commercial to journalistic, finally into market-research. Girl triumphs as a pop-singer. Boy moves in with girls. Girls come between couple. Girl becomes pregnant. Boy loses life examining a new tower-block flat for them. Girl tells police it was an accident.

NOTES

'One of the 121 French-speaking films,' ran the credit-titles, 'of which only 3 or 4 get made.' A pity this was one of them. Jean-Luc Godard failed completely in trying to comprehend, or even give free rein to, the children of Marx and Coca-Cola, of James Bond and Vietnam, in some '15 precise acts'—with Brigitte popping up in Act 10 for 85 visual and 18 audible seconds.

Godard's 11th feature, two years and five films on from *Le mépris,* began when Argos film chief, Anatole Dauman (producer of *Hiroshima mon amour*), required a double-bill companion piece for his revival of Alexandre Astruc's film of de Maupassant's *Le rideau rouge/The Crimson Curtain,* 1952. Godard proposed more de Maupassant with a film of *Le signe/The Signal,* and Dauman suggesting using *La Femme de Paul/Paul's Mistress* as well. Bargain struck, rights obtained, the project was heavily advertised at the 1965 Cannes festival: Michel Piccoli and Jean-Pierre Léaud in *La femme de Paul, avec le sourire.* That film was never made, although this script is still credited as being based upon the two stories. His aping of Bergman's *The Silence* as his Swedish film-within-the-film could be *The Signal* in miniature; but the publishers agreed that the completed film was far ('so far') from de Maupassant, that they allowed the Argos rights to be held in abeyance for later screen adaptation.

Godard himself admitted before, during and after shooting, that he did not have the slightest idea of what he wanted to do. After *Alphaville* and *Pierrot le fou,* he was dried out in the classic Fellini situation. 'I chose young people,' he told the French Press, 'because I no longer have any idea where I am from the point of view of cinema. I am in search of cinema. It seems to me that I have lost it.'

If he was, as he says, in search of youth as well, he used his own only, forcing philosophical portions of his own generation's adolescence upon a cast which he clearly had nothing in common with. Nor contact with. Of his starring foursome, he knew one alone, Jean-Pierre Léaud, Truffaut's alter-ego in *Les Quatre Centre Coups,* and Godard's own *stagiaire* in *Une femme mariée,* and his second assistant director on *Alphaville* and *Pierrot le fou.* The rest of the line-

Rehearsal. Of a rehearsal. Jean-Luc Godard (left) explains to Bardot and company how he wants their improvisation to work, among the tables of Le Zoo bar in Vincennes. For BB: 65 words!

up was unknown (mainly to Godard, even though he selected them): young singer Chantal Goya, and fledgling thespians Catherine-Isabelle Duport and, the only one of the three to have succeeded since, Marlène Jobert.

Casually, one could say crudely shot (it was Godard's first feature without Raoul Coutard on camera), the film, again, has to be listened to: conversation is even more incessant than in *Le mépris,* more monologue and interrogation than dialogue, and all convoluted, inter-related and continually punctuated by gun-shots and pin-table noises.

Bardot is heard—'Sequence 35, it doesn't come off'—before being seen. She is in Le Zoo bar at Vincennes, discussing a play, *The Prodigies* by Vauthier, with actor-director Antoine Bourseiller. (She also guested in his first film as a director, *Marie Soleil,* the year before.)

Her sequence climaxes the tenth act of Godard's little farce, where Léaud and Jobert are joined in the café by Goya. The camera remains on this trio as several voices, ultimately BB's, intrude from other tables. Jobert notices her: 'She looks exactly like Brigitte Bardot, doesn't she?' Indeed she does, with finger-combed tresses and black sweater, as she is finally seen on-screen in Scene 128, an 85-second shot of Brigitte and Bourseiller checking the pace of a script at their table. He wears a Beatle cap, drinks wine; she has tea and they both smoke.

In all, Bardot speaks 21 words on-camera, including *oui* four times, and 44 more words follow in her voice-over rendition of a speech from the play. But to what ends . . . for why . . . few people—Godard included—have ever made apparent.

Andrew Sarris, *Village Voice,* presented the theory that Bébé was recruited to assist in a parody of playwrights who seek to control every intonation of an actor's reading. 'But this sequence, like so many others, ends on a note of detached lyricism.' (Brigitte reading the passage from the play, over shots of construction sites, parks, cars, busy, brightly-lit streets and the neon glow of the Montreuil Métro station.)

Archer Winsten, *New York Post,* found a more cruel *raison d'être,* noting that in her cameo, Bardot was 'looking considerably older' than the other girlish chicks in the scene—and film. Bosley Crowther, *New York Times,* felt that the meaningless dialogue of the scene had nothing whatsoever to do with the film.

Actually, Bardot was in the film simply because, like Everest, she was there. And Godard asked her. According to the fourth youngster in the unhappy cast, Michel Debord, the small Godard team were planning *'nature'* (improvised) scenes at Le Zoo bar, when suddenly in she strolled. *'Voilà!* BB arrives,' he told *Ciné-monde.* 'We all have a little chat and she agrees to read a little piece to please Godard. Smiling, as fresh as a rosebud, *naturelle* too: otherwise with Godard it does not work! *Gentille,* laughing with everyone like a friendly novice. He makes her read a little bit of text. She chews on it for two minutes. Then *hop!* she says it marvellously all at once—one take. She plays her own rôle: BB. And, of course, because it's Godard . . . there is no great fuss.'

Any further criticism of the film is pointless; even the youth turned it down, Godard's youth having naught in common with them. Anyway, Godard's script said all that needed to be said. Paul, watching the Swedish movie in Scene II: 'This wasn't the film we dreamed of. This wasn't the total film that each of us had carried within himself, the film that we wanted to make, or more secretly, no doubt, that we wanted to love.'

No, it wasn't.

A coeur joie

1966

Heartful of Joy. Franco-British. Francos Films-Les Films de Quadrangle-Les Films Pomerue (Paris)/Kenwood Films (London); 95 minutes. UK: *Two Weeks in September,* Rank Film Distributors, 1967. US: No release on record. Franscope. Eastman Color. *Director:* Serge Bourguignon. *Producers:* Francis Cosne, Kenneth Harper. *Script:* Vahé Katcha, Pascal Jardin, Serge Bourguignon; *English adaptation,* Sean Graham. *Photography:* Edmond Séchan. *Editor:* Jean Ravel. *Music:* Michel Magne. *Sound:* William Sivel. *Art Director:* Rino Mondellini. *Costumes:* Tanine Autre. *BB make-up, hair-styles:* Odette and Jean-Pierre Berroyer. *Production Managers:* Ludmilla Goulian, Jack Hanbury. *Assistant Directors:* Georges Lussan, Ernest Morris. *Shooting:* from September 5, 1966, Studios Billancourt, locations in Scotland and London.

CAST

Brigitte Bardot	*Cécile*
Laurent Terzieff	*Vincent*
Jean Rochefort	*Philippe*
James Robertson Justice	*McClintock*
Michael Sarne	*Dickinson*
Georgina Ward	*Patricia*
Carol Lebel	*Monique*
Annie Nicolas	*Chantal*
Murray Head	*Dickinson's assistant*

STORY

Magnetic model Cécile arrives in London for a week's work—and separation from publisher-lover Philippe. Time enough to take a long, cool look at their relationship. She is chased by photographer Dickinson, a typically swinging London trendy, but is far more amused at the persistence of geologist Vincent. He has followed her from Paris where they danced, briefly, during July 14 street celebrations: now he shadows her every move, from photo set-ups at the Tower and the zoo to staying in her hotel. A caprice develops. After modelling a bridal gown, Cécile steps into Vincent's car and like honeymooners they speed off 'to the end of the world'. Scotland, actually: consummating their love in the straw-strewn idyll of a ruined castle owned by the local laird, McClintock. Love abounds; why though, they ask, is the happiness of one always at the expense of another—why is it impossible with three? Back in London's reality, Cécile has to choose. Home to Philippe or Hong Kong with Vincent. She dallies too long. Vincent goes east, love goes west.

NOTES:

BB: 'Love is the greatest illusion . . . At the instant you seem to share the whole world with someone else, you are, in fact, completely alone. It is the supreme expression of egotism. Your Graham Greene puts it well: wildly in love, one sees in the eye of the other person nothing but the reflection, enormously magnified, of yourself. This emotion, *un coup de foudre,* is ecstatic, painful, and hopeless at the same time . . . and this is the theme of this film.'

And of her life, *circa* '66. When this Franco-British co-production was first mooted by London producer Kenneth Harper and one of BB's favourite Paris producers, Francis Cosne, Brigitte's current lover, Bob Zaguri, was firmly ensconced in home and heart—in on the action, too, as an associate producer. When filming began in Scotland on September 2, 1966, however, Bardot had been Mme. (indeed, Countess) Gunther Sachs von Opel for seven weeks. Zaguri, poor fellow, never really knew what hit him!

Once again in the Bardot life it is impossible to ascertain which came first, the scenario or the reality. Zaguri was lolling around La Madrague, much akin to the similarly pedestrian boyfriend in the film, while Bardot sped off to 'the end of the world'. Las Vegas, actually: marrying the dashing Sachs, with the help of Teddy Kennedy. 'I thought she was shopping in Paris,' was Zaguri's remark when the wedding news broke. All the same, he dutifully turned up in Britain for the locations; each time Sachs appeared on the set, Zaguri disappeared. Enmity was strong . . . and not just between the vanquished and the victor.

Sachs was not around that often, providing the first chinks in the seven-week-old marriage by his jet-setter's indifference to the consolatory needs of any working actress, much less a sex-symbol in need of constant, consistent and close reassurance. For the first time in her life, therefore, Brigitte, although just wed, had no man in tow when she began filming; Sachs preferred shooting of a more literal nature in Germany. He popped over during London locations, usually found golf more interesting and soon jetted off in search of pursuits more satisfying than applauding a working bride. The honeymoon was over.

Bardot often says, 'When I work, I work. When I love, I love.' She managed both in London, in fitful order, having a determined fling with British co-star Mike Sarne. He played the film's *Blow Up*-style fashion photographer, shouting orders to his models

Lovers. BB wanted Terzieff in *Viva Maria*; this time she won.

197

Cover-girl. Modelling (again), as a bride (again) in the continuing story of her Agnes/Chouchou/Brigitte/Babette/Virginie/Sophie/and now Cécile mannequin persona. In short: half-hearted Bébé. With matching direction á la sauce Bourguignon.

('Hate me a little!') and soon reporting on his (official) love scenes with Brigitte in Bardotese: 'When we kiss, we kiss.' As producer Harper recalls, the couple soon went underground for a few days: 'We had a bit of a job prising them out, actually.'

In comparison, the screen affair, another of her cover-girl romances, was a resounding flop long before it reached cinemas; indeed, it had looked a loser from the outset. Brigitte declared that the project, like all movies, was a collective enterprise. 'We all took risks together and together we assumed the collective consequences.' The truth of these consequences was that Bébé had to shoulder the major blame. She had found the story, from the work of a new *copain,* Franco-Lebanese writer Vahe Kahé, and she also chose the director, Serge Bourguignon.

A freak Oscar-winner in 1962 for his first feature, *Les Dimanches de ville d'Avray / Sundays and Cybele,* and a total disaster with his Hollywood début, *The Reward,* 1965, Bourguignon attempted to assuage his considerably bruised ego with rash over-confidence where controlling Bardot was concerned. 'There is nothing she won't do for me,' he bragged to the producers. She heard all; hence, he could not have been more wrong. It was obvious to everyone on the inside that, following preliminary script meetings, Bardot had scant respect for her director, which is how they blew the movie before a shot was fired in collective anger. Working in English, as well as French, did not please them, either. It was a very talky film—French films about love usually are—and the British end of the

co-production insisted on dual versions of every dialogue scene. 'We didn't want the English version to be just another dubbed or sub-titled film, but a film in English,' Kenneth Harper told *Showtime.* 'Carefully scripted English at that. Not merely a translation. Shooting the film this way added only a week or so to the schedule. And not very much to the cost. But we end up with two films for 75 per cent less than the average cost of two films.' Sound reasoning; but the sound was pretty terrible. What the producers finished up with were two equally banal movies, with scant appeal to anyone beyond fans of women's magazine fiction, few of whom would go to see a Bardot film at any price.

Bardot's co-star, Laurent Terzieff, was another let-down. He is a more fervent performer on stage, but she wanted him and got him. He had tested in 1960 for the lead in *La Vérité*; BB, insisting then upon Trintignant, turned him down flat. In 1965, she asked Terzieff to join her in *Viva Maria*: he turned her down flat. This time, producer Cosne persuaded him to sign; he need not have bothered. In fact, both producers should have bothered more about their film than their leading lady. Minus her approval-stipulations of director, co-star and scenario, the production could have remained no less a typical BB venture, light, airy, an *amour de fou,* instead of the badly made potage of sauce Bourguignon: trendy tragedy and wearisome beyond redemption. (In English anyway; apparently the French language version holds together rather better.)

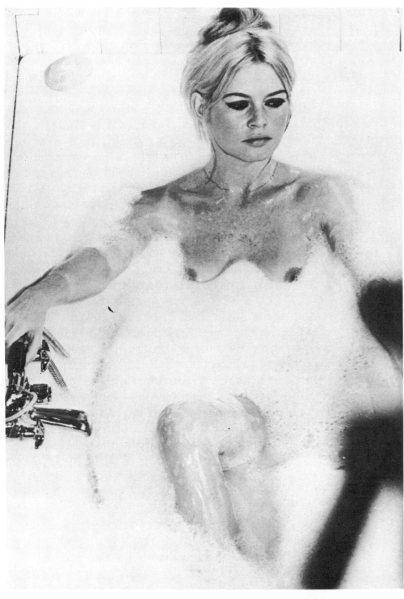

199

Francis Cosne defended Bardot manfully. 'She likes me. We work well together and there is a mutual trust between us. She's not just a beautiful girl but a good actress, too. I've found she throws fewer tantrums than many lesser-known actresses in France. She's always willing to co-operate.' (He has, all the same, never made another film with her.)

Trust, co-operation, interest—everything!—flew out of the window on this lamentable production. What else when the leading lady is summarily deserted by a new husband exactly when she required what com-fort he could bring her . . . picks up with a new lover, a young man of calculated indifference, who felt so much out of his depth when joining her in Paris, that he made her move in with him in London . . . plus a discarded lover mooning around on the sidelines still wondering what befell him exactly, and why. As with *Vie privée,* the BBetter story was happening off-camera, and Bourguignon was out to lunch.

It would also be true to say that Brigitte was nervous of the film, her first full-length production after two many cameos and a lengthy lay-off. She had originally found the script amusing; Bourguignon, who said the BB label lacked dignity, obviously felt the opposite. She explained her rôle: 'I'm a cover-girl, living in Paris with my lover. The affair has become banal, day-by-day, I might as well be married.' In Vahe Kahel's story, the lovers ran from Paris to Amsterdam; BB suggested Scotland instead. 'For us French, England is a bit humdrum, but Scotland, our old ally against the English, the lost causes of Prince Charles le Beau, is like love—the lands of dream unrealised.'

The setting also provided a third appearance in a Bardot film for the popular Scots character actor, James Robertson Justice. He required little assistance with make-up or costume for his kilted laird, a nature-lover using his estates as a sanctuary for birds (and the film's lovers) and his broken-down old castle as a centre for tape-recording bird sounds. Although by now well used to the vagaries of BB scripts, Justice seemed embarrassed, as well he might, when having to apologise to the screen-lovers for his tape equipment being activated during their love-play. His recorders were set off by a certain high-pitched frequency noise emitted by birds, 'and it would appear, madame, that you made exactly the same noise'!

The film had no conclusive ending; Brigitte says this abruptness was planned. 'The audience must decide what I do next. Perhaps I marry my lover and spend my life with the dirty dishes, tortured by memories of Scotland. Perhaps I find someone else. To marry while blindly in love is dangerous; to marry without it maybe fatal. It's a choice everyone must make for themselves.' Then she added: 'Of course, love has nothing to do with marriage or children or washing the dishes.' Not if your name is Brigitte Bardot.

The name seemed fading in allure for all that. Locations were accomplished in London with none of the *Ravissante idiote* troubles; a two-hour Press reception helped, not that the Press left her alone. The production's publicity man, Bob Herrington, told of one columnist trying hard for an interview—but not quite hard enough. He sent up a bunch of roses with a note asking Brigitte to see him at her hotel. The maid returned with a negative reply. Back went another note: No interview, no flowers. He left the hotel with an empty notebook—and his bouquet.

Tub. The high-point in any Bardot picture is generally a fond relationship to her bath-towel. Which, naturally, would mean a bath-scene first . . . or sometimes, at least.

Rub. As with Delon, the planned chemistry did not always work. Bébé and Terzieff looked good, although Laurent appeared uncomfortable. With reason. The risible script.

Rank released the film in Britain with a bright poster, soiled by a tired sales slogan: 'Sulky, sexy, pouting and provocative—it's the one and only Bardot.' Rank refused a Press screening, however; critics saw it in their own time, one reason why their attack was so vociferous.

Monthly Film Bulletin: 'Supremely ludicrous amalgam of all the clichés of women's magazine fiction, flashily photographed and directed . . . at a snail's pace in style that matches the insanities of the plot . . . and a whole succession of close-ups of Bardot in various stages of undress including one of her in a bubble bath opining that "happiness is just a drop of water". It might almost be a parody. But a film which signals a passionate love scene on a bed of straw in a ruined castle by a cut to waves pounding on a beach is obviously in deadly earnest.'

Ian Christie, *Daily Express*: '. . . the affair between Bardot and Laurent Terzieff that occupies the entire film is about as exciting as the relationship of a Darby and Joan . . . They talk a lot about love and very tedious it is too, for the script is hardly worth the paper it's badly written on.'

Patrick Gibbs, *Daily Telegraph*: '. . . it's not really as bad as all that . . . but the pace is so slow that commonsense keeps cranking in to tell us that sleeping in the nude in the North is more likely to result in pneumonia than ecstasy: and the film which started off as merry ends up as merely silly.'

Histoires extraordinaires

('William Wilson' sketch)

1967

Tales of Mystery and Imagination. Franco-Italian. Les Films Marceau-Cocinor (Paris)/PEA (Rome); 120 minutes. UK: *Tales of Mystery,* Cinecenta Film Distributors, 1973; 121 minutes. US: *Spirits of the Dead,* American International Pictures, 1969, 118 minutes. Wide screen. Eastman Color.
Director: Louis Malle. *Script:* Malle, Daniel Boulanger, *from the story by* Edgar Allan Poe. *Photography:* Tonino Delli Colli. *Editor:* Franco Arcalli, Suzanne Baron. *Music:* Diego Masson. *Art Director:* Ghislain Uhry. *Special effects:* Joseph Natanson. *Assistant Director:* Michel Clément. (Other sketches: *Metzengerstein*—director, Roger Vadim; script, Vadim, Pascal Cousin, Daniel Boulanger; photography, Claude Renoir; starring Jane Fonda, Peter Fonda, Françoise Prévost, James Robertson Justice, Philippe Lemaire, Carla Marlier. *Don't Bet Heads*—director/script, Fédérico Fellini; photography, Guiseppe Rotunno; starring Terence Stamp, Salvo Randone, Franrizio Angeli, Ernesto Colli, Marina Yaru, Anna Tonietti, Aleardo Ward, Paul Cooper.) *Shooting:* from March 20, 1967, Rome.

SKETCH CAST

Alain Delon . . . . *William Wilson*
Brigitte Bardot . . . . *Giuseppina*
Katia Christina, Umberto d'Orsi, Danièle Vargas, Renzo Palmer.

STORY

Nineteenth-century Italy. A young Austrian army officer rushes into a church and forces a priest to hear his weird confession. Throughout his life, all his most evil desires have been thwarted by the appearance of a stranger who is his exact image: his *doppelgänger*. Finally, this twin exposes the officer's cheating tactics at cards with a strangely hedonistic and masochistic woman. In a fit of rage, the officer murders the stranger: his conscience, of course. Unable to bear the truth, he jumps from the church tower into emptiness.

NOTES

BB: 'Sacha Guitry said that certain scenes are sometimes as valuable as a principal part. Let's hope that it will be like that in my sequence.'
It was. This second sketch-teaming of Bardot and Delon contained all the fire lacking in their more romantic work in *Les amours célèbres*; mainly because Delon is best when showing a malevolent streak—and ego-wise, he was playing with himself as first and Bardot as second co-star.
Unfortunately, the film has rarely been seen anywhere, winning limited releases only (six years after production in Britain), despite being a fairly lavish production of Fellini, Vadim and Malle *v.* Poe. Final score: Fellini won. Malle won, too. Vadim and Poe: nil.
Far more comfortable (and comforted) than in Scotland and England, Bardot had Sachs by her side and deep into production thoughts of his own. They rented the villa recently used by the Burtons during *The Taming of the Shrew,* along the Appian Way—just an appian stance away from the villa taken by Vadim and his third wife, Jane Fonda, who fared less well in her sketch than Bardot in hers. (Then, Brigitte did not have a brother for Malle to force her into love situations with, the way Vadim enjoyed spinning Jane and Peter Fonda incestuously together.)

Gene Moskowitz, *Variety*: 'Alain Delon has the callow but underlying viciousness for the part while Brigitte Bardot is used as a headstrong woman who engages in a card game with him to be won and used for sadistic rather than carnal pleasures. Though done with solid academic assurance, it rarely achieves insight into living *sans* a conscience or transcends its colourful but rote limning of this sombre parable of Poe.'

John Mahoney, *Hollywood Reporter*: 'The best accomplished segment of the trilogy is Louis Malle's . . . Richly Teutonic in style, it still provokes unintended laughter after the third or fourth time the evil Delon is squelched in the act by the appearance of the saintly Delon. The ultimate destination of Delon's embodied schizophrenia is never in doubt, though he and Malle sustain interest and movement in the tale. Brigitte Bardot, her beauty marred by a black straw wig, is very good as his adversary in a prolonged and taunting hand of cards.'

Success. Making BB/Delon chemicals fuse: Louis Malle.

Shalako

1968

British. Kingston Films/Dimitri de Grunwald Productions; Warner-Pathé distribution, 1969; 113 minutes. US: Cinerama Releasing Corporation, 1968. Franscope. Technicolor.
Director: Edward Dmytryk. *Producer:* Euan Lloyd. *Associate Producer:* Hal Mason. *Script:* J. J. Griffith, Hal Hopper, Scot Finch, *from the novel by* Louis l'Amour. *Photography:* Ted Moore; *second unit,* John Cabrera. *Editor:* Bill Blunden. *Music:* Robert Farnon; *title song lyrics,* Jim Dale. *Sound:* Keith Palmer. *Art Director:* Herbert Smith. *Production Manager:* Ronnie Bear. *Assistant Directors:* Peter Price, Joe Ochoa. *Shooting:* from January, 1968, Almeria, Spain.

Twogether again. Bébé and Irish cowboy Stephen Boyd.

CAST

Sean Connery . . . . *Shalako*
Brigitte Bardot . . . . *Countess Irina Lazaar*
Stephen Boyd . . . . *Bosky Fulton*
Jack Hawkins . . . . *Sir Charles Daggett*
Peter van Eyck . . . . *Baron von Hallstatt*
Honor Blackman . . . . *Lady Daggett*
Woody Strode . . . . *Chato*
Eric Sykes . . . . *Mako*
Alexander Knox . . . . *Henry Clarke*
Valérie French . . . . *Elèna Clarke*
Julian Mateos . . . . *Rojas*
Donald Barry . . . . *Buffalo*
Rodd Redwing . . . . *Chato's father*
Chief Elmer Smith . . . . . *Loco*
Hans De Vries . . . . *Hans*
Walter Brown . . . . *Peter Wells*
Charles Stalnaker . . . . . . *Marker*
Bob Cunningham . . . . . . *Luther*

STORY

New Mexico, 1880. The latest ritzy group of European aristocracy on safari in the West is deliberately led into Apache country by their iniquitous trail-boss, Bosky Fulton, seeking easy pickings from their jewels and gold plate. Lone cowhand Shalako saves them from attack, and in particular he rescues fiery blonde Countess Irina Lazaar. He makes a deal with the local tribal chief, promising to lead the safari out of Indian territory by sun-up. The aristos refuse to budge until an Apache ambush kills off some of their number, Fulton runs away with Lady Daggett, and the survivors scale mountains to prepare for a last stand on a high plateau. Once again, it's the cowboy with the Apache name (He Who Brings Rain) who saves them, engaging the Apache chief's son in ritualistic combat. The group leaves, minus Irina. Instead of joining her fiancé, Baron von Hallstatt, her path follows on that of the man called Shalako.

NOTES

BB: 'I have never made a cowboy picture. I like to try something new.' Which puts paid to the idea that *Viva Maria* was a western. Besides, it was time she made a full feature again and saved her box-office

rating, which was low and getting lower. There was, however, no lack of offers if and when she felt like filming. As the producer surmised, if she did not create queues, she was an invaluable publicity asset. Bardot could not make a film—especially one co-starring Sean Connery out of Bondage for once—without making front-page news and magazine covers galore. Her fee, £350,000, half down, the rest over three years plus 15 per cent of the profits, equalled several million dollars' worth of publicity to Euan Lloyd. Quite a few problems as well.

In 1966, Lloyd's idea had been Henry Fonda and Senta Berger; Fonda knew his name would not be readily bankable and was willing to withdraw. Connery became available when refusing the sixth 007 movie, *On Her Majesty's Secret Service*. Lloyd felt Bardot was the natural female for Connery—the world saw it as Bond and BB. And Bond producer Harry Saltzman wanted her opposite his makeshift new superspy, George Lazenby. She fell for the Western and Connery; he, too, for all his Scots reticence of comment which rarely went beyond 'Bloody marvellous!' Hardly the description for the ensuing shooting in dusty Almeria . . .

Brigitte arrived with her entourage—'my bon-bons, because we stick together like candy'. Gunther Sachs

Encounter. The casting made sense. Sean Connery, free for a while of inhuman Bondage, and Bardot, the acknowledged blueprint for each and every Ian Fleming heroine. (Just check his girl portraits: androgynous, polymorphic, perverse, every last one.) Hollywood film-maker Edward Dmytryk, however, was stuck with an odd mission. Get them to get it on—but please remember, it's for family audiences...!

was a notable absentee from the group, and as with *A cœur joie* Bardot began living it up, causing nervous headaches for all and sundry, producer Lloyd and publicity man Kenneth Green in particular. Said Brigitte: 'A movie is quite another affair, like a pregnancy, except that instead of nine months it usually lasts only three. In both cases, that's the end of all freedom.' Not her way.

She complained about Gunther to the gathering Press hordes, and proceeded to play the field, becomingly annoyed—bitterly—when linked yet again with co-star Stephen Boyd. An odd cause of complaint, even to insist upon denial statements; Boyd, or his Hollywood publicity man, had been steadily issuing false items about the couple's 'togetherness' in Hollywood gossip columns for the last five years.

Watching her activities on the fraught locations Kenneth Green told writer Peter Evans: 'She suddenly seemed to become obsessed with the idea of proving that she was ageless, a perennial teenager who wanted to show that she could go dancing, singing and whooping it up all night.' As far as her country's teens were concerned, she succeeded. In a survey carried out around this time, French 16-year-olds—four when *Et Dieu créa la femme* opened—voted Bardot as their ideal woman. There were those on the *Shalako* strength who felt otherwise. Everyone handled her with kid-gloves, though, except for the Hollywood cowboy stunt-riders, who often taunted her unmercifully.

The screen was not exactly scorched by Connery and Bardot, for reasons more concerned with winning a family rating for the Western, than either Bardot's lazy English or off-set fatigue. The big clinch came in Scene 664 as the hero came across a primly topless Countess Bardot washing her chemise in a pool of water and when, as the synopsis phrased it, 'the sympathy and understanding between Irina and Shalako now builds steadily into love, as she realised the strength and courage of the man whose help they rejected . . .'

Still-cameras of the world clicked in unison as Bardot dropped her rehearsal blanket, revealing more than she did on the screen. And BB was still in superb shape. This surely was how the West was won! Connery moved in on the countess-turned-washerwoman. Even faced with his co-star's ample and unfettered charms, he remained a true man of the West and said nothing: actions speaking louder than words. Quite a coup for Britain's first Western (unless one really rates Kenneth More and Jayne Mansfield in *The Sheriff of Fractured Jaw*).

The tragedy about *Shalako* was that it dealt with a completely new factor in Western history—the chic safari parties from Europe. All four scriptwriters bypassed the potential of such a premise, to make a saddle-sore scenario with about as much impact as a Johnny Mack Brown serial. For 19th-century aristocrats of Europe, Texas and Mexico represented the lasting hunting ground. Buffalo and Indians were the target, and the parties dressed for dinner and brought their own servants, cooks, and even furniture. A certain Sir St. George-Gore, for example, led such a safari with six wagons, 21 horses, 12 yoke of cattle, 112 horse, 14 dogs and 40 servants. Princes, dukes, barons, viscounts and their ladies, plus celebrities of

the day—Rudyard Kipling and Oscar Wilde among them—joined the sport. Invariably Buffalo Bill Cody acted as guide. The film's publicity matter supplied all this background; the film, alas, had none of it. As Penelope Mortimer hoped in the *Observer*: 'Perhaps somebody will take it up and make the hilarious satire that it ought to be.'

Cecil Wilson, *Daily Mail*: 'You have not really lived until you have seen [BB] in this epic British answer to the American Western, wearing an immaculate top-hatted riding habit and galloping across the Spanish mountains into Sean Connery's arms.'

Renata Adler, *New York Times*: 'Miss Bardot clearly has a lovely time speaking inflected English in an American Western, and Sean Connery's obviously relieved to be, and very strong, outside James Bond.'

Dilys Powell, *Sunday Times*: 'A United Nationed Western, perhaps, sometimes delivered in a kind of Esperanto: "Doz eet conn-tin wottair?" asks Brigitte Bardot, offered a bit of cactus. Mr. Connery may be a fugitive from James Bond country, but he still knows, as Miss Bardot remarks, a lot about everything . . . Perhaps one should not complain of the constancy

of Miss Bardot's eye-shadow during a trudge across New Mexico or the scaling of a cliff . . . Undeterred by the chill of night in the Mountains, she offers the statutory view of her pleasing torso, and thus supplies one of the few moments during which I was able to forget the constant, sometimes deafening, musical accompaniment.'

Alexander Walker, *Evening Standard*: 'Alas, its aim is never again as sure as Bardot's in the opening scene . . . Bardot acts as if she could do with a week's sleep. And in spite of Connery's randy memories about washing down his squaw women, not much happens between them when she does an incredibly coy strip to the waist at the old water-hole. Miss Blackman has far more sex-appeal.'

Bardot used to strip, and please, for far better motivation. Although most of Scene 664 seemed to have been staged for the magazine cameras and not Ted Moore's. She was cast for her publicity value only. Euan Lloyd admitted it and, no fool she, Bardot knew it. She merely took the money and laughed all the way to the *banque*. She had made enough to take another year off.

Go West. And that's exactly where the script went, a sad waste of an intriguing slice of little-known Western history—the aristocratic safaris of the 1880s. Bébé loved the idea of a cowboy movie, though enjoying herself more off the set than on, surrounded by her entourage of *bon-bons*—'we stick together like candy'—including her double, Monique.

Les femmes

1969

The Women. Franco-Italian. Lira Films (Paris)/Ascot Cineraid (Rome); 90 minutes. US/UK release: none on record. Eastman Color.
Director: Jean Aurel. *Executive Producer:* Raymond Danon. *Script:* Jean Aurel, Cécil Saint-Laurent; *dialogue,* Ann-Marie Coteret. *Music:* Luis Fuentes Jr. *Sound:* Jean Petit. *Art Director:* Armand Labussière. *Production Manager:* Ralph Baum. *Assistant Director:* Meyer Berreby. *Shooting:* from March 24, 1969, Paris, Versailles.

BBoy. Patrick Gilles, the first lover to win a film rôle.

CAST

Brigitte Bardot . . . . *Clara*
Maurice Ronet . . . . *Jérôme*
Tanya Lopert . . . . *Louise*
Patrick Gilles . . . . *Raphaël*
Jean-Pierre Marielle . . . . *Editor*
Christina Holm . . . . *Marianne*
Annie Duperey . . . . *Hélène*
Carole Lebel . . . . *Gertrude*
Honore Bostel . . . . *Mayor*
Maurice Bernard . . . . *Géo*
Guy Michel . . . . *Wagon-lits Inspector*

STORY

Clara is a secretary, proud, young, carried away by sensual emotions, and fed up with fiancé Raphaël; he does not love her as much as she feels he should. Jérôme is a Prix Goncourt-winning writer, *un homme à femmes,* yielding easily to the temptations of all women. He needs peace and quiet to write his new book and advertises for *une secrétaire particulière.* Clara takes the job, though appalled at the contract: she must be equally ready to work by day or night and sleep with him if he feels so inclined. Soon after Raphaël takes her to the train. Jérôme is very much inclined. Sexual obligations alternate with the dictation of his amorous memoirs. A strange intimacy grows between the couple, enlivened by Clara's reactions to his bedroom ventures which comprise an initiation in love rather than another rake's progress. In her dual capacity as servant and mistress, Clara becomes aggressively insolent and eliminates her two main rivals, Hélène and Marianne. Jérôme boasts he has never met two women alike; in Clara he meets his match, a woman to dominate him and make him suffer. Yet he does not love her. He loves women in general. He is sure she loves him, perhaps the first woman genuinely to love him. He's right—and it's for this reason she runs away. She loves him too much not to. Jérôme discovers a new emotion; despair. But the book has to be finished. The new secretary is Livia. Pretty, too.

NOTES

BB: 'I would do exactly the same in real life. I would

AOK. After 41 films, three husbands and innumerable lovers in 17 years, Brigitte Bardot at 35—still looking good.

leave with good grace, even at the very summit of our love, before love began to tarnish. This is the only victory one can have in love—knowing when to quit. It's a principle I have followed all my life. Painful? Of course! But that's what love is—uncomfortable and beautiful at the same time.'

Once more, the scenario matched (which is better than aping) BB, or her view of her image, to the extent that another new lover, young Patrick Gilles, played the rôle of the fiancé discarded at the beginning of the film—as Gilles himself was for Christian Kalt before the year was out.

This 43rd assignment meant a complete return to normal French features, parochial only in as much as *Les femmes* hardly travelled to other than French-speaking territories; six years later it has still to be seen in Britain or America. The BBox-office bubble had definitely burst. Though far from her best work, of course, this happens to be an intriguing slice of Bardolatry, containing perhaps more home truths about its lady than many of her more triumphant scripts.

Her co-star was Maurice Ronet, Louis Malle's suicide from *Le feu follet,* and then riding particularly high at the home box-office. His part was described in

Team. *Les hommes* for *Les femmes,* left to right: producer Raymond Danon, co-star Maurice Ronet, director Jean Aurel.

French publicity as being a Don Juan '69. Vadim cast them together again later with Ronet as the victim of Bardot's *Don Juan 1973.*

Les femmes was Bébé's debt to the 44-year-old director Jean Aurel—one of the *Une Parisienne* script-writers and the man she unceremoniously sacked from the Vadim-rescued *La bride sur le cou.* Aurel had since come of age with *L'Amiel* with Anna Karina, and *Manon '70* which features Vadim's Bardot Mk. III, Catherine Deneuve, with one of BB's cast-offs Sami Frey.

French critics hardly bothered with the piece at all. Mediocre they dubbed it unanimously, although as *Cinéma 69* added, it was somewhat satisfying mediocrity: a sinking film with ridiculous dialogue, pretentious voices and systematically ugly photography, saved only by Annie Duperrey as Ronet's Hélène. 'Towards the end of the film [BB] invites us to verify that her famous profile, while sunbathing, as in *Et Dieu créa la femme,* has not grown old. Plentifully reassured you can forget the rest.'

Together with his usual script collaborator, Cécil Saint-Laurent, Jean Aurel took as his theme one of the thoughts of Balzac: 'Ill luck to him who tells all in Love as in the Arts.' Or indeed, ill-luck to her . . . and Bardot took the philosophy with a pinch of salt and talked, during shooting, most fully about love, sex and screen eroticism, since she opened the doors of freedom in 1956.

'I'm always faithful while I am in love. When I cease to love and even before that, I quit, because it would not be at all nice to deceive someone you love. My own moral code puts love above duty. No one will ever persuade me that one must love just for the sake of duty.'

As for eroticism, yes, she had read erotic literature, everything from Arentino to the Marquis de Sade.

'I hope one day our erotic films will be as good as the books. I think it calls for considerable talent, to make good erotic films. It is not enough just for the people who make them and act in them to live in a country where there are no sexual taboos and where you are allowed to portray physical love on the screen. I don't think the Swedes are necessarily good at sex films, just because they have taken the mystery out of sex. Sex needs a little mystery. When all the taboos have been lifted they will no longer have an appeal.'

She maintained she had rarely been censored—in France. 'That's because the scenes in which I wore very little were never indecent or shocking. They were just nice to look at. Eroticism is used and abused. For a long time no one dared. Now everybody dares and they, of course, go too far. But on the whole, it's for the good. Perhaps it will help to establish common sense and balance in our love problems. Me? I just happened to come in at the moment when these things were in the air as it were, and people wanted to ventilate things a bit. Vadim, who I'd already known for some time [sic], helped me with this. But it's wrong to say he created me. Believe me, I was already there! I existed and I existed as I had already decided to exist. That is, in a way of life I had made up my mind to follow . . . after thinking a lot about it. One never really gets rid of one's upbringing and education; one only gets over it. I don't regret any of the things that remain from my upbringing. They come in useful.'

Finally, she denied, for the umpteenth time, that she could ever be considered (or any more) a sex-symbol. 'Oh, I would say I symbolise purity rather. My films are mother's milk compared with what is shown on the screen today.' And in the face of Russ Meyer, American King of Nudie Movies, and his ilk, that milk was suddenly going sour around the world.

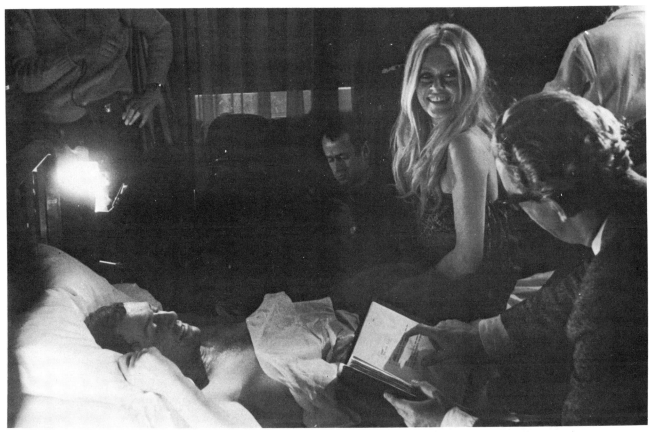

Style. 'She is one of those rare people who are able to achieve almost physical impact upon audiences through the medium of camera and screen. In her case, the impact is especially disturbing because even at her silliest, she can force spectators to rediscover in themselves those subterranean facets of human character which humans spend a great deal of their time denying. No one denies these facts more vigorously than her critics—professional and amateur, male and female—who stolidly imply that she leaves them unmoved ... Actually, Brigitte seems to be able with only a few insolent motions of her body—or with one flat and sullen stare—to provoke the embarrassment of the most basic emotions: envy, lust, guilt or anger.'—Paul O'Neil, *Life* magazine.

L'ours et la poupée

1970

The Bear and the Doll. French. Parc Film/Mag Bodard/Marianne Productions; Paramount release in France; 90 minutes. UK: no release on record. US: *The Bear and the Doll,* Paramount, 1971. Eastman Color.

Director: Michel Deville. *Producer:* Mag Bodard. *Script:* Nina Campaneez, Michel Deville; *adaptation, dialogue,* Nina Companeez. *Photography:* Claude Lecomte. *Editor:* Nina Companeez. *Music:* Rossini, Eddie Vartan. *Sound:* André Hervé. *Art Director:* Claude Pignot. *Costumes:* Gitt Magrini. *Hair-styles:* Jean-Pierre Berroyer. *Production Manager:* Philippe Dussart. *Assistant Directors:* Jean Lefebvre, Alain Tourroi. *Shooting:* from May 29 to August 6, 1969, Paris and Chevance.

CAST

Brigitte Bardot	*Félicia*
Jean-Pierre Cassel	*Gaspard*
Daniel Céccaldi	*Ivan*
Xavier Gélin	*Réginald*
Georges Claisse	*Stephane*
Patrick Gilles	*Titus*
Olivier Stroh	*Arthur*
Patricia Darmon	*Mariette*
Sabine Haudepin	*Julie*
Valérie Stroh	*Charlotte*
Sally	*The dog*
Nina Companeez	*Woman in white*

STORY

He is a 'cellist with a radio orchestra, absent-minded, uncouth, caring only for music—Rossini, mainly—flowers, living in the country with his little family, one son, three nieces and a dog. She is a snob from an ultra-snobbish side of Paris, beautiful, flirtatious, spoilt, insufferable, irresistible, very rich, very fashion-conscious and very, *very* surrounded by hangers-on she constantly maltreats. One fine day (actually, it's raining), she drives off in her Rolls to collect a divorce, her second—as he drives off in his homely little *deux-chevaux*. At a crossroads near Bougival, they meet. Which is to say, they crash. And it's the Rolls which cracks up. Thus begins the confrontation of two sexes, two worlds: of the Bear and the Doll. They have abso-

lutely nothing in common except instant dislike. So much so they just have to meet again in order to tell each other. Unused to resistance to her charms, she is excited by the challenge of captivating this grumpy old bear. They're both obstinate, but the age-old game goes on. The doll and her city, her husband, smart friends, split-level apartment and Rolls *vs.* the Bear and his kids, dog, flowers, music—Rossini, mainly—his country home and little *deux-chevaux*.

NOTES

So near and yet . . . Here was France attempting to rekindle some of the comedy sophistication of Holly-wood past, a mite too early for the sex 'n' violence era, as the glossy triumph of *A Touch of Class* showed in 1973. Once more though—despite never being bought for Britain—a most creditable effort, from a trio of ultra-polished film-makers.

Producer Mag Bodard's team of director Michel Deville and his co-writer and editor Nina Companeez had made some of the most sophisticated and certainly most visually stunning movies in all France. Grim realism was not for them, their screen shone with all the hues of a TV shampoo commercial. The results,

Re-tread. The idea began with Deneuve and Belmondo in mind; then Catherine and Delon. Finally, Bébé and Cassel (below). 'Luck guided us,' said director Michel Deville. 'Not the ideal combination—but good. There are no rules in cinema ... this is what supplies its charm.'

Benjamin for example, were beautiful and most relaxing in what was becoming a rather grimy decade of full-frontal ultra-violence elsewhere.

Michel Deville started in movies as apprentice to director Henri Decoin, working his way up from trainee to assistant director during 13 films. He made director status in 1958 and began this shining partnership with Nina Companeez in 1960 with *Ce soir ou jamais,* leading up to *Benjamin* in 1967. Music plays an integral part in their scripts, chosen usually before their stars. Certainly Rossini (including the *Thieving Magpie* overture) was selected for this project long before the right stellar combination was secured.

Deville waits to write with an exact star in mind. 'I think of an actor and it is necessary for me to have him.' Neither does he like to waste time. Together with Nina Companeez, Deville pens a film exactly as it will be shot and edited (by Nina). 'We don't want to make literature, we don't write anything which won't finally be in the film. For my part, I think Nina is the best dialogue writer in France. I feel I'm very spoiled.' (Not any more; Mag Bodard moved Nina to director with *Faustine ou le bel été,* and indeed it is Nina who directed what Bardot claims to be her final film: *Colinot.*)

Mag Bodard did not take to the first treatment of *L'Ours*; Deville and Companeez made a ritzy *policier* instead, *Bye Bye Barbara,* while re-tooling their comedy with Catherine Deneuve and Jean-Paul Belmondo in mind. Both stars declined. The team thought again: Deneuve and Alain Delon. Again: *non.* Deville recalled the last time he could not obtain the stars he wanted. In 1963 he had devised an unusual musical comedy—'the people did not sing, but movements developed the action; the characters had to dance. There was a lot of imagination and a number of dream-like quality scenes, very stylish.' He intended it for the *West Side Story* find, George Chakiris and Brigitte Bardot. The project collapsed due to their unavailability. Now he went back to Bardot to stave off another collapse. And the story goes she read the script and said yes the same day—which later prompted Joseph Gelmis, in *Newsday,* to suggest a speed-reading course if she intended to continue making such hasty decisions.

Bébé's agreement ruled out trying Belmondo one last time; and Gene Kelly's discovery, Jean-Pierre Cassel, became the Bear. 'And the film gained in truthfulness and artistic skill, if I may say so,' adds Deville. 'You can see the film was not only the match between two opposites, but also the opposition of two worlds ... the star and the anti-star. Bardot–Belmondo would have been a match between two stars. Luck guided us to good casting, which was not this time the ideal combination—but good. There are no rules in cinema, no laws. This is what supplies its charm.'

An intriguing cast-note, and one underlying the ever-ageless imagery that is Bébé: the young actor chosen to play her fiancé proved to be Xavier Gélin, 24-year-old assistant film director son of film-star parents, Daniel Gélin and Danielle Delorme, who were the closest friends of the teenage Bardot and the lean and hungry Vadim in the early 50s. In fact, Bardot's third screen appearance (see page 100) had been as a witness, along with Vadim, to the marriage of the Gélin couple in *Les dents longues* (1952). Xavier was then six years old . . . now here he was, 18 years on, playing BB's lover and looking well enough in the part. As did she; looking delicious and young enough at 36, to cope with what, for other sirens of a like age, would have appeared cradle-snatching.

She was, of course, eminently well versed for such generation-gap affairs—considering the similar age of her current lover, Patrick Gilles, who was also in the cast; his second successive film with Brigitte.

As far as French critics were concerned, the film's highspot came in BB's inevitable bath, ending with her leaving her oval tub, fully dressed up, saying: *'Ces cochons de bonshomes, ils n'y verront rien!'* Which can be roughly translated as meaning, 'Those male chauvinist pigs won't see anything!'

In *Variety,* Gene Moskowitz, still no great BB fan, understood her delight in the script, but found the

film overwrought and precious. She was 'trying to change her sex kitten status to that of a light comédienne in zany situation love comedies. Her choice of vehicle has not been happy and her lack of comic poise is against her . . . Miss Bardot's dim-witted rich sexpot is just whimsy and Jean-Pierre Cassel's good-natured musician borders on caricature. Miss Bardot's pop culture parties are tame and her evening in her new staked-out man's country house is forced slapstick and tries too hard for charm, which eludes it. She sometimes looks lovely and sometimes shows her age. A brief bit of longshot nudity has her obviously clad in all-over tights. So this comedy of different types united by love just misses a true comic flair and gets repetitious. Only fanatic Bardot fans can relish this one and there may not be enough of them to give this rambling comedy much foreign chance.'

Even so, Paramount, who had bankrolled the film in France, decided to release it in the United States; it flopped after more harsh reviews, aimed as much at Bardot's age as the film's near miss. Joseph Gelmis called it a supposedly frothy adult fairy tale.

Donald J. Mayerson, *Cue*: 'Now aged 36, the sex symbol has not altered her kittenish appearance, not has she improved her acting ability. She is unable to play comedy . . .' (Arrant nonsense.)

Vincent Canby, *New York Times*: 'A witless romantic fable about two perfectly mismatched lovers . . . that only the talent of the late Ernest Lubitsch might have elevated into fabulous farce . . . Charm is the ingredient that is in singularly short-supply . . . largely, I suspect, because Miss Bardot, once a sex kitten, [is] now approaching middle-age with all the grace of a seasoned predator.'

For once it took a woman fully to appreciate the earliest women's liberationist in France. Wanda Hale, *New York News*: 'Bardot is my favourite Gallic good-bad girl . . . even more beautiful today—and still all female.' There was and is still no denying that.

Les novices

1970

Franco-Italian. Les Films La Boetie (Paris)/Rizzoli
(Rome); 95 minutes. UK: *The Novices,* Scotia-
Barber Distributors, 1971; 90 minutes. US: none on
record. Eastman Color.
Director: Guy Casaril. *Producer:* André Genoves.
Script: Guy Casaril; *dialogue,* Paul Gegauff. *Photo-
graphy:* Claude Lecomte. *Editor:* Nicole Gauduchon.
Music: François de Roubaix. *Sound:* Guy Chichig-
noud. *Art Director:* none listed. *Sets Designer:* Alain
Belmondo. *Costumes:* Tatine Autre. *Hair-style:* Jean-
Pierre Berroyer, Patrick Gomez; *make-up,* Odette Ber-
royer. *Production Manager:* Georges Casati. *Assistant
Director:* Marc Picaud. *Shooting:* May 26–June 10,
1970, Paris and Brittany.

CAST

Brigitte Bardot . . . . *Agnès*
Annie Girardot . . . . *Mona Lisa*
Lucien Barjon . . . . *Ambulance Client*
Angelo Bardi . . . . *Village Client*
Jean Carmet . . . . *Dog Client*
M. Deus . . . . *Priest*
Jacques Duby . . . . *Ambulance Driver*
Jess Hahn . . . . *American Client*
Jacques Jouanneau . . . . *Client*
Clement Michu . . . . *Stuttering Client*
Antonio Passalia . . . . *Playboy*
Jean Roquel . . . . *Taxi Driver*
Noël Roquevert . . . . *Old Client*

STORY

Nuns from the Convent of St. Opportune file on to
a deserted Brittany cove, set up picnic baskets and,
under the vigilant eye of Mother Superior, strip off
sombre habits for bathing suits and a swim. Sister
Agnès buries her robes deep into the sands and swims
strongly, far out to sea—to freedom. Obtaining
fashionable clothes and sunglasses from a bathing hut
on a nearby crowded beach, she also steals a bicycle
and makes off—for Paris, where the bike is soon
smashed between two cars and she winds up in jail
for the night. A colourful tart called Mona Lisa takes
the demure girl back to her flat where Agnès hides
in the bathroom when Mona's stream of duty calls.
With no job or qualification, Mona attempts to teach

the ex-nun the tricks of her trade. Ten years of convent abstinence are hard to wipe out and she flees her first client—takes up ambulance driving instead. Idea! Mona Lisa's business picks up fast as Agnès drives her around Paris, turning the ambulance into a portable bordello. Unfortunately, one of her clients works at the hospital, recognises Agnès and the ambulance, and the girls flee . . . Back in the small cove near the convent, the swimming Sisters of St. Opportune fall to their knees in thanksgiving as the presumed Sister Agnès emerges from the sea again. And with a new novice: Mona Lisa.

NOTES

BB: 'I have come to a turning point in my career. I had to give myself a shake—my last films have not been very successful. Then, with *L'Ours et la poupée,* things began to change . . . In future I shall pay much more attention to the scripts I choose.'

Guy Casaril, a TV arrival with *L'Astragale* under his belt two years before, based his often hilarious story—and his memorable opening sequence—upon fact. 'One day when I was in Normandy, by a little creek not far from Cherbourg, I saw a really colourful sight. A coach, full of nuns, stopped nearby. The next moment, the whole coachload was running down to the sea and changing into black bathing costumes . . .' This incredible vista, coupled with Casaril's admitted fascination with the old idea of the tart with the heart of gold, led him to want to make a film about friendship: 'A really sensitive, warm friendship, not the kind of male camaraderie that turns up so often in films'.

As with the previous BB picture, the friendship emanated from another meeting of two people as different from each other as possible. A nun and a prostitute. 'But the film doesn't attempt to deal with problems of love,' explained Casaril. 'Neither the nun nor the prostitute has problems that are in any way sexual. *Les novices* is not at all meant to scandalise people. It is not satirical, nor is it anti-clerical or erotic in intention. In most French comedies, the people are funny and the situations realistic. Here it is the people who are real and the situations imaginary. I'm more interested in producing a few smiling faces than laughter.'

He wrote his story with a couple of amateur actresses in mind. Chabrol's producer, André Genoves, put up the money and one of Chabrol's scriptwriters, Paul Gegauff, supplied dialogue exclusively tailored for Bardot and Girardot. After another series of films with less than chemically responsive male co-stars (Connery included), Bardot wisely decided to repeat the *Viva Maria* experiment and hit it off, on and off screen, with the superbly talented, if less internationally known, Annie Girardot, as she had done with Moreau. 'It's wonderful to be with Annie,' BB said. 'I like her as much as an actress as I do as a person.' Girardot soon felt like Brigitte's mother. 'I love looking after her, doing little things for her. I make sure she has at least ten hours sleep a night . . . and I plan little menus for her.'

The movie was the best meal of all—Bardot's best success, in Paris at least, since *Viva Maria* (and for almost the same reasons): it was also her first British release for two years. Good news for Britain's loyal BB fans until they heard the unimproved examples of dubbing which had Bardot mouthing unsynchronised Franglaise and Annie turning Brooklynese. Casaril never had time to be nervous of his imposing

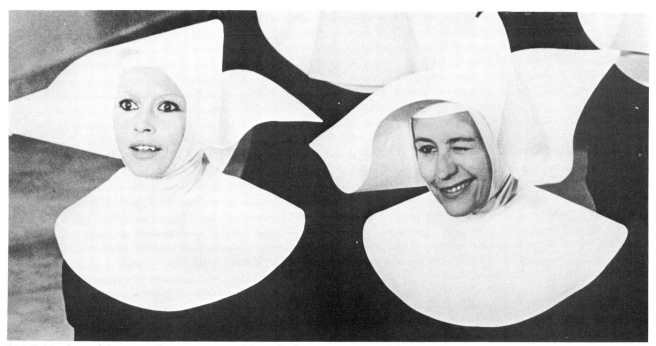

Old Habit. One of the screen's strongest traditions is that any actress with an earthy reputation must, one day, wear the wimple: Sophia Loren, Ingrid Bergman, Ursula Andress, Sylvia Syms, Barbara McNair *et al*. Now, Bardot and Girardot.

leading ladies. 'It does not seem as I'm working with two famous stars. It is much more as though we are three friends who have got together to make the film. It is far better working with good actresses than bad, you can rely on them so much more. And anyway I don't like the word: direct. What one is doing, above all, is placing the actor in a situation from which he can express himself. I try to get everything to conspire to make Brigitte and Annie really want to act . . . and I do that as discreetly as possible—my actors aren't horses showing off their paces. As it turns out, Annie Girardot has perhaps five times as much to say as Brigitte and Brigitte Bardot is actually on-screen perhaps five times as long as Annie. Both of them understand that a film has to have balance; it's not a question of rivalry between a couple of buskers.'

Gene Moskowitz, *Variety,* remained difficult to please. He thought it a one-track, good-natured if fairly insane charade without much sales potential, except at home where its vulgarity seemed to please. 'It had to happen. Ageing sex-kitten [BB] is now playing a novice nun. But this meandering, one-joke affair about her mating up with a pro joy-girl lacks the irony, point, satire, comic invention or even saucy eroticism for much foreign ploy or play . . . Miss Bardot, well made-up and with her long bleached hair under a severe nun's head-dress . . . plays it in a wide-eyed style which does not quite show whether she is simple-minded or just plain dumb, while Miss Girardot is bouncy, pleasantly vulgar and full of gusto as the prostitute with a heart . . .'

Nigel Andrews, *Monthly Film Bulletin*: 'Despite some neat comic ideas, Guy Casaril's film never quite

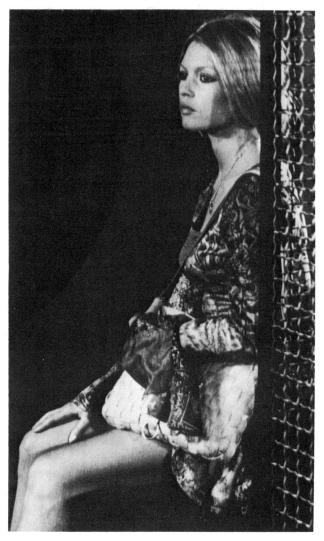

gets up enough steam to provide an effective vehicle for the pairing of Bardot and Annie Girardot. Perhaps Casaril is too preoccupied with laying on the charm (the heroines winking saucily at the camera as they rehearse their trade walk up and down the bedroom; Bardot's poutingly innocent début on the street, complete with auburn wig and ugly-duckling walk).'

Guy Casaril, and Brigitte, were sufficiently entranced by the double femme teaming, to try it again in 1971: *Les pétroleuses* opposite Claudia Cardinale. But she committed herself to three more first. 'Robert Enrico has offered me a very good part in *Boulevard du rhum,* a 30s star pursued by a naval captain. Then I shall be acting with Annie Girardot again in Luchino Visconti's next film, *A la recherche du temps perdu.* And Roger Vadim has offered me a nice part, a teacher in an American university.' Of that trio, she only ever made the first; Visconti's ill-health, to say nothing of finance, closed down his venture; and Vadim went on to America for *Pretty Maids All in a Row* in 1971 without Brigitte, utilising the luscious-limbed Angie Dickinson in her place. Angie, to quote the old cliché, had never looked better, nor been so freed from what usually passed for sex in Hollywood: Bardot, though, had still managed to avoid the Hollywood trap, even with Vadim at the helm.

Boulevard du rhum

1970

France. SNEC Gaumont International production;
125 minutes. UK/US release: none on record. East-
man Color.
Director: Robert Enrico. *Producer:* Alain Poiré.
Script: Pierre Pélegri, Robert Enrico, *from a novel by*
Jacques Pécheral. *Photography:* Jean Boffety. *Edi-
tor:* Michael Lewin. *Sound:* Christian Forget. *Art
Director:* Max Douy. *Production Manager:* Paul Joly.
Assistant Director: Serge Witta. *Shooting:* from Sep-
tember 21, 1970, locations in Spain, Mexico, British
Honduras.

CAST

Brigitte Bardot . . . . *Linda Larue*
Lino Ventura . . . . *Cornélius Von Zeeling*
Bill Travers . . . . *Capt. Gerry Sanderson*
Clive Revill . . . . *Lord Hammond*
Guy Marchand . . . . *Film Star*
Jess Hahn . . . . *Big Dutch*

STORY

1920. Prohibition. Rum-runner Cornélius Von Zeeling,
45, a man's man, coarse by appearance, buccaneer
by spirit, gentle by nature, loses his boat to the US
coastguard patrol. Beached, he risks his life in a Russian roulette version of blind man's buff in which he's
the target for gamblers shooting at him in the dark.
At the sixth shot, he is wounded; at the eleventh, he
gives up: rich enough to buy the ship of his dreams,
the 'Queen of Hearts'. He meets his vessel's namesake
in a cinema: Linda Larue, biggest star of the age,
beautiful enough to take one's breath away. Cornélius
is spellbound, hopelessly in love and follows all her
films, as he voyages from Mexico to Jamaica, forget-
ting smuggling until Captain Sanderson reminds him
of an obligation. And there she is, out of the blue,
on a deserted beach, emerging from the seas, tall,
blonde, stunning, the object of his passion: Linda
Larue in person. He approaches. She runs, laughing.

She invites him to a party and is won over by his masculinity. Inseparable, they make a lovers' cruise. Sanderson's worst fears are realised: the coastguards pursue them and a bloody sea battle takes place. A white yacht intervenes: Lord Hammond's. Within a few days, Linda is Lady Hammond. Cornélius confidently awaits her return. Instead she is spirited away by film-friends suggesting a film of her life. Shooting begins. Prohibition ends. Amnesty for rum-runners. On the movie-screen, Linda Larue cavorts. In the audience, Cornélius Von Zeeling watches, waits.

NOTES

Brigitte's best work for five years. Sadly this too remains unseen outside her normal French-speaking export territories. The blame belongs to distributors, not to Bardot.

Of any category within the multifarious film industry, it is continually distributors who are religiously least likely to put their money where their cigar-chomping mouths are. Rarely will they take the kind of financial gambles that are, more often than not, the very life's blood of the more creative elements in movies. Producers, directors, writers, cameramen, most technicians, certainly actors and even occasionally producers will, when needs, artistry or career insist, gamble their talent and their instincts—and a personal investment. Distributors are dyed-in-the-wood traditional cowards, happy only when repeating proven formulas: a kind of *status quid pro quo*.

Hence, Robert Enrico's *Boulevard du rhum* gathers dust upon French shelves, despite a genuinely sparkling performance from Brigitte as a 20s movie queen (a persona she had already shone with in various song set-pieces in her New Year's Eve TV spectaculars in Paris). Lino Ventura, of course, like Annie Girardot before him, did not—in distributors' jaundiced eyes, at least—have sufficient international kudos to help bolster the fading ticket-selling allure of Brigitte and risk a wider release. He provided, all the same, a grittily perfect counter-balance in the film, as BB's most effective (and first believable) male co-star since Henri Vidal . . . 11 years and some 21 films before. Usually backing Delon and Co. as cop or crook, in any number of the Parisian gangster thrillers, Ventura (born Lino Borrini in Parma, 1919) is the logical successor to the immortal Jean Gabin. He shares the same effortless humanism and honesty of a Gabin, of Tracy, Hackman and Belmondo, before and after him.

The story derived from the first novel of 63-year-old Jacques Pécheral, a French adventurer who was condemned to death in three different countries, when accused of plotting to overthrow the governments of Honduras, Turkey and Italy, as well as getting (and escaping from) 20 years' hard labour under the Vichy

Superb! If sight unseen around most of the globe. Bardot as 20s movie siren (with Guy Marchand, below) is won by the infectious buccaneer, Lino Ventura . . . the new Gabin and finally being recognised by Hollywood directors.

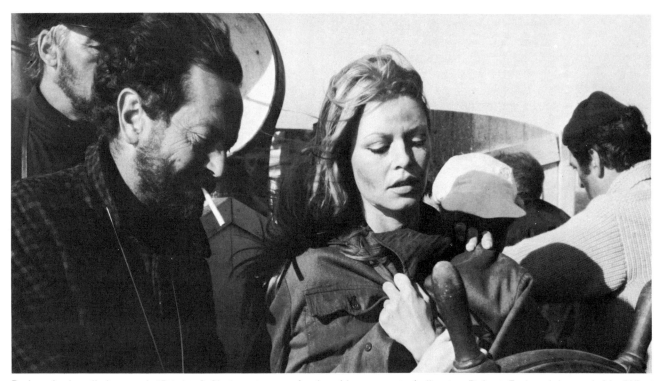

Praise. And well deserved. 'Brigitte? She's a true professional,' commented director Robert Enrico (above, left). 'What other actress could slip so easily into the skin of an actress of the Gay Twenties. And with Ventura—a sensational couple.'

Government back in France during the war. Pécheral
led a life every bit as fantastic as Henri Charrière:
and as Gabin was too old, Ventura would have been
the screen's perfect *Papillon* when the Charrière book
was filmed. This very rum-runner rôle underlines my
point, as once again his lack of global credibility was
against him since Steve McQueen won the Charrière
story.

Director Robert Enrico, who first made news with
his début shorts, *Thaumetopea,* 1960, and in particular
La rivière du hibou/Incident at Owl Creek, had tried
for four years to film the Pécheral book. He made
seven other features instead, two with Lino Ventura,
one with Belmondo, and another turning French-
Canadian Joanna Shimkus into a star (*Tante Zita,*
1967).

'I think patience must be one of my best qualities,'
Enrico remarked during location treks from Spain to
Mexico and British Honduras. 'I've always believed
that eventually I would get what I wanted. Now it's
happened thanks to Gaumont. Pécheral's novel
appealed to me for two reasons. First, it's a good
adventure story. Secondly, it's set at the time of Prohibition in 1920—a period I've always been particularly
fond of.' The director had garnered a reputation as
being best fitted for adventure stories—'men's films'.
He refused any specialisation or theorising, although
it was his image, and the usual masculine style of
his films, that was probably the root cause of such
a rejuvenated Bardot performance.

'Brigitte? She is a true professional,' praised Enrico.

Siren. Brigitte apes Pearl White and Fay Wray ... in *The Perils of Linda Larue*!

'She really knows her job. What other actress could slip so easily into the skin of an actress of the Gay Twenties ? Lino Ventura is the same as ever. We know each other well as we worked together on *Les grandes gueules,* 1965, and *Les aventuriers/The Last Adventure,* 1966. The relationship of a Hollywood vamp and a 45-year-old buccaneer makes very good viewing. With the two of them, indeed thanks to them, the classic theme of Beauty and the Beast takes on another dimension. A sensational couple.'

The French agreed—audience and critics. Guy Allomberty, *Image et Son*: 'People are singing, laughing, dancing in *Boulevard du rhum* and the suspicion of melancholy is only a zest in a cocktail. Taste, as a bonus, is that of old rum. One takes, by finding again Bardot, following Ventura, an extreme pleasure.'

Gene Moskowitz, *Variety,* felt otherwise—intractably. The film was amiable and picaresque, yet with a campy period air; also repetitious, rather naive, overwrought and redundant; an overlong, parody of a parody. 'It sends up silent films and aims at a good-natured, knockabout comedy in the old Hollywood manner. Robert Enrico is one local director who can stage a fight and also brings off some deft sea battles. Miss Bardot is fetching in her period attire and Lino Ventura has a craggy bonhomie . . . and Miss Bardot is going through her slim, pert thirties with a better command of diction, though tastes and erotic outlook have changed so drastically that it is hard to see why she was ever deemed a sex kitten or erotic temptress for that matter.'

Les pétroleuses

1971

The Oil Girls. Franco-Spanish-Italian-British. Franco Films (Paris)/Coper Cines (Madrid)/Vides Films (Rome)/Hemdale Group (Great Britain) co-production; 95 minutes. UK: *The Legend of Frenchie King,* Hemdale Film Distributors, 1974: 96 minutes. US: no release on record. Eastman Color.
Directors: Christian-Jaque, Guy Casaril. *Executive Producer:* Raymond Eger. *Script:* Clément Bowood, Guy Casaril, Daniel Boulanger, *from an idea by* Marie-Ange Aniès and Jean Nemours; *English dialogue,* Clément Biddle Wood, John Bird. *Photography:* Henri Persin. *Editor:* Nicole Gauduchon. *Music:* Christian Gaubert; *lyrics,* Hal Shaper, Francis Lai. *Sound:* Bernard Auboy. *Art Director:* José-Luis Galicia. *Production Managers:* Ignacio Gutterez, Enzo Boetani. *Second Unit Director:* Jean Couturier; *Assistant Director,* Denise Morlot. *Shooting:* from June 18, 1971, locations in Madrid and Burgos, Spain.

CAST

Brigitte Bardot	*Louise King*
Claudia Cardinale	*Maria Sarrazin*
Michael J. Pollard	*Sheriff*
Patty Shepard	*Petite Pluie*
Emma Cohen	*Virginie*
Térèsa Cimpera	*Caroline*
Oscar Davis	*Mathieu*
Georges Beller	*Marc*
Patrick Préjan	*Luc*
Rocardo Salvino	*Jean*
Valéry Inkijnoff	*Spitting Bull*
Micheline Presle	*Aunt Amelie*
Denise Provence	*Mlle. Letellier*
Leroy Hayns	*Marquis*
Jacques Jouanneau	*M. Letellier*
Raoul Delfossé	*Le Cornac*
France Dougnac	*Elisabeth*

STORY

New Mexico, 1880. Bougival Junction, where the locals retain their French language, character and customs as resolutely as the matriarchal Maria Sarrazin rules her four brothers, welcomes a new family. Five stunning sisters led by Louise 'Miller'. The girls' Pa is the hanged outlaw Frenchie King and, unknown to the town, these demure-looking daughters keep Pa's criminal legend alive—in a gang dressed as men with Louise playing Frenchie. They've stolen Doc Miller's deed to the Little P ranch and move in. Maria tries to buy the spread after finding Doc's map showing the land is rich in oil. Louise suspects her motives and the matriarchs become bitter rivals, although their brothers and sisters prefer to make . . . friends. The town marshal/sheriff/dogcatcher loves both clan leaders and gets caught in the middle of their fist-fight showdown; Louise using cunning to combat Maria's strength. When Doc Miller arrives to snatch back his land, the families are jailed. Louise and Maria escape and blend wits to free their now married kinfolk from the train taking them to trial. Doubled in size, the King gang ride off into legend as the marshal hands in his badge: 'The West ain't no place fer a man!'

NOTES

Back in *Shalako* country and period . . . as the French supplied the reason why *Shalako* did not excite as

Punch-up I. Luckless sheriff Michael J. Pollard gets caught in the centre of the BB/CC initial assault.

231

Jump. Brigitte leaps aboard her Trigger-stand-in. She jumped well, but rode little in the actual screen chases.

Jerk. Michael J. Pollard had not had so much luck since *Bonnie and Clyde*. Except he mugged himself off the screen.

planned. Bardot should have played Shalako. She attempted much of the Connery rôle here, as well as re-enacting both Marias from *Viva Maria*. The actual formula was so crowded and clouded, however, that its targets, of which there were many—too many, from Jesse James to *Destry Rides Again*—were rarely hit on-centre.

Since the initial rise of BB, her rivals had been built up, and in most cases knocked down, by the score or more. One alone made rapid headway and clung tightly to a similarly up-and-downish career, replete with Press adulation, speculation and eternal comparison to Bardot—Claudia Cardinale, Italy's Sardinian-born second-string Loren. The initials aided the headlines and even Bardot followed the line when making the polite enough comment: 'CC comes after BB, *naturellement.*' Naturally! Cardinale chased Bardot since her *déjà vu* beginning of early sex-pot rôles and British importation by Betty Box, the Pinewood producer who had found Bardot for *Doctor at Sea*.

Therefore the idea of production chiefs in Paris, Rome and Madrid seemed sound enough. A BB/CC match in the style of Bardot/Moreau, Bardot/Girardot. Cardinale, however, proved more chauvinistic than either French actress, and rather than metaphorically bowing to the queen on-screen, she struck out for herself and won—handsomely—the round, the day, the movie and the match.

So she should have. She had the positive advantage of the more straightforward rôle in strictly delineation terms. Bardot had to attempt to exemplify both the quiet femininity of Louise and the sado-masculinity of Frenchie King, a dual rôle she was extremely capable of on paper, except that in this instance the script suffered overkill from *six* writers and one director too many. Guy Casaril, who had worked the Bardot/Girardot oracle so well, started *Les pétroleuses* and is credited, alone, with the BB/CC casting. On location, however, he ran into certain differences with the trio of production companies and quit. Christian-Jaque, the *Babette* director, took over the reins. No broncobuster he, for all his enthusiasm.

'I think it's a lively and eventful story that does justice to the talents of its heroines,' declared Christian-Jaque. 'It's a more a satire than a parody. Zany but not exaggerated . . . with all the trappings of the Western, Sheriff, Indians, saloon, chases and fights. Brigitte was very brave because she hates physical pain. Claudia is a real tomboy—up in the mornings early to ride and shoot.'

He was also richly fulsome in praise of the major sore thumb of the project: Michael J. Pollard, the New Jersey actor with the mashed-potato face, best remembered as the getaway driver for *Bonnie and Clyde*. What Arthur Penn had controlled so adroitly in that instant-stardom performance, every other director had allowed to go unchecked. Consequently, Pollard was drowning in his own overworked facial mugging. In the French release print Pollard's lawman was the only character speaking English. Indeed, *Variety* suggested he made up his rôle as he went along. Christian-Jaque definitely allowed him far too

Punch-up II. Zap hands, here comes BB v. CC in the one sequence where the film came close to being alive. 'A lot has been said about their fight,' says director Christian-Jacque. 'I was in a cold sweat over it. It had to look authentic and I asked the two actresses not to hold back. They set to with such a will that I was afraid I'd have an invalid on my hands. But it was all right in the end, nothing worse than a few bruises.' And nary a one on the ego.

much leeway, because he thought him a superb comedy performer; he was also in awe of the Oscar he kept mistakenly insisting Pollard had won for Penn's film.

'It was enormously satisfying working with him,' said the director. 'He does so much with a character that might have been quite ordinary. To me, he is as important as the two women.' In fact, he was totally dispensable; and ridiculously young for the rôle, which ached for a veteran of the Hollywood or spaghetti West; Lee Van Cleef or Jack Elam would have added immeasurable impetus to the tin star and thereby the stars. Too many possible and plausible conflagration points like this were totally wasted, and *Viva Maria* was never topped, or even matched. The usual fate, then, for a hybrid mixture of international finance.

Producer Raymond Eger was convinced he had a family entertainment winner. Children would adore the comedy and the action, fathers would certainly appreciate the blouses that never quite fastened and the skirt so innocently torn in the fighting. And mothers . . . well, among the more fatuous reasons Eger put forth for his potential success, was the brittle contention that *Pétroleuses* was a feminist film—as if this was anything new or rare in BB vehicles.

Christian-Jaque took the same view, however. 'If you're given the opportunity to direct a film where

the men's parts are played by women, then you just play all the feminine trump cards. There was nothing in the script against it, so I put the emphasis on two versions of natural beauty. Even in the great Westerns, I've never liked heroines to look as though they've stepped straight out of a beauty salon somewhere in the middle of Texas. Claudia and Brigitte are shown as they are, with very little make-up, messy hair and frequently messy clothes as well. And I may say they look all the more pretty and desirable as a result.'

He took over the film (his 74th) when the English title was announced, which caused a major misunderstanding in film trade papers. From the news in Spain, it seemed the BB/CC combination was such a success that two films were being made back to back: *The Legend of Frenchie King,* a Western by Christian-Jaque, and *Les pétroleuses* by Guy Casaril, which to make everything more complicated was also known as *The Oil Girls* and sounded like a feminist re-make of Gable and Tracy's 1940 *Boom Town*—not a bad idea, that.

Instead of which it tried hard to be *Viva Maria et Louise,* which never came off. On Spanish locations, the initial sex-symbols got on remarkably well (Cardinale talked more about her son than Bardot mentioned hers), and they were photographed together

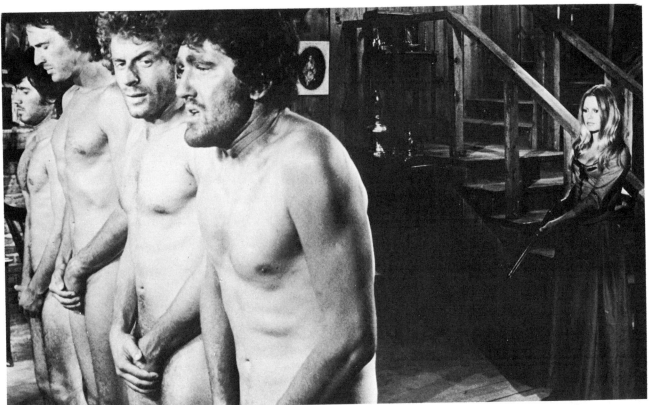

Hands *Down*? Gunslinger Bardot turns the tables on her foes—and audience. In a complete switch of her *La bride sur le cou* scene with Subor, she has the gun and the orders. Strip!

in happy moods as often as their twin-parked, sun-shaded Rolls-Royces: BB's white 3-WR-75 and CC's grey model, 877479. Both cars and stars deserved hours in the broiling sun for a better cause than the non-legendary *Frenchie King*. French reviews were cool and cold. *Image et Son* wryly mentioned that the promised conflict of BB/CC was resolved explicitly only in the last shot of the film: 'four white riders, four black riders, nobody has a sex any more'. Actually there were five riders per colour, but no matter . . . there was heavier acidity to come.

Jean-Loup Passek, *Cinéma 72*: 'Resolving the equation BB + CC is a kind of Christmas present for dunces . . . Cardinale as a missed boy (remarkably missed, the voyeurs can be assured of that!) has at least the merit to do her job conscientiously. But [BB], who looks like a cat thrown in a bath of cold water each time one asks her to do a few movements or to jump on a nice horse (on the horse, it is not her who takes the risks but her double), proves once again that her knowledge is of the most limited. She, who could have become our Judy Holliday, is from now on simply a pair of initials for which the dealers of the temple are still fighting over. For how much longer?'

Gene Moskowitz, *Variety*: 'Simplistic oater has a couple of gimmicks going for it via a U.S. Western town founded by French people and speaking French

Poster. The names tell all. And for once, it's not the stars who will undress—but the anonymous starlet in the corner.

Encore. Christian-Jacque, director of *Babette s'en va-t-en guerre*, returns to the BB fold at 67—for his 74th film.

and [BB] as a sort of female Jesse James and [CC] as her enemy with both fighting over an oil claim. But otherwise, pic is too predictable, naïve and gauche to get a needed note of satiric dash into the proceedings . . . Misses Bardot and Cardinale supply some pulpy and fading pulchritude, but the film remains chaste except for a long-shot nude scene.'

Tom Milne, *Monthly Film Bulletin*: 'Crudely directed and unpleasantly dubbed—everybody he speak ze English in this French township—this is a drearily unfunny attempt to repeat the formula of *Viva Maria*—the girls this time toting their guns in a Western

setting. All the jokes miss fire, the performances are as flaccid as the script.'

Derek Ellery, *Films and Filming*: '. . . the BB-CC teaming has all the potential allure of a Newman-Redford tandem . . . The English title leads one to expect a narrative based on the thrilling exploits of Bardot, rather than the confrontation and battle of wits between the two women. This is all the more unfortunate when one considers Bardot's disappointing performance: though representing the feminine side of the film, she has none of the abandon or sheer sense of fun which is needed to keep such an idea alive; she never for a moment matches Cardinale in strength or authority. Her talents lie more in mindless fields— witness her excellent *Les novices* with Annie Girardot—not in such straight battles of will.'

Depending on scenario and direction, that is. While watching the movie creak along during its Paris première run, I was constantly frustrated by the magical chances missed, messed up or completely misunderstood and kept wishing Serge Leone had handled it. Then another fantasy, hope, sprang to mind: Leone directing Bardot in a re-run of *Johnny Guitar* . . . If only.

Don Juan 1973 ou Et si Don Juan était une femme

1973

If Don Juan Were a Woman. Franco-Italian. Film-sonor Marceau-Paradoxe Film/Filmel (Rome); 87 minutes. UK: *Don Juan* or *If Don Juan Were a Woman,* Hemdale Films, 1974; 94 minutes. US release: none on record. Eastman Color.
Director: Roger Vadim. *Producer:* none credited. *Script:* Jean Cau, Roger Vadim, Jean-Pierre Petrolacci; *dialogue,* Jean Cau. *Photography:* Henri Decau, Andréa Winding. *Editor:* Victoria Spiri-Mercanton. *Music:* Michel Magne; *orchestration,* Magne and Claude Germain. *Sound:* Jean-Louis Ducarme. *Production Manager:* Paul Veillon. *Assistant Director:* Jean-Michel Lacor.

CAST

Brigitte Bardot . . . . *Jeanne*
Maurice Ronet . . . . *Pierre*
Mathieu Carrière . . . . *Paul*
Robert Hossein . . . . *Prévost*
Jane Birkin . . . . *Clara Prévost*
Michèle Sand . . . . *Léporella*
Robert Walker Jr. . . . . *Guitarist*
Laurent Vergez . . . . *Student*

STORY

Vadim: 'The Don Juan of our day is the woman—Brigitte Bardot in real life.'

Jeanne confesses murder to her cousin Paul, a young priest. Aware of the woman's consistent immorality, he refuses to listen until reluctantly persuaded to visit her extraordinary home: a Hefneresque bathyscape apartment under the Seine. She coolly regales him with a list of men she has driven to destruction; targets picked with a tranquillity bordering on *ennui*. Pierre: respectable, well-to-do, well wed, well set in government circles, well led astray from home, hearth, wife, child; reduced to drunken victim in an idyllic affair which Jeanne soon finds sour enough to drop him and his career into a Swedish student orgy. Prévost: vain, millionaire, crude, savage, sadistic; Jeanne deflates his ego by subverting his timid young wife Clara's fear of him, by arranging for Prévost to find the two women in bed together and refusing his randy proposal to join them. And the Spanish guitar player, so smitten by Jeanne that he agrees to her offer of herself in exchange for the highest price possible—his life. He slashes his wrists after coitus—the murder she confesses. Shattered by all this perdition, Paul is likewise unable to resist Jeanne's sensuality. Willing to confront her retribution, Jeanne meets Pierre again, and due to her one act of sympathy—rescuing him from the blazing house he had planned for them to die in—she meets destiny and death in the flames.

NOTES

Ten years since *Le repos du guerrier,* sixteen since *Et Dieu créa la femme,* and Bardot and Vadim come

Bleue? Hardly. The over-publicised bed-sharing of Bardot and Birkin seemed more like a sketch dropped by the *Monty Python* crew.

Blues. Robert Walker, Jnr., played the smitten Spanish guitarist, with one expression throughout: the blues. 'My price,' says Jeanne, 'has gone up each time. Soon they won't be able to afford me.' Walker insists he can pay: 'no matter what it costs.' *Jeanne:* Your life. *Guitarist:* That's all? Why, that's nothing.

Blown. Mathieu Carrière was better served in Vadim's next film, *Charlotte/La jeune fille assassinée.*

together again—after marriages, divorces and ever-heated headlines of love-affairs apiece, departures into new fields (TV *chansons* for her; Hollywood for him), plus 16 movies for her and half as many for him. If their never-ending friendship brought them together, so did their common urgency for a resounding commercial, or even artistic hit. This was not it.

The screen they had so joyously liberated in 1956 had long since caught them up and passed them by. BB, certainly; he was to recover his old, bold, splendidly erotic form with *La jeune fille assassinée,* 1974. Film-makers and actresses (sex-symbols already being *passé*) from Munich to Melbourne had followed through on the Vadim-BB team's once revolutionary variations upon the sexual themes and schemes of life, subtle and otherwise, in differing adagios of cause and effect. From John Schlesinger and Ken Russell socio- and fantasia-dramatics to Russ Meyer and David Friedman rudie-nudies. All of which had pushed the door even further into true blue pornography with Gerard Damiano being hailed by American Establishment critics as the Ingmar Bergman of porn for sexplicit productions like *Deep Throat, The Devil in Miss Jones* and *Memories Within Miss Aggie,*

Reincarnation. Bardot as Don Juan *circa* '73. Why a female Don? 'Because,' explained Vadim, 'concerning eroticism and conquest, we can no longer be shocked by a man. But with a woman, it's still possible. The Don Juan of our day is the woman—Brigitte in real life.'

and his audiences voting the ex-Mme. Vadim, Jane Fonda, as the actress they wanted most to see on the new, blue screen.

The French couple's once biggest market was just not there any more. To Americans in the porno-chic 70s, sex-dramas meant either the *Emmanuelle* soft-core sensation from Paris, or the home-made hard-core pornography productions. The names with box-office power now belonged to Linda Lovelace, Harry Reems, Georgina Spelvin, Eric Edwards, Darby Lloyd Rains; producers like Summer Brown, a bright San Francisco girl; directors like Radley Metzger in New York—and a whole new home-grown BB in the sensuality personified (and explicitly realised) shape of Barbara Bourbon from Los Angeles.

Bardot was plainly—from this film—not sure if she wanted to compete. As she neared 40, she was, for all her lovers, reverting to her bourgeois status. Eroticism, she was saying now, equalled pornography: the commercial exploitation of the gestures of love disgusted her. Was this the thrusting Juliette of *Et Dieu créa la femme* speaking? 'That,' she said, 'was simply the story of a liberated girl, free, really nothing unhealthy.' Linda Lovelace said much the same about *Deep Throat*.

Vadim often wondered if she would complete the film at all. Her latest romance had broken apart after three years; boyfriend Christian Kalt, feeling he belonged to her like a puppy, quit his plush kennel. 'And for BB,' reported Vadim, 'a rupture, even if it is her own fault, is always a drama. Thank God, my Petit Messiah arrived in time.' The nickname belonged to 24-year-old medical student Laurent Vergez, on call for a possible part in the Swedish locations. 'I only asked him to come to Stockholm for a try-out,' says Vadim, 'but when I saw how things were going for him and Brigitte, he was quickly engaged. Vergez saved us. We were undergoing a real tragedy. BB would leave and then come back. Vergez, who knows medicine, tried to calm her.'

She needed calming—with a script packed with insane homilies like: 'Seducing is easy. It's conquest that's difficult. Why seduce if you don't destroy. I know no other way to live. I am, after all, a man.' And perhaps, closer to home: 'One thing I can't stand is people treating me the way I treat others.'

Don Juan had all the essential elements of a typical (i.e. old-fashioned) Vadim sexuality treatise; complete with Bardot nude on-screen for the first time for 15 films (*Le mépris*), and fully frontally so for the first

241

time in anything except the occasional *Lui* magazine pose. Vadim even managed at long last—more for him than the audience—to fulfill his old dream of showing Bardot in bed with another woman, though the Lesbian congress was low camp of a schoolgirlish order. The film, therefore, became little more, or less, than a sumptuously overdressed, and naively underdressed series of intermingling sketches in search of, if not an author, then at least a director.

Even in the dubbed British release print, it is obvious that while Bardot is up to the games in hand (and keeping them there), Vadim had lost interest, style and, above all, his elegant *élan*. From tame beginning (Bardot entering a church, smoking) to the *Liaisons dangereuses* ending (Bardot trapped by fire), the *longueurs*-riddled *Don Juan* reminded one of Jacques Charrier's old accusations, long after his marriage to Brigitte had collapsed and he could comment with hindsight replacing trauma: 'I believe she made Vadim rather than Vadim making her.'

Vadim had lately turned autobiographical with his film of *Hellé* (starring his third American discovery, Gwen Welles) and seemed bent on similar traits when outlining his new/old theme, seduction. 'And the way it destroys love—something that is possibly more poignant in a woman.' He wrote the script with Jean Cau, the prize-winning novelist who had celebrated

Bébé's 35th birthday in *Paris-Match* by dubbing her Aphrodite-Bardot, a blonde witch, '*une cascadeuse* [stuntwoman] *de la vie, de l'amour et de la morale*'. Neither Cau, nor Vadim, proved so eloquent in their film.

'If Don Juan were a woman,' Vadim declared, 'he would be Brigitte Bardot—or at least the character I've asked her to play. A woman who affirms her personality through her conquests, without thinking of the consequences for other people or for herself. For she destroys herself through the game she plays.' In films, he felt, it was still possible—with a woman—to shock in terms of eroticism and conquest. Not that his film should be taken as simply a libertine fantasy: 'It's about a woman who sets no limit on her passions and doesn't realise that she is going too far.'

Tempered, perhaps, by Jean Cau's 1969 comment that Bardot would be lost if she joined the sexplosion which she and Vadim had unleashed upon America, Vadim never went far enough with scenario, camera or star. He had the services of his best and most trusting leading lady, a script hinged for good or ill on her redoubtable sexuality and upon his extemporisation of it—and he flunked it.

Early views of the script showed two other 'confessions' by BB's Jeanne character. One had Bardot forcing another pillar of respectability into bed with her—

on his wedding day; the other had her disguised as a man in order to seduce a younger girl. Neither episode was seen, or referred to, in any copy of the final production prints. Vadim considered he had gone far enough in pitting Bardot against Maurice Ronet and Robert Hossein—hardly casting of all-fired public interest as both had appeared with her before, in *Les Femmes,* and the last BB–Vadim outing, *Le repos du guerrier.* Vadim relied for new sparkle, too heavily so, on the pairing of Bardot and Robert Walker Jnr., in the simply ludicrous episode of the guitarist (met with loud guffaws every time I've seen the film). Vadim also felt the thought, indeed the climatic sight, of Bardot making love to a priest (an ill-used Mathieu Carrière) would be sensational enough to cause the old queues around the block. Only in Vatican censorship chambers, perhaps.

'I think eroticism has always appeared in my films without vulgarity: elegant,' said Vadim. 'One should give the spectator some precise indications, which means being a little daring, but something that enables him to go beyond the image. Eroticism is what exists beyond what is shown ... I feel that *erotisme* is developed on the screen more by directors than actors. I could take, I think, some actress whom nobody would ever suspect of being erotic in any way, and I could make a very erotic film with her.'

And yet when faced with Bardot and Birkin naked in bed—a sequence which appears to have been largely shot with *Lui* magazine in mind—nothing half-way erotic exists, happens, either on-screen or in the mind; in Vadim's subconscious maybe, but not in any audience's. He had forever attempted to feature Brigitte in bi-sexual situation with a female co-star in their past, notably in his continued overtures to her with regard to *Le vice et la vertu,* 1962.

She balked at the suggestion, as it was usually his current girl he was hoping to match her with, first Annette Stroyberg, and then Catherine Deneuve (who made the film with Annie Girardot, minus the scene in question). Vadim had earlier implicated his second wife, Annette Stroyberg, into heavily hinted Lesbianism with Elsa Martinelli in *Et mourir de plaisir / Blood and Roses,* 1960; and later, in both *Barbarella* and his sketch in the Poe trilogy, *Histoires extraordinaires,* he shot his third wife, Jane Fonda, in feminine entanglements with Anita Pallenberg and Clara Merlier. The urge to do likewise with Bardot never left him. 'Men are *passés,*' he had her say as Jeanne. 'Useless.'

But was the dream-wish of this 44-year-old movie director merely to show Brigitte Bardot hiding most of her celebrated body behind that of another girl, intercutting with close-ups of BB's feet rubbing the other's toes while intoning such passionate rejoinders as 'That tickles, doesn't it?' or such triteness.

Confession. Bardot tells her cleric cousin Carrière about destroying the lives of politician Maurice Ronet (centre) and Robert Hossein (bottom), a crude, vain millionaire.

Refuting any theory that he was implying, or even underlining, a factual Lesbian streak in Bardot's sexual make-up, Vadim maintains the sequence was not his invention, but that of his scenarist, Jean Cau. 'It happened,' further explains the director, 'that he did for me, some of the dialogue in *La curée* (1966). But really a few lines; not a lot. Because *La curée* was a success, the producer decided to use him to write this script. He had always wanted to write a film. But, you know, Jean Cau is somebody very, in a way, puritan—aggressive to and frightened by women. His approach to *érotisme* is strange. And so, all the love scenes—*all!*—were . . . sort of strange, *non?* I cannot say if the Bardot–Birkin scene was a joke in his mind, but you can believe me, it was most certainly a joke on the set!'

Jane Birkin shared the bed. The leggy British girl had become something of a *cause célèbre* in 1966 as the screen's first full-frontal female nude in a feature film—together with the '59 Vadim discovery, Gillian Hills, as the swinging London teenagers in search of photographic glory in Antonioni's *Blow Up*. Invited a few years later to France for one film, *Slogan,* opposite singer-composer-actor Serge Gainsbourg, Jane never left Paris. She stayed Gainsbourg's lover and protégée on disc and screen, attaining the early BB front-cover success and popularity

Gainsbourg had figured among the men in Brigitte's life; he wrote various of the TV spectacular songs, and albums, and appeared with her on both. Indeed, the song he helped make Jane Birkin (in)famous with, *'Je t'aime, moi non plus'* was originally written for Bardot. Serge had recorded it with her, and part of his/her legend is that they were both asked to leave the recording studio at the time, because of the heated audioerotic effects they were waxing. Their tapes were confiscated: or at least never released.

And so in the way of all Vadim *copains,* everyone—Vadim–Bardot–Gainsbourg–Birkin—knew everyone long before filming began. Jane Birkin insists she agreed to the film, and thereby the shared nudity with Brigitte, only because she knew and trusted Vadim. 'He's not a destructive director, like some I've known.' As far as Bardot was concerned, she trusted him as

well; 'I like him a lot . . . he's a stranger I know well.' Vadim commented: 'Brigitte has always had age, aggression and vulnerability.'

Verina Glaessner, *Monthly Film Bulletin*: 'A decidedly foolish film which efficiently sidesteps any serious consideration of Don Juanism, let alone the feminisation of Don Juan. The related idea of the lethal, vampiristic seductress and its relevance to the Bardot myth—acknowledged in the script in lines like "You'll never change"—is similarly left unassimilated on any level. The three tales fail to conjure up any sense of depravity or sin on the one hand, or liberating subversion on the other . . . Almost twenty years after *And God Created Woman*, however, Bardot sails through the nonsense, myth intact, without a chink in her armour.'

Gene Moskowitz, *Variety*: 'As usual, despite these more permissive days, Vadim mainly veils [BB's] charms and suggests the love bouts, but finally does show her fully nude in her big seduction scene of a priest who is also her cousin . . . Chalk this up as a rather quaint tale of a woman finally punished for her ways by burning alive. [BB], at 38, still looks good but is not up to giving this the outright *femme fatale* or tongue-in-cheek quality that might have made this attempted Don Juan distaff fable more palatable . . . As it is, it could catch some off-shore fancy as an antidote to the more hardcore fare of today . . . Vadim's direction is as decoratively garish as usual.'

Thus the latest example of the old firm—Vadim and Bardot—is more than likely to remain their last. 'I don't see how she can continue to act if she does not want to change,' maintains Vadim. 'I mean, if she accepts to mature the way Elizabeth Taylor has done, sure, why not? But Brigitte cannot continue to play Bardot the way she was five or ten years ago. There is a moment when it doesn't work any more. I hope for her that she is not going to make any more movies—unless she really finds something and accepts to play a different game.'

She never has, though she did try just once more . . .

L'Histoire très bonne et très joyeuse de Colinot Trousse-Chemise

1973

The Gay and Joyous Story of Colinot, the Skirt Puller-upper. Franco-Italian. Parc Film-Mag Bodard (Paris)/PECF-PIC (Rome); 105 minutes. UK/US release: none on record.
Director/Script: Nina Companeez. *Producer:* Mag Bodard. *Photography:* Ghislain Cloquet. *Editor:* Raymonde Guyot. *Music:* Guy Bontempelli. *Sound:* André Hervé. *Art Director:* Claude Pignot. *Costumes:* Anne-Marie Marchand. *Make-up:* Alex Marcus; *BB make-up,* Maggy Vernadet. *Hair-styles:* Huguette Lalaurette. *Production Managers:* Philippe Dussart, Charlotte Fraisse. *Assistant Directors:* Jean Lefebvre, Christiane Gratton.

CAST

Francis Huster	*Colinot*
Brigitte Bardot	*Arabelle*
Ottavia Piccolo	*Bergamonte*
Nathalie Delon	*Bermade*
Bernadette Lafont	*Rosemonde*
Alice Sapritch	*White Lady*
Muriel Catala	*Blandine*
Francis Blanche	*Vagabond*
Henri Tisot	*Tournebœuf*
Jean Le Poulain	*Brother Albaret*
Guy Grosso	*Lucas*
Rufus	*Breadwinner*
Jean-Claude Drouot	*Mesnil Plassac*
Maurice Barrier	*Executioner*
Antoine Baud	*One-Eye*
Laurent Vergez	*Knight*
Mike Marshall	*Lord*
Guy Bontempelli	*Troubadour*
Claude Brosset	*Inn-keeper*
Yves Elliot	*Lord Aubin*
François Florent	*Lord Corentin*
Philippe	*The Herald*
Michel Motto	
François Nadal	} *Monks*
Paul Muller	

STORY

Fifteenth-century France. Colinot Trousse-Chemise, so called for his incurable and often successful habit of lifting the skirt of any pretty wench, is hunting his sweetheart, Bergamotte, carried off by three brigands during their bucolic betrothal. From his Northern France peasant stockade, he journeys to Pays d'Oc in the South learning about life, wealth, misery, brutality, food, and hunting as he meets thieves, assassins, poets and women . . . Rosemonde, rich and bored; Bertrade, rebellious wife; Dame Blanche, an ugly, indomitable warrior and her lovely niece, Blandine; and the most beauteous and disturbing of all, Arabelle, surrounded by a court of elegant, subservient courtiers and lovers. Arabelle is her own mistress in matters of love and Colinot's teacher in the most important lesson of all: that a woman's body is far easier to possess than her heart.

NOTES

BB: 'This will be my final film.' She had said it so often in the past; this time, in her 40th birthday year, she insisted she meant it. Two days later, eternally feminine, Brigitte pointed out she was perfectly capable of changing her mind. And midway through her ten days' work, she called *Colinot* 'the first film I'll be sorry to finish'.

Mag Bodard and Nina Companeez, producer and writer-editor of *L'ours et la poupée*, had won her interest; and I would suggest their filming methods will help to persuade Bardot to continue her career, if and when she feels like it. She enjoys their scripts, set-up and style—her *Colinot* rôle was scheduled within ten tight days—and they, in turn, understand her completely. Companeez recognised Brigitte's sincerity about quitting the screen. 'It gets harder for her to start new films with new directors, new crews and fresh problems. She's a woman driven wild by life.'

The would-be farewell film marked a return to the kind of costumed rôle Bébé had only enacted before in sketch-films. Arabelle is a medieval courtesan, remarkably close to the omnipresent BB image: seducing, never seduced, living with her own hand-picked retinue of lovers and other hangers-on. (Her *chevalier*-servant in the group was her own latest lover, since *Don Juan 1973*, Laurent Vergez—her second lover,

Final Faces. Brigitte Bardot in what she claims to be—perhaps—her farewell film rôle. Among her courtiers—boyfriend Laurent Vergez, since superseded by a new *amour*: the multi-named Miklos/Mirsolav/Kirco Brozeck, a Czech sculptor, using the stage name Jean Blaise for his film work: Jean Gabriel Albicocco's *Le grand Meaulnes* (1967).

incidentally, to appear in two films with her.)

Since Brigitte's previous film for Mag Bodard, Nina Companeez—the 37-year-old daughter of the late scenarist Jacques Companeez—had graduated from being Michel Deville's dialogist and editor to making her directing début with *Faustine et le bel été*. She worked with a group of predominantly unknown young actors, the film was a triumph and the actors are no longer unknown: two transferred admirably into *Colinot,* including Francis Huster, of the Comédie-Française, in the title rôle. This was, though, a far more ambitious undertaking, moving on from the realms of adolescent sensibilities (which she also explored within *Benjamin*) to a picaresque tale of adventure and romance.

Nina Companeez has no desire to make fashionable films, merely to entertain with perhaps a hint of satire in the fun. Like Ken Russell, she also enjoys allowing her camera to tell one story, independent from the narrative. Both tales will be her own. 'Naturally. I could never direct somebody else's scenario—it would be like being in love and asking somebody else to make love for you.'

She devised her scenario from intriguing extracts of Middle Ages literature and ballads, also making considerable research into costumes and customs of the era—a favourite of hers as she says it showed the first emergence of women as a power in history. Bar-

dot's Arabelle, for example, is based less on Bébé as most critics suggested in their instant-label fashion, than on Nina's impression of Eléanor of Aquitaine, the wholly emancipated wife of Louis VII of France and, later, of Henry I of England. Whether Katharine Hepburn, who last played Eléanor in *A Lion in Winter,* would recognise this fact has never been ascertained.

The rest of the impressive French cast featured at least two of Bardot's Parisienne rivals: Bernadette Lafont, who began her career with the *nouvelle vague* helped into motion by BB and Vadim; and Nathalie Delon, an adventurous entrant into movies when still married to Alain Delon, who had amazed herself (and no doubt, M. Delon) with her acting ability and sexual verve. Further down the cast-list is Nina Companeez's original discovery for her *Faustine* film, Muriel Catala, of whom it has been said, and admittedly by this writer perhaps more than most, that she is the closest newcomer on the French scene to the early BB since the early Bébé herself. Companeez agrees La Catala has a remarkable personality, 'as if she were an intriguing sort of little animal'. Now where has one heard that before . . . ?

Exquisitely shot in the slightly unreal traditions of all Mag Bodard's Parc films, the exteriors were chosen in the Périgord area of the Dordogne valley, and around the town of Sarlat in Provence. Bardot's palace is really the sumptuous home of the famous Bishop of

Couple. Nathalie Delon and Francis Huster.

Cambrai, the castle of La Motte Fénélon. Two priceless 12th-century tapestries hung in her ballroom; specifically designed costumes, more in a Renaissance style to accentuate her modern mode of life, were lavishly embroidered and bejewelled with a fantastic head-dress created by Pierre Salnelle.

Everything was sumptuous. But costumes, not even good intentions alone, do not a success make. Warner Brothers, connected with the financing in Paris, turned the film down for its Columbia-Warner releasing service in Britain; and the French reviews were far from generous.

Jean-Loup Passek, *Cinéma 72*: 'Colinot is supposed to be a Middle Ages Western, a revival of those typical French stories full of mirth and truculence... *Fanfan la tulipe* and *Tom Jones*. Here, alas, it is rather on the side of *The Decameron* that one must look for the inspiration . . . as [Colinot] parachutes into the arms or under the skirts of some pretties . . . and finally lands in *kitsch* with Brigitte Bardot, in the posture that one would expect. As for [BB], for whom

About *Fesses*. Unlike Colette's *Gigi*, BB never had to be taught the rules of the eternal sex game. She gave lessons herself. Smouldering on in her 48th film in 22 years, the love goddess can still hold her own classes. With one major difference. The boot is now on the other foot; so are the clothes. Brigitte is chastely covered and it is the leading man (Francis Huster) having to bare all, or almost all, for art. As for the rest of French screen sex—'the gestures of love' are now too explicit for her. She leaves it to *la nouvelle-vague-porno* directors, Jean-François Davy, Jose Benazéraf, and to the *bleue-BBs*, Claudine Beccarie, Frédérique Barral, as they bring Bébé's 1965 sexual revolution to graphic fruition.

it has been said, this is her goodbye to cinema, I regret to say that her presence alone, as radiant and congealed as it can be, is not worth the 12 Francs that spectators will have to pay to enter the lugubriously over-nice kingdom of Mme. Companeez.'

Gene Moskowitz, of *Variety*, was—ultimately—in beneficent mood; sentimental, perhaps, as he alone among the critics quoted herein has covered the BB screen career from start to apparent finish. 'Much nudity but not eroticism. In fact, the strained attempts to attain a Rabelaisian dynamism are only intermittently successful and this looks like a home item of some calibre. But it has [BB] as a free-living and loving noblewoman finally teaching the young quester about love . . . But it is nice to look at and Miss

Bardot is still in stately shape.'

Too much so to quit, one would hope. If *Colinot* is to be Brigitte Bardot's farewell—her 48th film in 22 years—she has chosen to go out basically as she came in with *Et Dieu créa la femme*—on a feminist note. Apart from the title rôle, all the major characters, a host of the technical crew, plus the producer and writer-director, are women . . . which I maintain bodes well for more Bardot appearances in future Bodard/Companeez material.

For the moment the big questions remain unanswered. Is BB merely 'resting'? Will she be back soon . . . or later, within ten years, playing Darrieux-like mothers and the like? Says Brigitte: 'Wait ten years! . . .' And who among us will not?

Bardolatrie

'I am a prisoner behind my own face ... I have had many lovers in my life. It has been said that I am wicked. But it is not a matter of wickedness, it is a matter of affection or tenderness ... I don't care about fame for its own sake ...

I never wanted anything. It just happened. I never would have believed it. Now it has swallowed me up. It's all business. In the beginning, it is a pleasant sensation to win first prize. Now ... if you only knew how much of a sham I feel. There are days when I feel absolutely rotten and I find myself cheap and showy all the time. In spite of feeling feeble and exploited, I believe that I have a certain strength. Strength of character. I don't run away. I commit myself.

Then, I have a certain talent for organisation. And finally, willpower. What I dislike is superficiality. I hate it—and I am a superficial person myself. Consequently, my fame, as you call it, rests on air and to a great extent on hate.'

—**Brigitte Bardot, 1962**

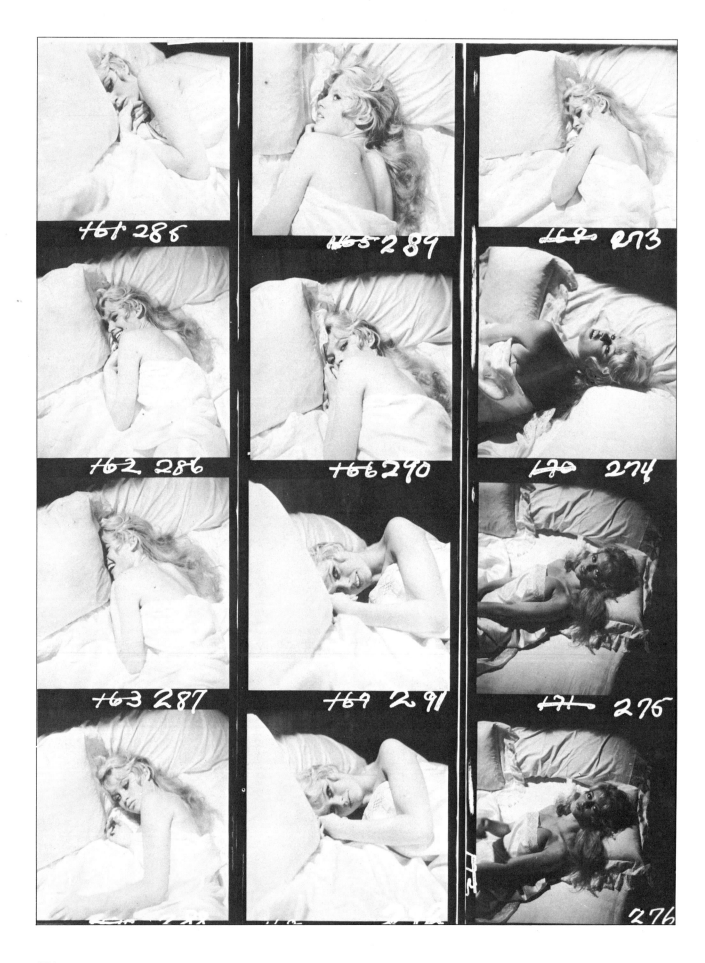